Scotland Rising

'This is a comprehensive, well-sourced and very wide-ranging discussion of the strengths and weaknesses of Scotland's independence movement, as it faces the challenges of a second referendum. Hassan shows how sterile the extreme arguments of unionist and nationalist can be. And he offers a fascinating projection of the impact of Scottish independence on the remnant UK and, in particular, on the "Empire State" delusions of England's elites.'

—Neal Ascherson, writer and author of *Black Sea*

'Gerry Hassan's forensic, incisive and also respectful account lays out the arguments for and against Scottish independence. The future of Scotland, Hassan rightly notes, will not be decided by true believers and activists for Yes or No, but by many hundreds of thousands of Scots who need to be reasoned with and convinced. This constructive, thoughtful, sharp- edged discussion confronts the choices for a new Scotland. It's also very readable as well as scholarly.'

—Gavin Esler, broadcaster and author of *How Britain Ends*

'A careful consensual account of how Scotland has come to be at the brink of independence, and of what this choice means for those who are not yet committed either way. A clear description of what has changed since 2014 leading to a forensic examination of the implications for impendence of the new context: a far less self-assured British elite. And a clear warning of just how nasty this debate is likely to become, across the UK.'

—Danny Dorling, Professor of Human Geography,
University of Oxford

'An important and timely contribution to the future of the Scottish inde-pendent movement.'

—Ruth Wishart, journalist and broadcaster

'Scotland needs this book. Read it. Give to your grandparents and grand-kids. Put it on reading lists for students. Make sure it's in the libraries. It's one of the new pillars which we need to structure our thinking.'

—Alison Phipps, Professor of Languages & Intercultural Studies
and UNESCO Chair for Refugee Integration through Languages
and the Arts at University of Glasgow

Scotland Rising

The Case for Independence

Gerry Hassan

First published 2022 by Pluto Press
New Wing, Somerset House, Strand, London WC2R 1LA

www.plutobooks.com

Copyright © Gerry Hassan 2022

The right of Gerry Hassan to be identified as the author of this work has been
asserted in accordance with the Copyright, Designs and Patents Act 1988.

British Library Cataloguing in Publication Data
A catalogue record for this book is available from the British Library

ISBN	978 0 7453 4727 1	Hardback
ISBN	978 0 7453 4726 4	Paperback
ISBN	978 0 7453 4729 5	PDF
ISBN	978 0 7453 4728 8	EPUB

This book is printed on paper suitable for recycling and made from fully
managed and sustained forest sources. Logging, pulping and manufacturing
processes are expected to conform to the environmental standards of the
country of origin.

Typeset by Stanford DTP Services, Northampton, England

Simultaneously printed in the United Kingdom and United States of America

To the memory of Nigel Smith (1941–2020):

My dear friend; a voice of insight and compassion and an exemplar of political empathy, learning and listening. We did not always agree on everything but we agreed on what matters. I hope the influence of Nigel lives on in the spirit of these pages and elsewhere.

Contents

PART IV: THE SHAPE OF THINGS TO COME

PART V: FUTURE LANDSCAPES

Acknowledgements

This book attempts to facilitate a more constructive debate on Scottish independence by exploring some of the specifics that independence has to address, considering the wider context of the Union, and interrogating Scotland's position in relation to the UK and wider world.

This is as much about profiling the human dimension, as well as about offering analysis, facts and figures. The book acknowledges that this is a debate about how people see the present, who they are and who they could be, and how they see the future – all of which brings forth a range of emotions including hope, fear, optimism, negativity, risk, loss, impatience and many more.

This book was planned, conceived and written to offer an explanation of the case for Scottish independence and to respect and understand those who hold different views. If some feel I have at points fallen short of this aim, this was not for the want of trying. We all need to keep listening, engaging, reflecting, understanding our political opponents, respecting those who disagree with us and in turn asking for respect, and pushing beyond our own echo chambers.

Numerous people have given their time, expertise and encouragement in the creation of this book. It would be impossible to thank each and every one of them, but in particular I would like to mention Kevin Albertson, Simon Barrow, Anne Bryce, Graham Bryce, Madeleine Bunting, Leon Cameron, Dougie Campbell, Karen Campbell, Aditya Chakrabortty, Carol Craig, John Curtice, Iain Docherty, Stephen Duncombe, Frances Ferry McKenzie, Richard Finlay,

Douglas Fraser, Isabel Fraser, Gregor Gall, Hannah Graham, David Heald, Eve Hepburn, Kirsty Hughes, Arianna Introna, Ben Jackson, Karen McCluskey, James McEnaney, Aileen McHarg, John McIntosh, Lynsey McIntosh, Phil McMenemy, Paul Mason, Eddie Rice, Philip Schlesinger, Mike Small, Jean Urquhart, Andy Wightman, and Richard Wyn Jones.

In summer 2021 I moved to Kirkcudbright in South West Scotland, where I wrote this book, and would like to give a special mention to Elizabeth and Stewart Parsons who opened Gallovida Books – a well-stocked and welcoming independent bookshop – one minute from my front door a couple of months after my arrival in the town.

I would also like to take this opportunity to thank all those who took the time to engage and reply to my queries about independence and other issues for this book. Thank you to Neal Ascherson, Anthony Barnett, Alex Bell, Marco Biagi, Kathleen Caskie, Malcolm Chalmers, Stuart Cosgrove, Iain Docherty, Danny Dorling, David Edgerton, Kenny Farquharson, James Foley, Jim Gallagher, Kathy Galloway, Doug Gay, Carol Gentry, Stephen Gethins, Pauline Gordon, David Greig, Gordon Guthrie, Kevin Hague, Craig Harrow, Tom Holland, Richard Holloway, Pat Kane, Sunder Katwala, Colin Kidd, Neal Lawson, Magnus Linklater, John Lloyd, Sue Lyons, Archie Macpherson, Robin McAlpine, Gavin McCrone, Val McDermid, Andy Mciver, Joyce McMillan, John McTernan, Ashish Malik, Ciaran Martin, James Mitchell, Laura Moodie, Lesley Orr, Sue Palmer, Alison Phipps, Adam Ramsay, Lesley Riddoch, James Robertson, Michael Roy, Kirstein Rummery, Anthony Salamone, Hillary Sillitto, Christopher Silver, Alan Sinclair, May Sumbwanyambe, Katherine Trebeck, and Dave Watson.

A sample of quotes and comments from this diverse group can be found throughout the book; an equal appreciation to everyone else who replied and said they would have loved to have answered my queries and in one case said 'my questions made them think too much' which I took as a compliment.

I owe a major debt of gratitude to all of the kind spirits who were generous of their time and intelligence to give endorsements to the book. Many thanks to Neal Ascherson, Danny Dorling, Gavin Esler, Hannah Graham, David Greig, Neal Lawson, Alastair McIntosh, James Mitchell, Alison Phipps, Katherine Trebeck and Ruth Wishart.

I would also like to take the opportunity to thank the entire team at Pluto Press who have consistently promoted and championed radical books throughout my adult life and who I am overjoyed to be working with. In particular, I would like to single out David Castle who worked on this book with myself from initial idea to its conclusion.

Finally, I owe the biggest acknowledgement and thanks to my partner Rosie Ilett who encouraged and supported me at all stages of this book's journey. She aided my thinking and specifically in the latter stages read the entire book in draft form, proofing, checking and commenting on the text. I am of course ultimately responsible for the text within these covers, but it has been made richer and sharper thanks to Rosie and her insights and expertise.

Having said all of the above, this vital subject is living and evolving. I hope I have done justice to its complexities, judged its long-term importance appropriately and that this book can play a small part in this critical debate for the people of Scotland and beyond.

Gerry Hassan

Introduction

The question of Scottish self-government and independence is a live and ongoing issue that affects, and has significant implications for, not just Scotland but also for the UK/rUK (rest of the UK) and internationally.

This is thus a question that deserves to be treated with respect and seriousness, and that requires substantive discussion and debate. Too often these qualities are found to be missing, crowded out by the noisier parts of how the independence question is expressed in public – a state of affairs which ultimately does no one any real favours.

This book is a conscious attempt to offer a constructive contribution to this vital and important debate and to recognise its wider importance by exploring and making the case for self-government and independence. It aims to offer some of the leading arguments for independence and to consider the choices and difficulties involved, with honesty and a respect for facts and all shades of opinion.

It does this in the context of recognising and respecting the argument for the Union and against independence. At points, it explicitly outlines the case for independence and the case for the Union, and argues that politics and public life would be better served if the main sides could recognise that there was a valid, rational argument on the other side as well as shades of grey in between.

Too often even in the senior levels of Yes and No there is a widespread propensity to caricature the other side. Yes advocates are posed by some pro-Union voices as hopeless romantic nationalists and No supporters by some independence advocates as scared – or in the pay of London elites. This is a complete disservice to what is a fundamental question for Scotland, democracy and the subject of independence.

This book is not a narrow, over-partisan, closed-minded account, or an attempt to advance any particular party perspectives. It does not offer a rationale for everything about the Scottish National Party (SNP), their policies and record in office, nor does it commend everything from the Scottish Greens or other pro-independence forces. Similarly, it does not offer a blanket dismissal of everything from the anti-independence parties: Labour, Conservatives, Liberal Democrats. Rather, it starts from the premise that we have to rise above such an outlook and recognise that wisdom, intelligence and ideas come from many disparate sources, including beyond political parties.

It is true that the claims of the SNP and independence are interlinked but they are not the same. The cause of independence would not be possible without the rise and role of the SNP, but it is possible and necessary to differentiate the two. The same is true on the claims of the Union. Whatever people feel about the politics of Labour, the Conservatives and Liberal Democrats, the argument for the Union is about more than the respective merits or not of these parties.

This book is for anyone with an interest in politics and the notion of challenging the mainstream. If you are for or against independence, unsure or don't know, or even do not see how this debate is relevant, then this book (while not an introductory text) aims to be as accessible and jargon-free as humanly possible. This does not mean that it is devoid of jargon and esoteric words, but that these are kept to a deliberate minimum – and when they are used, they are explained as much as possible. That has been the intention throughout; readers can judge for themselves how successful this has proven.

This book has not been written for those who think there is no need for further debate and that the subject is now closed. Such perspectives are found across the political spectrum – and include a smattering of independence supporters so impatient for change that they think any further discussion a distraction, and a larger group on the pro-Union side who think this topic was decided in 2014 and that is the end of the matter. Clearly, a large part of Scotland disagrees with these propositions and wants to explore the independence question further.

Those who will shape the future of Scotland are not those who take up much of the oxygen on social media, and are arguably the most passionate, committed and certain. It will not be those who wish everyone else would get in line with their thinking. The people who will determine the future have a very different rationale and way of seeing the world. This group include soft Yes and soft No supporters; the many who do not define themselves by their political identity or think about politics too much, as well as the floating and swing voters. These voters, which this book describes and listens to, will be the defining constituency of this debate. If you are one of this group (or more likely someone with an innate interest in politics), bear this in mind. The future of Scotland will be decided by people who do not live and breathe politics – and in particular party and partisan politics.

Running through this book is the notion that politics across the developed world has an empathy gap which magnifies the bitter divisions and divides which harm and distort democracy and political engagement. This is true of the independence question, and how Yes and No understand each other and frame the topic. Many people will agree and disagree with parts of this book and its assumptions, but this issue of empathy and reaching out and understanding and personifying respect is fundamental to how we think and act in public life and critical to the subject of independence.

All of this is made more urgent by the turbulent times that we live in that are shaped by crisis, turmoil and political upheaval. In the past few years, we have witnessed Brexit – the decision in 2016 of a UK majority to leave the European Union and which saw the UK finally leave the EU on 31 January 2020; the impact of the COVID-19 pandemic with millions of deaths worldwide, national lockdowns and international restrictions, and public services stretched to the point of exhaustion. If that were not enough, in March 2022 Russian President Vladimir Putin decided after months of escalation and brinksmanship to invade Ukraine, provoking an unprecedented political crisis: the first invasion of a sovereign independent European state by another in post-war times. At the time of writing the shape of this conflict is unfolding but looks likely to be long and bitter, involving significant fatalities, destruction and the displacement of large numbers of the Ukrainian population.

All of this is without mentioning the spectres of Donald Trump, Jair Bolsonaro, Viktor Orbán, Matteo Salvini, Marine Le Pen, Nigel Farage and others – the forces of right-wing populism who have proven so effective as forces of disruption, framing themselves as the new radicals taking on the liberal-left 'woke' establishment. Their counter-revolution has sadly yet to blow itself out or be defeated by organised opposition.

This is all of relevance in the Scottish debate. There are many people across the world who will say that they would just like a quiet life, and not to have to consider the big issues or radical change and rupture. There are also many who will say that against the backdrop of the above dramatic changes and upheavals there is need for a period of consolidation and healing in societies that have been stretched to breaking point.

This context has to be remembered in relation to Scottish independence. Scottish society and the rest of the UK have been through tumultuous, uncertain, fraught times in recent years. We have to respect the fragile and bruised fabric of our country and focus on bringing people together before any formal independence campaign is begun.

One comment on the writing of this book, the personal and the local. This book was written in the beautiful coastal town of Kirkcudbright in Dumfries and Galloway in south-west Scotland where I moved last year after living nearly 30 years in Glasgow. I have always questioned 'the Central Beltism' of too much of public life and media in Scotland and been aware of the over-focus on Glasgow and Edinburgh – a trend reinforced by the establishment of the Scottish Parliament. Living in Kirk-cudbright, this narrow bandwidth of what politics and power is in Scotland is much more noticeable and an issue which increasingly people mention in conversation and are concerned about, irrespective of their party allegiance and views on independence. This underlines the pointlessness of Scotland achieving independence only to replace Westminster with an Edinburgh that accrues even more power, status and influence and refuses to disperse decision-making across the length and breadth of the country. This is one more subject which shows the need for the independence question not to be about abstractions, and instead about how we make decisions in and within Scotland and nurture and support our own democratic institutions.

The search for common ground

In the tumultuous times in which we all live, where despite or maybe because of our huge challenges, there is a widespread fetishisation of small differences, this book starts from the premise that there are things which should unite us. There are rational, logical and instinctual arguments for both independence and the Union. We would benefit from recognising this, and both sides have to undertake serious work to convince voters in enough numbers in the future.

It is perhaps a little idealistic, but agreeing on some common ground across much of the political spectrum might help debates and how we shape the future. This would include:

- The UK domestically is in a state of political crisis concerning government, public institutions and public trust.
- Increasingly over recent decades, the UK has become a harsh, unequal country in terms of economic and social realities and divisions.
- These divisions affect nearly all public life, politics and society – with an unaccountable wealthy elite, millions in poverty and insecurity, and many more worried about their long-term livelihoods.
- The impact of Brexit has done untold damage to the fabric of the country, from how we do politics and take collective decisions to its impact on the economy and the UK's relationship with its European neighbours.
- The UK's geo-political position and influence is now seriously weakened – not just by Brexit, but by developments in the US and elsewhere; the current climate and rise of Putin's military aggressiveness does not automatically address this.
- Scotland's politics and institutions do not show the advanced state of atrophy, decay and corporate capture of the UK, but serious remedial work and rethinking is needed across all aspects of public life in Scotland.
- None of the mainstream political traditions, whether it be in Scotland, the UK or across the West – left, right, centre, green, feminist, nationalist, pro-autonomy, populist – has so far the answers to the huge challenges of our age: climate change, corporate capitalism, the march of AI and the global and national imbalances and instability which flow from these.

Any debate in Scotland should at least aspire to agree to some if not all of the above precepts. The Scottish self-government debate can only make sense and be relevant if there is some buy-in on this wider context and crisis – of politics, capitalism and the planet. Going beyond this, there needs to be some recognition that all the mainstream political parties, philosophies and outlooks, have up until now shown themselves inadequate in how they respond to the multiple challenges facing humanity and the world. We cannot pretend (whatever our view on independence) that continuing as we are is right, or that we have the answers either at a Scottish or UK level.

A word of explanation on some of the observations and testimonies cited in the book. Apart from conventional sources, three waves of contributors are included to widen the bandwidth of debate. First, there are the historic non-voters – 'the missing Scotland' and 'missing million' – drawing from focus groups undertaken in 2013–14. Second, there are voters who supported No in 2014 who by 2020 had shifted or were open to shifting, who were extensively interviewed. Finally, in February/March 2022, a group of nearly 60 participants in the debate, ranging from academics to opinion formers, businesspeople, entrepreneurs, community activists and campaigners. Their views covered the entire political spectrum – pro-independence, pro-Union, agnostic, ambivalent, don't know – and they were asked specific questions concerning views on independence; the reason or set of reasons for their views; and whether anything could happen that could change their mind.

As one caveat to this – and to the entire independence debate – too much has been framed around already privileged male voices who are used to being on platforms and being heard. This text tries consciously to counteract this, but all of us in Scotland have much work to do in this area – on gender, generationally, class, ethnicity, disability and more. I am more than aware of how a subject as important as this can be the preserve of a small coterie who congratulate themselves on how inclusive and welcoming they are. We need to recognise that such attitudes are part of the problem.

These are fast-moving, even bewildering and disorientating times. We are living through historic change that should make us pause and reflect on how we understand the world. This obviously includes how all of us see the Scottish debate. The future of Scotland is being created, made and remade by the multiple decisions and exchanges of all of us. We need to recognise this and act accordingly, understanding the responsibility that puts on each one of us who lives in Scotland for ourselves, and for the wider interest and ramifications this has for the rest of the UK and our friends, families and colleagues in England, Wales and Northern Ireland, as well as internationally. This book has been written with all such people in mind as a small contribution in addressing our collective future on this and other issues.

The structure of this book

This book is divided into five parts. The first begins by laying out the context and content of the Scottish question(s) and its rise in recent decades; followed by examining the changing notions of Scotland, stories about Scotland and the importance and power of collective voice.

The next part opens by putting Scotland's near-history into perspective in asking how independence came centre-stage. It then looks at the main arguments for and against independence, and for the Union, as presented in contemporary debates; making the case that supporters on each side need to better understand the rationale and logic of their opponents to enrich democratic debate.

The third part considers the choices that Scotland faces, the wider dynamics of the nature of the UK and in particular how they impact on Scotland. It explores the impact of the continuation of Empire State Britain not just internationally but domestically, and the fragile nature of the limited democracy that has been won in the UK, proposing that the UK is in many respects still not a fully-fledged democracy and how this, along with Scotland's own democratic shortcomings, impacts on our politics and public life. Subsequent chapters in this part address the nature of British capitalism and the economic inequalities which define the UK – and their consequences for Scotland. This is followed by an examination of social inequality, power and privilege in Scotland and the relevance of this for the independence question. The next chapter starts from the presumption that the framing of independence is too often presented as exclusively about politics and institutions, which inevitably narrows the debate, rather than addressing wider societal and cultural change. This is followed by a chapter on the international dimensions of independence that addresses Brexit, EU membership, the nuclear question and defence amongst a range of issues.

The fourth part explores the conditions in which Scotland has another independence vote. It then reviews the possible contours and challenges of a future referendum, potential implications for pro- and anti-independence campaigns, their messaging and the voters they need to target and listen to.

The final part addresses the future dimensions of Scotland and the UK, starting with imagining the environment after a successful independence vote. It does this by first looking at Scotland after such a vote, then UK/rUK, arguing that the creation of an independent Scotland is not only a momentous moment for Scotland, but also for UK/rUK with major implications for England, Wales and Northern Ireland. These consequences could have major democratic and progressive advances, if people in these three nations dare to take the opportunity provided by the crumbling of the *ancien régime*.

The book concludes by emphasising the importance of Scotland's right to decide its collective future being as widely accepted as possible. The final chapter stresses that this critical debate has to be seen as about more than politics and politicians, drawing from a richer well and tapestry including the stories that a society tells itself. In this, Scotland has moved and shifted dramatically over the course of recent decades, and will continue to do so in the near-future, irrespective of what is decided by the people of Scotland on the independence question. That is right and proper and similar to elsewhere, but the pressures to see this huge topic in a narrow frame – as somehow just being about the SNP, anti-Toryism, anti-Westminster or solely about parties and politicians – has to be resisted and does this subject a grave disservice.

A fundamental strand underpinning this book is the issue of what makes political opinions – allowing for change, and the importance of doubt. In an unpredictable and uncertain world, we have to avoid fixed mindsets and listen to the possibility of change from all sides and directions. It is critical to make spaces to hear those voices of doubt and not allow them to be shouted down to the detriment of us all.

The independence debate has many shades and layers; one that has to be given space and air is the psychological dimension. Independence brings up a profound range of responses from different voters: of enthusiasm and energy, of despair and deflation, and every emotion in between, including confusion and a search for great clarity and answers. This book tries to illuminate the debate, not just by discussing the institutions of government and governance, or even democratic legitimacy, but in thinking about how people see themselves and their collective future and stories and, in a fundamental sense, how they want to express being citizens and even human.

These big questions are daunting ones in a world of confusion, noise and threats, and it behoves all of us to try and engage with a degree of respect and humility, including those living in Scotland, in the rest of the UK and internationally. I have tried my best to honour that in the following pages.

PART I

The Terrain of the Debate

1
The Scottish Question(s)

Scotland is not a colony, a semi-colony, a pseudo-colony, a near-colony, a neo-colony, or any kind of colony of the English.

Tom Nairn, 'Three Dreams of Scottish Nationalism',
New Left Review, 1968

It can hardly be said about the Scots, as it used to be said unfairly about the Irish, that they are unworthy, or incapable, of self-government. They have been far too successful in governing other people (including the English) for this to sound plausible. Equally absurd would be the contention that Scotland is too poor and backward to enjoy the rights freely granted to other nations...

H.J. Paton, *The Claim of Scotland*, 1968

The independence question is one of the defining topics of modern-day Scotland. This was not always the case. In the recent past, independence was not seen by many as part of the mainstream, or as one of the defining subjects that would shape how we see and frame the future of the country.

To understand the nature of this topic it is necessary to comprehend how this changed and why this happened. How and why did independence come in from the cold? What does this tell us about the underlying reasons for this occurring – and how has this mainstreaming of independence changed it and the contours of public life? How might things evolve in the future in a world growing more unpredictable by the day?

The independence debate is about more than the merits, popularity and unpopularity of any political party. It is not just about the appeal or not of the SNP. Nor is it just about the unpopularity of the Tories or collapse of Scottish Labour. Much bigger factors are at work.

Fundamentally, what has changed, and that has fed into the rise of the independence question, is that the 'idea' of Scotland as we understand it – the sum total of the contributions, communications and exchanges of everyone who lives here over decades – has profoundly shifted with massive consequences. This is not to argue that there is one uniform, united version of Scotland or to pose an essentialist, singular notion of Scottish identity. That would be inaccurate and indefensible, as well as unhelpful in aiding greater understanding. Rather, across the post-1945 era Scotland became more explicitly defined as an identifiable space, place and territory, with its own distinctive characteristics not just politically, but how it saw itself economically, socially and culturally – the facets of which are explored in the next chapter.

One example suffices to make the wider point. There is now no sense in arguing that a distinctive 'Scottish political system' does not exist or that its existence is something which is solely predicated on the establishment of the modern Scottish Parliament in 1999.

'A separate political will':
a short tour from 1970 to the present

Not so long ago senior figures in public life used to argue about whether there was a 'separate political system' in Scotland or a distinct 'sub-system'.[1] Step forward as evidence the Labour Party in Scotland and the era when it was the undisputed dominant party in the land. In its submission to the Royal Commission on the Constitution (which became known as the Kilbrandon Commission) in May 1970, the party was unapologetic and absolutely sure of its view on Scotland and political autonomy.

W.G. Marshall (Labour):
There is, however, no such thing as a separate political will for Scotland...

Maitland Mackie (Commission):
Surely you must accept that there is a political will for Scotland?

Dr Hunt (Commission):
Where a Conservative Government was in power at Westminster, would you really feel under those circumstances that the Scottish Grand Committee or the Select Committee on Scottish Affairs would have adequate power of control over Scottish Office administration?

John Pollock (Labour):
If you accept the United Kingdom structure, as we do, such a situation may be the inevitable outcome of it. We must add that, as Scottish members of the Labour Party, we see our interest as being the same as members of the Labour Party in England and Wales on a vast range of issues...

Chair (Commission):
You cannot be in exactly the same position as English members of the Labour Party... In the extreme, but perhaps not entirely hypothetical case, that Labour held all 71 Scottish seats in Parliament, but there was a Conservative Government, how in these circumstances would Scotland exert any control over the Secretary of State?

John Pollock (Labour):
I think that situation is hypothetical and almost impossible...

Chair (Commission):
It could still be true that one party might gain a very large majority in Scotland.

Dr Hunt (Commission):
The odds are that with a Conservative Government for the UK, there would still be a majority of Labour MPs in Scotland.

John Pollock (Labour):
The only effective way of solving the Scottish problem is to have a Labour Government at Westminster, but we are prepared to put up with the short period in which a Conservative Government might be the administration, because we can more than make that good in our next administration. It is essential to maintain the kind of system in which a Labour Government at Westminster in the future is able to control the country in the interests of all the people in the UK.[2]

This evidence was given on 4 May 1970, and is a fascinating set of comments because it puts the clear Labour voice against Scottish autonomy and for centralisation and the notion of the British state as the unchecked force for progress. It was also, little did anyone know at the time, the dying embers of the old Labour faith in such shibboleths.

Within weeks of this exchange Labour Prime Minister Harold Wilson called an election; Labour was ahead in most of the polls and expected to win but when the results came in on 18 June 1970 Labour had lost to Ted Heath's Conservatives who won an overall majority of 30 seats. Not only that, the situation outlined above had come about: the Tories had won big in England while Labour had decisively won in Scotland, producing for the first time in post-1945 politics the question of how Westminster governed Scotland being a controversial subject.

Running through the Scottish Labour evidence is a barely concealed disdain for even the consideration that there might be a 'separate political will for Scotland', and that any damage done to Scotland by a Conservative government without significant popular support 'we can more than make good' by the actions of a future Labour government. Not only is this the politics of faith in British government and the state, the idea of a unified Britain which underpinned Labour unionism, and the regular alternation of governments with Labour incrementally making the UK more progressive. All that was to be blown away with the election of Margaret Thatcher in 1979 and the following 18 years of Tory rule, by which time Labour had abandoned the mindset outlined above.

The politics of difference

A major strand through the history of the above and subsequently is that of the politics of difference – and the notion that Scotland is or is not different from the rest of the UK and in particular, England.

In one corner are some pro-independence supporters who say that Scotland is becoming a distinct country and political system, separate from England and that overall, its people display a profoundly different set of political values. Former First Minister Henry McLeish articulated a version of this, saying in light of the 2016 Brexit vote, that:

> Scotland and England's politics are diverging. There's a growth of hard-headed nationalism in England, there's xenophobia, there's racism, there's an ugly politics developing that we're not part of.[3]

On the other hand, are those who say from a pro-Union perspective that Scotland is not that distinctive compared to England and the rest of the UK. They emphasise the shared pool of common values and ideas, and propose that any perceived differences are more at the level of party voting, something seen as more transitory.[4] As Alex Massie put it in 2014 looking at Scottish and English differences: 'Nice, kind, progressive Scotland is a myth as cherished as it is, well, mythical.'[5] The journalist Alan Cochrane goes even further charging that the politics of difference are 'allied to the view that bad things are "done" to the Scots by the English'.[6]

The narrative of difference – championing and contesting it – is one of the big dividers and defining issues of politics in Scotland which is about more than just understanding facts but about how Scotland is seen as a political community.

Academics and journalists often tend to interpret their data to discuss how small the differences are between Scotland and England. This often draws specifically from the Scottish Social Attitudes survey. An examination of the 2021 survey, for example, illustrates the degree of difference between Scotland and England. Asked if the distribution of income in the UK was unfair, 73 per cent of those in Scotland said it was, compared to 65 per cent of those in England; asked if it is wrong for people to buy private education and healthcare, 46 per cent of Scots said it was wrong for education and 42 per cent for healthcare; the comparable English figures were 34 per cent on education and 32 per cent on healthcare. And when asked to choose the kind of society they wanted to live in via the shape of an income pyramid, 78 per cent of Scots choose a more egalitarian society compared to 71 per cent of the English. These figures were undertaken with a comparison to Nordic countries, leading the analysis to summarise: 'Scotland appears once again to lie between the Nordic countries and England in its level of support for equality.'[7] All the above shows that there is some difference between the two nations but, as these measurements indicate, it is not large.

The pro-difference argument can draw attention to Scotland as a very different political system and culture compared to England. This is a political system shaped by a politics of the centre left post devolution which informs the contours of political debate across the public policy choices which Scotland faces in the current environment. This can be seen in the weakness of the Conservative vote in Scotland compared to England and the difference between the Conservative–Labour lead between the two countries when they were the two lead parties in both – which takes us up to 2015.

The first shows significant differences – with a Conservative vote in England of 47.2 per cent (1979), 39.5 per cent (2010), 47.2 per cent (2019) and a Tory vote in Scotland in the three elections of 31.4 per cent (1979), 16.7 per cent (2010), 25.1 per cent (2019). This produces a gap over the three of 15.8 per cent (1979), 22.8 per cent (2010), 22.1 per cent (2019) between Scotland and England in three elections which produced UK Conservative governments, two with overall majorities and one just short of an overall majority which went into coalition with the Liberal Democrats.[8]

The second indicator between Labour and Conservative leads in Scotland and England rose from 20.6 per cent in 1979 to an all-time high of 36.8 per cent in 2010. It then fell back as the SNP became the leading party in Scotland and the Labour vote slumped, the gap between the two main UK parties reducing to 18.6 per cent in 2015 and an even lower 6.7 per cent in 2019.

Other measurements dig deeper than the Scottish Social Attitudes material, such as a number of questions in large-scale public surveys from Ipsos MORI Scotland. Their survey in 2013 found that 58 per cent of Scots believed that 'publicly' owned and run public services were more professional and reliable, compared to 19 per cent who said this about 'privately' run services; in England and Wales the comparable figures were 30 per cent for publicly owned services and 29 per cent for privately owned services.[9]

One area where many Scots think there is a difference in attitudes between themselves and the rest of the UK is immigration. Yet in regular surveys of opinion there is no major difference between Scotland and England and Wales. The British Social Attitudes survey found in 2017 that more people in Scotland think that immigration is good for the economy (46 per cent) than bad (17 per cent): nearly identical to England and Wales (47:16 per cent). One interesting divide in Scotland is that nearly three-fifths of SNP supporters (59 per cent) in 2017 held pro-immigration views: a figure nearly matched by Scottish Liberal Democrat supporters, with Labour and Tories much less supportive – and the Tory figure (30 per cent) significantly below Tory supporters in England and Wales.[10]

This debate is then framed by pro-independence opinion as stressing the liberal credentials of Scotland and disparaging the policies of the UK, while pro-Union voices question the former and how different Scotland really is. On the latter, the policy choices and public preferences of Scotland on immigration would only fully be investigated by independence and the degree to which Scotland departed from the stance of UK governments.

What can be said is that there is a different political dynamic and salience of the issue in England which drives UK policy.[11] This can be seen in the impact in the 2016 Brexit vote, to the discrimination and xenophobia evident in the treatment of the Windrush generation, UK Home Office attitudes from the 'hostile environment' stance, toxic debate on asylum seekers and refugees, Nationality and Borders Act of 2022 outlawing people entering the UK and assisting them through non-approved routes such as the English Channel, and the less-than-generous UK attitude to refugees fleeing Afghanistan in 2021 and Ukraine in 2022. All of these point to a much more loaded English debate shaped by stigmatisation, 'othering' and elements of racism, which seem less prevalent in public debate in Scotland.

Dramatist and playwright May Sumbwanyambe recently expressed their dismay at the relentless stance of UK governments on this:

> The Westminster/Home Office position under successive governments has been that immigration/integration is a problem that needs to be solved. The current constitutional arrangement where Westminster policies override Scottish Government policies is highly unsatisfactory. The truth of how important immigrants are to our communities has been cruelly exposed by Brexit. As long as we don't have true accountability, there really feels like nothing Scottish citizens can democratically do, to impact callous Westminster policies like creating a 'hostile environment' for human beings, depriving people (and often refugees) of dignity simply because of the colour of their skin or place of birth. Enough is enough.[12]

The above illustrates that both arguments have grounds for making their case in relation to hard figures. In reality, Scotland is both different and at the same time has a lot in common with England and Wales. Posing this terrain in either/or terms is to do it a disservice. Scotland is both a distinct nation and place with its own traditions, values, institutions and stories but also shares a rich set of common experiences and interests with England and the rest of the UK.

The 'divided Scotland' argument

Another potent trope used about Scotland that is regularly put into the mix is to lament the existence of a 'divided Scotland' where the shared values and sociability of being part of the same community has supposedly been lost or significantly eroded – rent asunder and ripped apart by the zealotry of the separatist case, so the argument goes.

This 'divided Scotland' is defined by the two binary camps of Yes and No with apparently little room for other perspectives. While there is truth in Yes and No crowding out alternative views, what is missing from this take is that Yes and No are not fixed entities and closed tribes, but constantly changing and in flux, with people joining and leaving them all the time.[13]

The 'divided Scotland' mantra ignores the change and churn which is continually going on with voters and the huge number of voters who are floating, swing and don't know – as well as the 'missing Scotland' and 'missing million' explored later in the book, namely the voters who have been systematically disenfranchised by a politics that they have seen as not for them or about them.

The corollary of the above is the continual talk about the prospect of another referendum, describing it as a 'divisive referendum'. Numerous examples of this are available; two will suffice. Willie Rennie in his capacity as leader of the Scottish Liberal Democrats said of another vote that we need to 'stop the division, chaos, new borders and economic cost that independence would cause'.[14] Kezia Dugdale, then leader of Scottish Labour, took a similar tone: 'Scotland is divided enough; Nicola Sturgeon is wrong to attempt to divide us again.'[15]

Hundreds and hundreds of similar quotes are part of a concerted attempt to frame Scotland's debate in negative terms and to throw up a series of psychological barriers to how voters view independence and the prospect of a future referendum. It is an understandable attempt by opponents of independence to delegitimise and stigmatise calls for another vote. It is what opposing politicians do when trying to label in a negative way the topic, so shaping how many voters see the issue and their views on it. It should be seen as part and parcel of the political cut and thrust – listened to and challenged.

Scotland needs to aspire to a politics on this and other areas that is less divisive in how it is conducted, informed by respect and pluralism. Ideally, this is aided by a politics about substance, tackling real issues and all shades of opinion, and calling out and having 'zero tolerance' for those who want to bring hatred, bile and bigotry into this debate and wider politics. It is not acceptable, as occurred in the 2014 independence referendum, to call any politicians 'traitors' and 'quislings' as happened to the likes of then Labour MPs Jim Murphy and Margaret Curran.[16] This is a mindset which ends with the language of political violence becoming actual violence, as the UK has witnessed in recent times with the murder of Labour MP Jo Cox in the midst of the 2016 Brexit referendum campaign and Tory MP David Amess in 2021.

What drives and shapes the current debate has to be fully understood: is it all about the SNP, as some claim, and the desire by politicians for more power? Is it about being anti-Tory or anti-Westminster? Is the main issue the principles of democracy, or as some claim, 'identity politics', or are there other factors at work?

Take the notion that one of the drivers of independence is identity and the distinction between Scottish and British identities which is a common explanation. The reality is more complex and nuanced. Scottish and British identities are so prevalent in the present, not exclusive and overlapping, that this is less of a clear predictor of how people stand on independence than is often commonly thought. When forced to choose a single national identity in 2014 in the Scottish Social Attitudes survey, 65 per cent of respondents said that they were Scottish and 23 per cent British. Yet it is also true that a significant majority of voters in Scotland recognise being Scottish and British – with the former being more strongly felt. When people are allowed to choose both identities, 62 per cent said they felt some combination of Scottish and British identities. As the academic and psephologist John Curtice of Strathclyde University puts it:

> although the more strongly someone felt Scottish, the more likely they were to back independence, the fact that many voters had mixed loyalties meant that for many their sense of national identity alone was not necessarily decisive in deciding how they were going to vote. Instrumental considerations mattered too.[17]

Numerous other considerations were at play in 2014 and are in the present. There is the democratic question; there is Brexit. And then there is the issue of economic prosperity and assessing the prospects of the future. The first of these worked in favour of independence in 2014 and since; the Brexit vote has worked in favour of independence since 2016, while this has also brought numerous complications including that one-third of independence supporters backed Brexit in the 2016 vote. And there is the question of economic prosperity which worked to the advantage of No in 2014 and has continued to since.

If all of these factors remained broadly the same, and no new factors emerged and gained in salience, any foreseeable vote would on existing trends be close to call and more competitive than 2014. That is a challenge and also a worry to both the pro- and anti-independence camps. It represents progress by the forces of independence compared to 2014 but not decisively so, and underlines further that the outcome of a future vote cannot safely be predicted. And that also means that the case for independence or the Union could shift the debate in their favour by seriously working on its offer and also that the entire debate could be altered and reframed by external forces, given we have already had in the years since 2014, Brexit, COVID-19 and the Russian invasion of Ukraine.

Beyond the barricades

There has to be a greater understanding of the different perspectives in Scotland, on the independence question and indeed other issues. There are parts of independence opinion who think there are no valid reasons for the Union, which can then in the extreme lead into a dismissive attitude for why 55 per cent of voters endorsed the Union in 2014, two million of our fellow Scots. This is a variant of a trope familiar to many who have come through left-wing politics and rejects the verdict of the people when they come up with what is obviously the wrong answer in the eyes of the elect – the narrow stratum of a pure left who know the right answer. This is the world of seeking refuge in false consciousness and conspiracy theories, such as that somehow the 2014 vote was altered and that really Yes won, a view which fortunately only exists on the outer margins of independence.

There is a view on the pro-Union side which does not even understand why Scotland has been having such a debate, why it arrived at it and is continuing to have it. It sees the idea of independence as irrelevant to Scotland's needs when it already has devolution, seeing 'separatism' as completely irrelevant and even damaging in an age of interdependence.

I know people who take both these outlooks. Pro-independence people who cannot understand the case for the Union;

who think the UK main political parties and establishment have no real understanding or commitment to Scotland and just view it like a piece of property or real estate: something they feel they have a right to own and can't quite let go of. I know lots of pro-Union people, including many Labour MPs past and present, who have no grasp of independence and why it has become such a key topic in the politics of Scotland. This nearly always involves the fact that they have never really thought about the subject seriously beyond party tribalism, instinctively opposing it because it originates from the SNP.

Many English Labour MPs, with one or two obvious exceptions, are against it because they are 'against dividing people', worry about 'putting up barriers' and argue for 'the politics of people coming together'. Whether or not you have sympathy with such sentiments, it is clear the politicians saying them have given no substantive thought to the subject and are instead clutching at slogans. This reflects some deep-seated emotional commitment in the Labour Party and labour movement about the British state and Britishness, but even more damningly its unwillingness to move away from the dominant Tory and right-wing versions of these critical ideas and to dare to articulate their own counter-story.[18] What would be wrong within the Labour tradition in daring to embrace and articulate a radical socialist idea of self-government for Scotland? It could even help the bigger picture and assist Labour in challenging the Tory idea of Britain and address the English dimension.[19]

We all have to do better than that, whatever our views on the subject. We have to dig deeper. Ask difficult questions. Confront uncomfortable facts. Listen to people who we disagree with and listen and discuss beyond our respective echo chambers. That means in particular listening and engaging with those who are unsure on this subject and treating them with respect and humility.

The future of Scotland will not be decided by the most committed of true believers on the Yes or No side speaking in the most self-certain way, evangelising the merits of their faith. In many respects, that is following in the footsteps of a long-established Scottish tradition – preaching to the faithful and hunting for heretics – which was never a very attractive part of our character and is no way to contemplate running a country and deciding on a collective future.

2
Nation, Stories and Voice

Nobody can be a power in their age unless they are part of its voice.

Naomi Mitchison, novelist and poet,
wartime diary, 2 March 1941

Scottish civic nationalism is the product of Scottish civic society and its admirable humanist tradition… In Scotland, we have been fortunate and we therefore owe it to ourselves, as a society, to always question herd behaviour and group-think, even when it feels seductive, which it often does.

Kapka Kassabova, author and poet,
Scottish Review of Books, February 2018

The changing notion of the Union and self-government

If we look at the long view of Scotland's constitutional debate, many of its core assumptions have been continually in flux. This is obvious when it is remembered that independence was until recently not part of the mainstream but now clearly is.

It is true that what has been meant by independence and self-government from the SNP has evolved. The party's understanding of these constitutional areas in the 1930s and 1940s represented a kind of supra-home rule. It explicitly stated, and was party policy, that Scottish self-government would be in the context of the country enjoying Dominion status in the British Empire and then the Commonwealth.[1]

The party emphasised examples of self-government within the Empire such as the Isle of Man and Northern Ireland with their unquestioning loyalty to the Crown – trying to avoid comparison with the Irish Free State – a stance the exact opposite of 'separatism'.[2]

Notions of what the Union represents and how it is presented by its advocates have also continually shifted.[3] This is not a criticism; merely an observation. In the 1950s the Tories were at a historic high in their popularity in Scotland that gave them confidence in expressing their unionism and the form it took. They felt comfortable talking about and championing Scottish difference and distinctiveness, underlining the case that this was one of the strengths and benefits of the Union.

Winston Churchill, when leader of the Tory opposition, visited Edinburgh a week before the UK general election of February 1950 and in a speech in the Usher Hall railed against Labour centralisation. He declared that he 'should never adopt the view that Scotland should be forced into the serfdom of socialism as the result of a vote in the House of Commons'.[4]

This was not the exception. When in office from 1951 the Tories continued to present the case for the Union as one of Scotland enjoying a degree of autonomy against the march of a uniform UK advanced by socialists. Harold Macmillan, who later became prime minister, said as housing minister in 1954:

> For generation after generation, unity of purpose has been achieved by the Union of our two great Kingdoms and of the Principality of Wales. But it must be the Union of the wedding ring not the handcuff.[5]

This was the language of a Union of consent which celebrated tradition, difference and autonomy against the leviathan of the central state. All of this contributed to the Scottish Tories invoking the Union as an expression of the Scottish nation which was then aided by the post-war direction of the party in office, accepting Labour's reforms and under Harold Macmillan advocating what amounted to a social contract between the working and middle classes sharing the fruits of affluence. Subsequently, as the constitutional question rose in importance in the 1960s, Ted Heath when Tory opposition leader presented his party's new pro-devolution stance as the 'Declaration of Perth' – as it was made to the Scottish Tory conference in Perth in 1968 – consciously invoking the Declaration of Arbroath of 1320.[6] Nothing concrete came of Heath's devolution pledge even though the party entered government in 1970, but this remained formal Tory policy until Margaret Thatcher, newly installed as the new Tory opposition leader, ditched it in 1976.[7]

This confident strand of unionism has slowly withered since then and become almost totally extinct. In recent years, unionism has more and more made the mistake of conceding the argument about greater substantial self-government and distinctiveness to the forces of independence and finding it difficult to articulate on the Union and even finding parts of its base turning away from such an outlook. In particular, it has been poorly placed to present a vision of the Union against the onward march of the central state – hamstrung by the increasing centralisation of successive UK Labour and Tory governments – and which talk of 'levelling up' and the creation of more regional mayors by the Tory government will do nothing to reverse.[8]

Such has been the struggle for contemporary unionism to find an appropriate language that they have even retreated from the language of championing a flexible Union, such as talking of 'the four nations' of the UK. Alister Jack, Secretary of State for Scotland, in a collection *Strength in Union* published in 2021, said: 'I am no fan of the "four nations" expression, for the Union gives us one great nation.'[9]

Similarly, Tory MP for Vale of Clwyd James Davies took a swipe at the rise of this term in response to the COVID pandemic:

> Early on in the pandemic... it became convenient parlance for nationalist leaning politicians to refer to the UK as 'the four nations' – a divisive term which pretends to equate our single nation state with an association of sovereign states. The term successfully found its way into common usage, including via the BBC and wider media.[10]

One of the biggest factors in this has been that of Scottish nationalism. But like every other perspective in this debate, it too has morphed and evolved over the years. It may seem contradictory to many from today's vantage point but being a Scottish nationalist and invoking its icons, images and leitmotifs, was once completely compatible with being pro-Union. Hence, for most of the period of Scotland's experience of Union the likes of Robert Bruce, Robert Burns, Bannockburn and the Declaration of Arbroath were cited as pro-Union facets because they had contributed to Scotland becoming a distinct nation which then chose to join in a Union with England; this was the age which at its height saw the evoking of a 'unionism-nationalism' – a unionism comfortable invoking Scottish traditions and nationalism.[11]

Scottish nationalism can fit into Michael Billig's concept of 'banal nationalism' meaning that it can be seen as widely held across society, moderate and mainstream – although this does not mean it is completely uncontested.[12] With its belief in Scotland as a nation with a sense of national identity, it has a wide array of variants and strands. There has been a diverse social and apolitical nationalism which informs these tenets and does not read anything political or important into it. There is a cultural nationalism which has at times had a significant impact – one we will examine in later chapters (and in particular Chapter 10). And then there has been the rise of contemporary Scottish nationalism which has become synonymous with self-government and latterly independence.

In the 1980s there was a growing home rule consensus for a Scottish Parliament and against the Tory government of Margaret Thatcher. At this time Labour were the leading party of Scotland and often evoked nationalist language and politics in opposition to the Tories. The high point of this was when Labour MPs (bar Tam Dalyell) signed *A Claim of Right for Scotland* asserting 'the sovereign right of the Scottish people', the politics of which we will examine later in Chapters 12 and 15.[13]

The evolution of Scottish nationalisms

This political landscape undoubtedly had an impact on Scottish nationalism.[14] It brought it more explicitly into the orbit of centre-left politics, the ideas of social democracy, and brought about a combination of the politics of class and nation, which might have been simply articulated by some but was to prove enormously influential.

This of course did not meet with universal agreement including figures in senior positions in the Labour Party. Subsequently, when Labour came to power in 1997 a host of prominent figures such as Gordon Brown and Douglas Alexander took aim at Scottish nationalism seeing it as being the equivalent to supporting the SNP and independence. In this they were trying to make the case for a new progressive, inclusive Britain and Britishness, but in relation to Scotland it often sounded jarring and partisan.[15] They were motivated by trying to steer their party back from what they regarded as the excesses of the 1980s, but were also embarking on a dangerous exercise. In trying to tar Scottish nationalism with the sins of nationalism everywhere, and latterly, with the likes of UKIP, they gifted the terrain of Scottish nationalism to the SNP and independence, a mistake which was to lay the ground work for future trouble for Labour and the Union.[16]

A Scottish Labour Party which considered the idea of 'no mandate' against the Tories in the 1980s was in the 1999 Scottish Parliament elections running with the campaign slogan 'Divorce is an Expensive Business' showing the Scottish nation being graphically torn off from the rest of the UK.[17] That represented quite a political shift in a short period of time and represented a defensive unionism trying to reclaim lost ground.

Labour politicians, and indeed most non-SNP politicians, like to pontificate about the evils of nationalism and how it has been a force for destruction the world over. Much rarer has been any senior Labour figure who has outlined its positives. One example is provided by the work of the London Scots Self-Government Committee, a pro-home rule group active in the 1930s and 1940s that included many prominent Labour members and MPs. Herbert Morrison and Clement Attlee were known to be sympathetic and attended occasional meetings. Attlee as Labour leader endorsed its publication *Plan for Scotland* in 1937 saying in its foreword:

There was at one time a tendency among Socialists to underrate the force of national sentiment. Today we ought all to recognise that nationalism has an immense attractive force for good or evil. Suppressed it may poison the political life of a nation. Given its proper place it can enrich it. The London Scots Self-Government Committee and Mr. Tom Burns are to be commended for having got down to practical proposals as a basis of discussion.[18]

This is an unusual take from Clement Attlee, universally seen as the greatest leader the Labour Party has ever had and Prime Minister of the most radical Labour government in the party's history. This outlook is not just endorsing the principle of self-government but locating it in an understanding of the positive attributes of nationalism as well as their negatives.

In the 1980s, as Scottish Labour emphasised its home rule credentials and opposition to Thatcherism, it was still unusual to see Scottish nationalism being positively invoked. One exception was Ernie Ross, Labour MP for Dundee West and then a prominent left-winger, who wrote in 1983 in the aftermath of Thatcher's second election victory:

> The Scottish nationalism of the labour movement has recognised the difference in social class in the community, unlike the right-wing leadership of the SNP who tend to ignore this aspect. Part of the traditional message of the Scottish labour movement has always stipulated the need and the demand for Scottish self-government to attack social inequalities in Scotland – together with the view that socialism would win the argument in Scotland before it did it in England.[19]

Another exception was the late Donald Dewar, who served as First Minister, who was clearly pro-Union but comfortable in seeing himself as sympathetic to Scottish nationalism in the broadest sense. He once said in a *BBC Scotland* debate with myself at the outset of the Scottish Parliament: 'I am a Scottish nationalist with a small "s".'[20] This was a typical Dewarism – getting a phrase slightly wrong but acknowledging a deeper meaning, invoking Tom Nairn's 'upper case' and 'lower case' nationalisms.[21]

The prevailing response of most Labour figures has been to disparage Scottish nationalism as an ideology diametrically opposed to internationalism and solidarity, and hence the values of the Labour Party and wider labour movement. This has been the stance of numerous Labour figures who have called Scottish nationalists 'small-minded fanatics', 'one-dimensional' and that 'solidarity and internationalism are our core Labour values not separatism and nationalism' — the first two comments from former Labour MP Brian Wilson and the last from trade unionist Kate Wilson.[22]

Labour leader Keir Starmer in a Fabian Society pamphlet in 2021 wrote:

> The Conservatives and the Scottish National Party may define themselves against each other, but their politics is symbiotic, requiring one another to sustain and grow... Both the SNP and Conservatives use culture to distract and deflect, creating division between people of these islands. The business of effective governance and improving people's lives comes second to ideology. Both use nationalism freely to whip up fear of the other.[23]

The Labour MP Jess Phillips commenting on Boris Johnson's habit of misnaming the SNP 'the Scottish Nationalist Party' stated:

> They don't want to be called nationalists but that is what they are; I am not saying they are the racist type, as a rule, but they are nationalists, and I will never think of nationalism as anything but dangerous populism that breeds hatred and division.[24]

The power of story

Another key dynamic that has informed the Scottish question down through the ages has been the power of stories we create and tell ourselves. As Ben Okri powerfully said:

Stories are the secret reservoir of values: change the stories individuals and nations live by and tell themselves and you change the individuals and nations… Nations and peoples are largely the stories they feed themselves. If they tell themselves stories that are lies, they will suffer the further consequences of those lies. If they tell themselves stories that face their own truths, they will free their histories for future flowerings.[25]

This is not some frivolous exercise for affluent societies but goes to the core of being human. The historian Yuval Noah Harari pointed out in the immediate aftermath of the Russian invasion of Ukraine in February 2022 that: 'Nations are ultimately built on stories. With each passing day, more stories emerge that Ukrainians will tell not only in the dark days ahead, but in the decades and generations to come.' He concludes at a time of stark international crisis and an assault on democracy by Russian military forces on an optimistic note:

This is the stuff nations are built from. In the long run, these stories count for more than tanks… The last few days have proved to the entire world that Ukraine is a very real nation, that Ukrainians are a very real people, and that they definitely don't want to live under a new Russian empire.[26]

Such profound truths about the tragedy of Ukraine not only illustrate the power of story but also put the Scottish question and the future of Scotland into a proper context, where we are fortunately not faced with such stark and black-and-white choices. It is true that the dramatic events in Ukraine change many of the assumptions that the idea of the West has been built upon in the past 70 years and will have implications for the Scottish independence debate which we will explore later.

In the concluding chapter the potential stories of Scotland's future will be addressed and what they could be and how we give real meaning to them. But in an age of increasing complexity, instability and risk, stories matter more not less in how we make sense of our lives and societies.

Scotland has a rich history and tapestry of stories which have helped define us as a nation. There is the story of the Enlightenment Scotland, which aided intellectual inquiry, the advance of ideas and rationalism and in so doing assisting in the creation of the modern world; there was the account of the Scottish Empire and the role the country played in imperialism, colonialism and conquest including slavery, parts of which Scotland is only beginning to fully come to terms with; there is the Scotland of enterprise and invention that saw many of the critical discoveries of the industrial revolution made here; and there has been education Scotland and the belief in the power of knowledge and spread opportunity.

As well as this, there has been the story of egalitarian Scotland which resonates into the present and has deep roots in the Presbyterian tradition as well as the socialist movement. These have all been presented by some as positive stories but there have also been negative accounts such as the divided nation we have already cited which argues that Scotland is too disunited to be able to govern itself and determine its own future.[27]

Scotland's stories, like the ideas which define us, come to the fore at a given time and have dramatically changed through the centuries as in nearly every nation in the world. Once upon a time there was a powerful resonance to the idea of Scots (and Scots men) as a fighting people – from Scottish soldiers at war through the Empire, World Wars and the myth of 'Braveheart'. But that is now much less evocative and captivating a story and indeed has become noted as problematic in a world still defined by systemic violence whether domestically or internationally.

Scotland's voice and the relevance of exit and loyalty

One useful way to understand Scotland's changing status and place in the Union is to draw from the political scientist Albert Hirschman's influential *Exit, Voice and Loyalty* (1970). He defines these three concepts in the following ways: loyalty is the power of solidarity and co-operation; exit is consumer choice, approval and disapproval; voice is the power of collective organisation and opinion. The first two have been associated with the politics of the left and right respectively, yet it is third – voice – that Hirschman judges has the greatest potential and power and which he believes conventional politics most fears because within it is the power of self-organisation.

From late Victorian times there was an evolution of Scottish 'voice' in the Union which led to a period of 'loyalty' where Scotland's place in the UK was based on an expansion of the state and an implicit idea of citizenship and social contract between government and citizens. Once this political settlement began to weaken and be more contested in British politics, a significant part of Scottish opinion began to move to consider the potential of 'exit' from the Union – first embracing a partial autonomy in the form of a devolved Scottish Parliament and then considering formal independence.

Whether the Scots embark in the future on a formal 'exit' or more gradual process of withdrawal remains to be seen. Hirschman viewed that states can erect a high price for 'exit' and that this, as well as the perceived cost of entry, can affect the balance between 'voice' and 'exit'. He assessed that it is possible that 'the huge price of the "unthinkability" of exit may not only fail to repress voice but may stimulate it'.[28]

This set of relationships – voice, loyalty and exit – within the UK can be identified in the expression of 'voice' at play domestically within Scotland and how it then represents itself in institutional form and conveys itself beyond the country.

This brings forth concerns about what Scotland is being included in the notion of 'voice', whose are the dominant voices, and who is being excluded, deliberately and by oversight.

There is a contradiction in this between the desire of numerous Scottish institutions and bodies such as those historically associated with 'the Scottish lobby' and how it operated in relation to government and in particular Westminster pre-devolution. This organised group felt it had more influence if it could stress its unanimity and widespread consensus on an issue spreading from the forces of business (Confederation of British Industry (CBI) Scotland, Scottish Council for Development and Industry (SCDI)) to local government (Convention of Scottish Local Authorities (COSLA)) and trade unions (Scottish Trades Union Congress (STUC)). Such strength and breadth of opinion it was felt gave Scotland more clout in the corridors of power. This was historically how Labour politicians such as Tom Johnson and Willie Ross operated in the high politics of Westminster and Whitehall much to the envy of many of their other non-Scottish Labour politicians. But this also brought with it a tension about representation and democracy and the plurality or not of voices claiming to speak for organised opinion in the country.

It should be obvious in this set of analogies that recent decades have seen a shift in the balance between some of these forces. For example, the politics of access of 'the Scottish lobby' which served institutional opinion for the immediate decades after 1945 began to work less impressively in the Thatcher era. Although Margaret Thatcher reflected in her memoirs: 'In Scotland the Left still formed its own establishment which intruders challenged at their peril', in her opinion believing in the 1980s it still operated too effectively frustrating her agenda.[29]

The weakening of this approach is one element in the equation which led to the rise of the home rule question and then independence. Pivotal to this is the notion of 'voice' as laid out by Hirschman which saw in the 2014 referendum the collective power of people coming together, self-organising and remaking the contours of public debate and the public sphere.

This is surely a set of developments which, allowing for the retrenchment since, will have long-term consequences in how people in Scotland do politics, democracy and see their future. In the key concepts of this, the meaning of the Union and self-government alongside the relevance of story, will continue to adapt and change. But to understand how things might evolve in the future we need to understand how the wider idea of Scotland beyond the constitutional question has shifted post-1945 and it is to that we now turn.

PART II

The Story So Far

3

The Road to the Independence Debate: How Did We Get Here?

There is another radical quality in the Scots. It is their self-respect, and from this self-respect comes the most valuable element in the movement for Scottish home rule, an element not usually to be found in a small nation struggling to reassert itself. The Scottish movement is not built upon a sense of inferiority, upon fear or upon hate, but upon a desire for full self-respect.

Moray McLaren, *The Scots*, 1951

The background to the independence question is critical to understanding it, where Scotland is and how we got to this point, and from then to assess the lay of the land and future terrain of the debate. This is about a whole host of factors that are more fundamental than the ebbs and flows of successive Westminster governments, the appeal and lack of individual political parties and personalities and in particular Conservative governments and the nature of Thatcherism; all of these are in the mix but underpinned by longer-term dynamics which mean this debate is not going away.

In the first place is the historic experience of Scotland as a nation – once independent and which never stopped being a nation post-1707 – both in the imagination, institutionally, and legally. Secondly, consequences flow from this reality. Hence, post-1707 Scotland was a political and administrative entity which did not only not disappear or face conquest or complete assimilation into 'a Greater England' (as was the case with Wales in the sixteenth century), but existed at the level of an 'idea' or rather 'set of ideas' given there were, throughout history, contested versions of Scotland, all of which bought into the notion of this territory being a distinctive, communicative social space and political community.

A third factor has been the re-emergence of the modern constitutional debate about Scotland's future which has existed in its current form from the mid-1960s, dating it to the emergence and breakthrough of the SNP as an electoral force. However, its roots go back to previous eras, in particular to the National Covenant in the 1940s and to the forces of self-government in the Labour and Liberal Parties in previous decades.

Fourthly, what has underpinned many of these debates, informed and contributed to their momentum was an idea and concept of Scotland which went well beyond the constitutional and gave it a wider salience to what could be called 'bread and butter politics'. This was a point long misunderstood in the years running up to the setting up of the Scottish Parliament in 1999, when in the 1980s Tories opposing change tried to argue that talking about the constitution was a minority position of a small number of mostly middle-class campaigners, unconnected and without an understanding of 'the real world'.

Informing this debate then was a growing reawakening of Scotland as a political, democratic and civic community where government and administration should be held as directly accountable to the people as was humanly and practically possible. Part of this was a concern about the effectiveness of UK government, and how it could oversee and aid economic policy, growth and prosperity. Linked to this was a long-running discussion led by a variety of institutions with responsibilities in Scotland including a host of agencies and bodies who wanted to address a Scottish-specific agenda and prospectus.

The sum total of this activity is that institutions, expert opinion and the general public began to shift their focus and become more aware and conscious of Scotland as a distinctive territory, with its own characteristics, economic and social challenges and own set of problems. Many, if not all of these, were Scottish manifestations of wider UK problems but they were experienced differently in Scotland and the debate looking for solutions slowly began to deviate from the rest of the UK.

A fifth observation is that the Scottish question has been informed and significantly shaped by the electoral rise of the SNP. At such points, as its initial breakthroughs – with Winnie Ewing winning Hamilton in 1967 and the 1974 February and October UK general elections – this was aided by tapping popular discontent with the British state, government and the traditional political parties and order.[1] The SNP mined a terrain then which built on this growing awareness of a Scottish dimension and drew from the same headwind which in England gave the then Liberal Party major surges of support – particularly leading into the first 1974 election. But in Scotland, all of this was also about much more than the appeal of political parties and transcends the nature of the appeal of the SNP and its rise and fall as fortunes change as all parties do.

Sixthly, connected to all of the above is the observation that while part of this debate is about the re-emergence of Scottish nationalism, this debate should never be seen as just about Scottish nationalism or through the eyes of nationalism. This is a mistake and caricature which can happen from all sides. The most passionate pro-independence supporter might think that is only about Scotland's status as a nation and nationalism's role in reclaiming statehood. Similarly, some pro-Union voices may see the only assertions of independence as being the forces of Scottish nationalism. Many other strands need to be recognised and championed – as Scotland's debate cannot and should not be reduced to claims and counter-claims of whether 'my nationalism is better than your nationalism'.

Finally, the Scottish question has obviously been about the people that inhabit this country, but it has never just been about Scotland on its own, claiming our essentialism and unique character. It is true that it is about a degree of difference with the rest of the UK, but that does not imply separateness. Rather, the Scottish question has been informed by the nature of power and authority in the UK, and the nature of how UK governments and the British state have acted and in whose interests they have acted.

In particular, there are historic concerns about the character of the British state – its lack of nurturing and embedding progressive values (even after and including periods of Labour government), its lack of democracy and indeed contempt for democracy, and in recent decades, its regression into an even more reactionary form of politics. This latter development has seen over the past 40 years a ratcheting of UK politics to the right under Conservatives and Labour, and an increasing chasm between Scotland and Westminster politics, particularly when the Tories are in office at a UK level. Even more, the entire gravity and values of the political centre of the UK has become a set of advocates for 'global class Britain' – an unsustainable anti-social corporate capitalism which has served the people of the UK appallingly.

Why did the modern-day Scottish question come to the fore?

This shifting of Scotland over the arc of the post-war period (and over a longer time span than the usual takes of going back to Thatcherism, or the discovery of North Sea oil, or the disappointments with Westminster governments in the 1960s and

1970s) cannot be over-stressed. One question seldom asked in this entire debate is: why did the Scottish self-government debate come back in the way it did? And why did it then express itself in voting for the SNP in significant numbers? Looking at the reasons for this via a longer lens aids seeing the independence issue over a wider time frame.

In 1950s Scotland in the aftermath of the failure of the cross-party National Covenant which had seen a mass petition of up to two million Scots support home rule, the Scottish question on first examination seemed dead and buried. This was an era of very British politics, from the most northly point of Scotland to Devon and Cornwall and nearly every part of the 'four nations' in between. This was a time when in the 1951 election the Tory and Labour parties won a combined 96.8 per cent of the popular vote with the Liberals reduced to 2.6 per cent and six seats and the SNP 0.3 per cent of the Scottish vote standing a mere two candidates.[2] And this was not a one-off aberration: in the following election the two main parties won 96.1 per cent of the vote, the Liberals 2.8 per cent and six seats and the SNP 0.5 per cent of the Scottish vote with two candidates. This was an era of 'national swing', where 'class was thought to be everything' and the homogenisation of British politics thought permanent. There was discussion about whether the SNP should fold or whether the SNP and Liberals in Scotland should join forces. As the mainstream parties thought this new 'golden era' of pan-British consensus politics providing supposedly the best of Labour and Tory policies was permanent, underneath the surface change was afoot – in Scotland and across the UK.

In the period of Tory dominance that was 1950s Britain, Tory Prime Minister Harold Macmillan boasted that 'you've never had it so good' about an age of affluence, rising living standards and full employment. In Scotland, towards the end of the decade, the situation was significantly different. Scotland too saw growing prosperity but in 1958–59 growing economic divergence with the rest of the UK saw unemployment hitting over 100,000 for the first time post-war. The subsequent October 1959 UK election saw Scottish unemployment at 3.9 per cent while overall UK employment was 1.9 per cent; Macmillan was returned with a 100-seat majority while Scotland deviated from this in swinging to Labour. Such was the hold of British-wide politics that contemporary analysis of the election contained only one reference to Scotland's bucking the swing to the Tories – a trend which was to continue after 1959 and began a period of dominance by Labour north of the border – describing 'the leftward trend of Clydeside'.[3]

This backdrop resulted in a public debate about Scotland's economic state and its relative performance to the rest of the UK, resulting in interventions from government and public agencies talking about Scotland as an economic unit. There was a growing concern about the increasing branch factory nature of the economy with a decline in Scottish-owned firms, rise in headquartering elsewhere, and post-war encouragement of foreign investment – much American – and much encouraged by the economic body Scottish Council (Development and Industry) which, pre-Scottish Enterprise, was the most influential economic development body.

The Scottish Industries Exhibition at Kelvin Hall, Glasgow in September 1959 opened by Princess Margaret saw this economic shift, with more foreign-owned companies compared to five years previous. Such was the growing concern in some places that *The Times* noted that industry was characterised by 'Scots caution at its worst' and that 'What is needed is more imagination and initiative to create more new indigenous Scots enterprises.'[4]

Most well-known from this period is the Toothill Report of 1961 that contributed to a growing awareness of Scotland as a nation and economic territory.[5] Toothill has now entered into the popular lexicon of post-war Scottish history, widely cited but now seldom read. Its prospectus, while advocating the need for change, was grim and thin: more air travel to link Scotland to London, higher council house rents to provide shock therapy to the country's working people, all the while declaring it had 'no panacea for Scotland's economic problems' but demanding an end to 'propping up dying areas and the undue concentration on looking to others for help'.[6] This was not quite Thatcherism, but government-planned intervention with paternalism and impatience.

Academic Jack Brand, looking back at this from the 1970s, observed that: 'For the first time since the late 1920s Scotland was the centre of her own stage undistracted by foreign wars or worries' and that the sum of these debates was that this 'made Scottish people more and more conscious of Scotland as an economic unit'.[7]

At the same time, the nuclear question had also emerged in UK politics, bringing significant impact for Scotland as the US authorities asked for UK basing rights in November 1959 and the first deployment of nuclear weapons at Holy Loch occurring in March 1961. This brought the Campaign for Nuclear Disarmament (CND) into Scottish politics, radicalised young activists, and brought some into the SNP who, given its small size at this point, were to have a major impact.[8] The connection of the economic debate alongside the nuclear question, and a growing restlessness among some of the younger generation, contributed to an increasing awareness of a distinctive Scottish political culture, with the SNP beginning to make small progress in by-elections and organisation.

This was happening in the context of UK politics, as the 1950s turned out to be the high point of British politics from which dissatisfaction with the two main parties would but only grow. It was not just that there was a growing discontent with Westminster and UK government and a desire for a wider palate of political choices, which in Scotland was to benefit the SNP, in Wales Plaid Cymru, and in England the Liberal Party, along with, in the 1960s, an explosion of dissent and rebellion from trade union activism to student unrest. The point was that the re-emergence of the Scottish question and rise of the SNP was grounded in a number of significant shifts about Scotland, society and the UK.

One astute observer J.M. Reid at the end of the 1950s surveyed what he called 'the management of Scotland' and saw a political system increasingly ill-equipped for the future:

> It cannot be said that many Scottish Ministers, even Secretaries of State, have taken a very high place in British politics in our day: essentially they are still managers of a country with an obstinately individual life of its own which is apt to fret against the increasingly rigid framework of modern government from a distance...

Addressing the arrangements of administrative devolution, he viewed them dimly: 'Devolution which is merely administrative begins to look more and more anomalous as the years go by.'[9] This was written in 1959, that critical swing year and moment in Scottish politics and its relationship to UK politics. It was to take a long time – 20 years to the first 1979 devolution referendum and then another 20 years to the establishment of the Scottish Parliament – but the cracks were already appearing in the old ways of governing Scotland.

It was to take a while for others to notice that Scotland was shifting with 'the UK politics was everything' mindset too comforting to some including many in Scotland. In 1965 the nationalist writer Moray McLaren could state with confidence that 'a national movement... [has] no place in the brief history of the Scottish nation' – despite his fervent desire to will one into existence.[10] Even as society and culture were shifting and the old high-bound Scotland of authority and conformity waning, James Kellas, a trailblazer in academia making the study of Scottish politics more respectable, could write in 1968: 'Only a leisured, wealthy society can support organised culture, and Scotland has never had such a society.'[11] So much for the flowering of culture going on then or the idea of 'the Swinging Sixties'.

Despite this, the context was dramatically shifting in the late 1960s and early 1970s with a host of commentary suddenly rediscovering Scotland as a distinct political community in collections such as *Whither Scotland?* and *Anatomy of Scotland.*[12] In 1975 former Glasgow Labour councillor and future Liberal Democrat leader Vince Cable wrote in the left-wing collection *The Red Paper on Scotland* that: 'Scotland could, in all probability, expect in the 1980s to be more prosperous as an independent country.' He continued:

> The political 'left' is on the defensive in this situation. A generation of particularly sensitive Labour dominated local government has destroyed many illusions and left a vacuum of local leadership.[13]

Cable noted that seismic long-term political shifts were occurring within Scottish society – the decline of traditional industries, a shift in growth and population from West to East, the hollowing out of the established UK political parties, alongside instabilities and disequilibrium in the UK economy and politics which were fuelled by major changes in the world economy and capitalism. All of these raised questions about the survival of the UK and issue of Scottish independence.

The shift in the 'idea' of what Scotland was and how people lived in it, saw it and acted, should not be seen as uniform, or as one set of changes which were imposed or created across the nation. That would be to jump from one homogenised account

– that of high British politics in the 1950s – straight into another one of a united, uniform Scotland when nothing could be further from the truth.

There are many Scotlands and many contested interpretations of Scotland, but the point is that the central debate is now about what the 'idea' of Scotland is and what it should mean for how we are governed and organise ourselves as a society. This is the long backstory which has led us to our current place.

The re-emergence of Scotland as a political, democratic, social and communicative space is a fundamental shift in this nation, with profound consequences and implications not just for politics, but for society, culture and how we live our everyday lives. In this it is a break from the old Scotland which was beginning to die off in the late 1950s and early 1960s, which was administrative, authority based and a society of male elders who kept a whole pile of subjects out of public conversation (such as gay rights and sex education[14]). Of course, nothing is ever a simple old/new distinction, and in present-day Scotland we can still see elements of institutional conformity, of authority controlling debates, and no-go areas in public life. No doubt some will think these characteristics are connected to the Scottish Parliament or the rise of the SNP, but they reflect a society which has changed and opened up dramatically over post-war times but that still has progress to make.

The independence debate has been shaped by this long-term change and all of the above factors. It has been informed by this fundamental shift in how people think of Scotland and the consequences which flow from this which is still very much a live, evolving debate in the here and now.

The creation of the Scottish Parliament gave a distinctive platform, a democratic voice where previously there had been none, and a focus and energy around home-grown politics, all of which gave a boost to the cause of independence. Thus the victories of the SNP – in 2007 narrowly and then winning a parliamentary majority in 2011 – came from a political dispensation which was growing more conducive to taking seriously ideas of self-government and which then contributed to independence being taken more seriously by supporters and opponents.

All of this meant that, looking back at the 2011–14 referendum experience, something far-reaching happened which we are still living with the consequences of and that is still very alive. Namely, that the long campaign and debate leading up to 2014 brought independence in from the cold and made it part of the mainstream of the fabric of Scotland. That shift has to be understood in the longer perspective of how Scotland has changed from the 1950s and 1960s, and will continue to change in the future. Independence is now part of modern Scotland and part of the democratic debate. We will now turn to outlining the main arguments put for independence.

4

The Case for Independence

I think the more thoughtful and reflective participants on both sides of the debate understand that the obvious reason why Yes couldn't make it over the line last time around was the weakness of the economic case. For the middling people, those who tend not to be party members or campaigners, or particularly nationalistic, the key question is: will me and my family be better off or worse off? And in 2014 the balance of risk just wasn't right. The campaign was very left-wing, which to a degree it had to be to get Labour voters on board, but it made it very difficult for the middling folk to make the leap.

Andy Maciver, public affairs adviser,
personal communication, March 2022

The case for Scottish independence is about more than Scotland being a nation and nationhood, it is about more than history and what happened in the past – whether the long distant past of 1314 and 1320 or 1707, or more recently in 1979 and 1999 – and it is certainly about more than flags and symbols.

Rather, in recent decades the case for independence has coalesced around the issue of democratic legitimacy and accountability, alongside the belief that the best place to make political decisions about Scotland is within Scotland and the best people to make those decisions are the people of Scotland. Of course, such sentiments then come up against, and have to navigate, the realities of an interdependent world and to develop an idea of independence which fits with these times.

Seven arguments for independence

It is critical in understanding and conveying the case for independence that its messaging can be distilled into a set of concise and key themes which can be widely understood and disseminated to address voters. And it is important that independence advocates understand the rationale for the case for the Union and vice versa. Below are seven of the main arguments for independence.

- *The democratic argument*

As previously said the Scottish people are the best placed to decide their own future. Scotland should not have Westminster governments it did not vote for imposed upon it, as this limits and distorts choices, possibilities and our future as a society and nation.

- *Economic justice*

The UK is one of the most unequal countries in the developed world in terms of socio-economic inequalities, between regions and nations and generationally. The UK as it is currently constituted does not work for the vast majority of people in Scotland and for the vast majority of people within the UK. Scotland has the opportunity to chart its own course, different from this.

- *Social justice*

Despite the UK being one of the richest countries in the world, it is grotesquely unequal and characterised by a so-called welfare state which is not only ungenerous by the standards of most developed countries, but has been deliberately hollowed out in recent decades and is brutally punitive on the poor and those needing support from the state. It is a moral affront in a country as wealthy as the UK for this to occur as a deliberate act of public policy. Scotland has the opportunity to chart a different course on this – one more humane and compassionate.

- *The psychological dimension*

Having decisions made for Scotland elsewhere harms the collective well-being of Scotland. The psychological impact of power decisions and the networks and discussions around them being taken in London to a different set of priorities to what best suits Scotland has a lasting impact. It inculcates a prevalent feeling of powerlessness, that Scotland is distant and removed from where decisions are made, and is consistently ignored – and cumulatively the direction of the UK being one most Scots do not want. Bringing political power back home to Scotland would reverse some of these negative psychological effects and reduce this sense of powerlessness.

- *The endurance of the British Empire State*

The UK is not on any measurement a fully-fledged political democracy. Rather it is an Empire State – one whose ethos and cultures have been defined by systems of dominance at home and abroad, the legacy of Empire, the continuation of militarism and conquest around the world, and which is not at its core about the well-being of the people of the UK. Scottish independence deals a profound blow on the post-imperial delusions of the UK and the mantra of 'the UK punching above its weight'.

- *The UK is not a modern country*

The UK is not a modern state or country. Rather it is one defined and trapped by a caricature of its past. This can be seen in the continuation of outdated institutions and attitudes including the relics of feudalism such as the House of Lords and constitutional monarchy which sits as an integral part of the British state. Scotland has the potential to become a modern, democratic, outward-looking nation, all of which are not exactly revolutionary values but which the UK state has refused to champion.

- *A new internationalism*

The UK has increasingly played a disruptive and negative role on the international stage, the endless wars and military interventions and deployments, Brexit, failure of leadership on a host of areas and retreat on the environment and international aid. Scotland can chart its own course on the international stage, becoming a force for co-operation and solidarity, and an advocate for human rights and democracy around the world.

Scottish independence beyond narrow politics

Related to all of the above – and explored later – are cultural arguments for Scottish independence which are rooted in the terrain of culture, identity and social change in Scotland, and the potential of cultural change. This is based in a political intelligence which goes beyond party and formal politics, and instead is grounded in how Scottish society has changed, the nature of the public realm and public sphere, and how government and public agencies can aid fundamental and lasting change which contribute to addressing some of the key challenges of our age.

One response to the independence question is to comment that the UK may have its problems, but are they really enough to break up the Union? A second point is to stress that while Scotland sometimes does not get the government it wants in the UK, this is true of nations and territories everywhere from England to Yorkshire. Additional to this, it could be argued that Scotland as a nation and political community has survived and, in many respects, thrived in the Union. One pro-Union perspective never expressed could even dare to say that a Scotland with the self-confidence to debate independence is a product of the success of the Union. A unionism confident of itself would dare to put such an argument.

Connected to this is an assessment about the political territory where it is judged most appropriate and possible to bring about effective economic and social change. The case made by UK supporters is that its size — economically, in its resources, and demographically in population — allows for 'sharing and pooling' and a degree of redistribution, along with the management of risk.

Independence supporters can counter that the UK is disfigured by the scale and depth of inequality and that the actual redistribution which does take place is not far-reaching enough to counter these underlying conditions. Instead, it can be argued in the positive that Scottish independence could aid the creation of a wide public consensus that could pursue an agenda which puts social justice and greater equality centre-stage; which it is not possible to envisage under devolution and within the UK. The potential of this and some of the detail will be addressed later on — but suffice to say creating the conditions for such an environment in Scotland requires political argument and intervention and is not axiomatic; germane here is the poor record of devolved administrations of all hues (Labour and Liberal Democrats; SNP) to progress a politics of redistribution.[1]

One central tenet running through nearly all anti-independence commentary is the charge that Scotland would have difficulty surviving on its own without the largesse of the British state and fiscal transfers of the Barnett Formula. This even descends in the right-wing press and elsewhere to lambasting the Scots. *Daily Telegraph* and *Daily Mail* readers offer the following comments on Barnett: 'time to dump these Scottish ingrate freeloaders', that it is 'a slap in the face for the English tax payer' and 'the English are getting pumped to give money to everywhere else'.[2]

However, there is another way of looking at Barnett and this defence of Scotland in the Union. Leave aside that lots of right-wing opinion does not seem to be based on mutual respect and a spirit of solidarity, but more on open loathing and dislike of Scotland. Park as well the fact that when Barnett was conceived in the late 1970s it was meant to be a temporary measure which may become germane in discussions on its future.

The bigger question on Barnett is staking your position on the Union on what the right present as pork-barrel politics pure and simple. If UK politics continues on its present trajectory rightwards this looks unsustainable and indefensible in the long run. Making Barnett central to your case, begs the question: what price the Union after Barnett? And is a territory that can work to the benefit of Scottish independence.

A fundamental factor in the independence debate is the character of the British state. For all the continual invoking of far-reaching constitutional change and the promise from the likes of former UK Prime Minister Gordon Brown and others of federalism or quasi-federalism, this misreads the nature of the UK. Even in 1999 with the establishment of the Scottish Parliament and Welsh Assembly some constitutional political experts were claiming that the UK was incrementally moving towards a federal model and 'a possible step toward federalism'.[3]

With regard to federalism, it is inarguable that the UK is not such a state, is not becoming closer to being such a state, and under the influence of Brexit, is actually heading in the opposite direction – namely, the reconcentration of powers in the UK political centre. The UK has seen over the past two decades numerous calls for greater federalism and even some voices claiming that the establishment of the Scottish Parliament and Welsh Assembly in 1999 warranted such a description. Such an interpretation of devolution always seemed more wish-fulfilment than hard analysis: a prognosis borne out by the past 20 years.

Yet it is telling in that period that no detailed, credible plan for UK-wide reform which can be remotely described as federalism has emerged. Any such plan has to deal with some significant challenges which have consistently thwarted reformers. There is the predominance of England in population; the question of an English Parliament or English regional devolution; the nature of the political centre of the UK; and how to accommodate any change with the maintenance of parliamentary sovereignty.

Another obstacle in this is the reality of Brexit and what 'taking back control' has turned out to mean: a return to the politics of the UK political centre retrenching and reasserting its primacy which has entailed it doing so in relation to any rival institutions and centres of power in the UK from devolved bodies, to the judiciary, Supreme Court, Electoral Commission and more. This is a regression back to absolutism: the practice of an undivided, indivisible expression of the political centre unconstrained by formal checks and balances.

One rarely explored facet of this is the extent of the fetishi-sation of parliamentary sovereignty. This is not as many think the exclusive property of the right wing and their ideological project for the UK. It can also be found on the left, who have their own tradition and perspective clinging to this mindset.

For example, the Labour Party has throughout its history been wedded to a unitary state politics of parliamentary sovereignty, witnessed in the politics of Clement Attlee's post-war administration and that of Harold Wilson in the 1960s and 1970s and which Tony Blair and Gordon Brown refused to abandon post-1997.[4] Similarly, the Labour left's traditions, from Michael Foot to Tony Benn to Jeremy Corbyn, have embraced such a political perspective.

The nearest Labour have come to championing such a break with the British state and embracing far-reaching democratisation was during the Corbyn leadership when they commissioned a detailed prospectus for 'radical federalism' which was postponed from official launch and only saw the light of day post-Corbyn.[5] Its far-reaching canvas and fate is a salutary warning to any future Labour or other mainstream attempts to come up with a comprehensive critique. The British state will need more than a policy document to fundamentally change.

Instead, the dominant Labour tradition from the inception of the party to the present has been to advocate an all-powerful central British state which has the power and authority to take on and defeat reactionary resistance. Despite the central organs of the British state being profoundly reactionary, undemocratic and a barrier to progressive change – something underlined by successive Labour governments – the British Labour Party still to this day clings to the wreckage of the British state.

Independence, choice and morality

Independence involves choice, and embracing that Scotland has strategic choices it can make about the kind of society we want to be, its values and priorities. This is often stated in the general by SNP politicians without getting too much into the detail and the consequences flowing from such choice. To take one case: if an independent Scotland decided it wanted to dramatically reduce and even abolish child poverty the choice of prioritising this would entail costs and delays elsewhere, but would mean that Scottish public opinion had agreed to this ordering of priorities.

Nor can independence be merely a slightly enlarged version of devolution whereby the Scottish Parliament gradually becomes more powerful, taking over area after area until one day Scotland wakes up and finds that it is independent. This is an independence which is presented as a continuity Scotland – a safety-first, risk-averse future – to not scare the middle classes and businesses which would minimise the prospect of change and rationale for the entire enterprise. It would reduce an independent Scotland to the equivalent of a 'little Britain' north of the border which would potentially embark on undercutting rUK on corporate taxation, deregulation and privatisation. A different logic on independence has to be presented, and a very different approach to winning over middle-class interests who worry about their pensions and assets, and see in independence a threat to the security that they currently have in the UK.

This scenario occasionally came to the fore in the 2014 campaign with James Foley and Pete Ramand putting the case for a radical Yes in contrast to an economic and social status quo Yes: 'If Scottish rulers, politicians and managers conform to consensus assumptions about national welfare ... we could produce many of Britain's current problems.' They conclude with the suggestion of an alternative path: 'Scotland could aim to copy the example of its non-British neighbours, and define a social citizenship against Britain's neoliberal citizenship.'[6] This is true but will require political prioritisation, agency and a widespread public debate before independence as well as afterwards.

George Kerevan assessing the terrain from 2014 to the present takes the view:

> In the popular mind, Scottish independence has come to signify both resistance to Conservative austerity policies imposed from London and a naïve hope that a separate Scottish state can manage globalism in Scottish interests.

This requires, he believes, serious work to address the question: 'how can a small, independent state maintain a balance between popular national control and global market pressures?'[7]

There is also a moral dimension to Scottish independence founded on a rejection of the British state and what it represents in the present as well as its past misdemeanours, and believing that Scotland could do better – by being more compassionate, supportive of solidarity, and playing a co-operative role in the world. This sentiment is sometimes explicit, but more often implicit, but it does have to be qualified.

This sentiment is about Scotland as a moral community and hence draws from deep and historic traditions of the Kirk and Presbyterianism as well as Christian and ethical socialism. In its assertions of morality and ethics it has to be careful not to adopt an attitude of superiority and rather ground any morality in facts and choices.

The independence supporter Stephen Maxwell put this in *Arguing for Independence* in 2012: 'The ethical dimension often embraces claims about the moral worth of the policies an independent Scotland would pursue' but as he points out there are rival ethical interpretations about the choices in an independent Scotland – on public spending, taxation, defence and every area.[8] There is to some a positive moral dimension to the UK and the case for it. There are thus many different and competing moral interpretations and independence, like the Union, does not and should not be able to claim a monopoly of virtue.

This underlines the pitfalls of a political debate which is dominated by the competing claims of two nationalisms – Scottish and British – which both embody an element of certainty and belief in the self-evident logic of their case. The grounds for independence cannot be predicated upon this terrain which negates the complexities, ambiguities and compromises inherent in the modern world and politics, including an independent Scotland. The same is true for those making the case for the defence of the UK which is explored in the next chapter.

The shape of independence and work needing done

It is obvious to everyone that independence needs to update and completely revisit its prospectus compared to the 2014 offer. Not only does this cover the substance and outlook of independence and how the world has changed since then, but how this is done which goes beyond process to how independence in the here and now embodies and champions democracy.

First, the nature of any Scottish Government White Paper cannot be just sprung on voters from the recesses of the civil service machine and SNP leadership as it was in 2014.[9] Then there was the excuse of an ongoing campaign, but it still frayed nerves and lost goodwill. Any future official offer has to learn from the shortcomings of the past and be created by a set of processes which allow it to be owned by a wider constituency and seen as emblematic of the kind of democracy Scotland aspires to at its best. To do otherwise, dropping a single huge tablet of received wisdom from on high will come at a cost and act as a disincentive for some. It is also important to learn from the UK government's 2014 response which involved a dozen-plus impact papers published over the course of more than a year which then gave them multiple hits while Yes were left waiting for the Scottish Government White Paper.

Then there is the content of that 2014 White Paper, its specific pledges, take on the world and outlook which was one that everything was going to be alright and that there were little risks in independence. Those who took an anti-independence position then and now believe that there needs to be significant work. Magnus Linklater, former editor of *The Scotsman* and *The Times Scotland*, states: 'Without honesty there is a lack of trust. Without trust no government merits support.'[10] John McTernan, who worked in Downing Street as Tony Blair's Chief of Staff observes: 'Post-Brexit, there is a higher bar for the credibility of claims of "sunlit uplands" by proponents of change.'[11]

Others sympathetic or pro-independence believe more work is needed. The academic Iain Docherty from Stirling University looks back at the shortcomings of the 2014 offer and its mindset, and need for a fundamental shift now:

> 2014 was all about 'we're already rich, it'll be easy'. I didn't like it at the time (and said so) but had zero influence. I think it's pretty clear now that the world is an increasingly fractious, unstable or even dangerous place. To my mind this reinforces the need for public debate to scrutinise the implications of the status quo as much as the proposal for change, because actually the choice is between two different *trajectories* that are dynamic.[12]

The academic Ciaran Martin was lead negotiator for the UK government in the creation of the Edinburgh Agreement which led to the 2014 vote. He makes a different point about the danger of what can happen when independence has to answer every eventuality about what could happen in the future:

> The whole attempt, as in 2014, to present a 'definite' view of what post-independence Scotland might look like is polit-

ically understandable in advance of a referendum, but a crazy basis for governing should a referendum be won by those seeking independence. A referendum is not a general election campaign with a 'manifesto' for implementation. No one should pretend that it is.[13]

The author and campaigner Paul Mason takes another tack:

The 2013 White Paper *Scotland's Future* was a fiction whose believability, like the best works of literature, rested on what it didn't say. A new White Paper for the 2020s has to be concrete: it has to spell out the pathways and the costs of fiscal and monetary independence. It has to contain not just numbers but a project plan, with clear phases and risk assessments. Its centrepiece has to be an explanation of how an independent Scotland would achieve the goals it is committed to by COP26, and how it ensures both sovereignty and national security in a world order characterised by volatility and power-grabs.[14]

Second, within the above the pathways of a new constitutional settlement has to be explicit. This would entail mapping out how the people of Scotland would become active citizens in the creation of their own country and democracy in ways which went beyond citizen's assemblies and juries. There are global examples of participative and deliberate democracy out there in constitution making, for example, in Iceland and Ireland, and combining that with the power of story and storytelling could make this aspire to a genuine national exercise.[15]

Third, for the above to have real power and meaning it has to be rooted in a culture and practice of more than nominal rights recognising the limited democracy within Scotland at the present. For example, in 2014 the Yes official prospectus took a benign view of the Scottish Parliament holding power to account and ability to do so even more in an independent Scotland when a more honest assessment would say this was an area where more work was needed. This is a view which Neal Ascherson, one of the most acute observers of Scottish society and politics over the past five decades, takes when surveying the present landscape. In his mind, the most important challenge facing Scotland is revitalising its democracy by:

> Resolving to give Scotland a completely new distribution of local power, with real authority at the local level. i.e.: the European model (look at German local government, for example). A diametrically different constitutional doctrine: abolish parliamentary sovereignty, replace it with popular sovereignty in which power rests at the base of the pyramid and is only leased upwards to the next layer of authority. People prate about how 'the people of Scotland are sovereign'. No they aren't. Not until we plan and build a detailed new power structure which makes it a reality.[16]

This is what Scotland needs to think about in how to make democracy real and relevant; to democratise our public life, institutions and public sphere; tackle concentrations of power, and decentralise.

All these three strands – the Yes offer, constitution building and greater democracy – have to be connected to a tangible, real politics which is about the Scotland of the future in which people feel they have a collective say and ownership. If it falls short of this at the first hurdle, or is seen as the near-exclusive property of one party, then it will undoubtedly have less appeal and raise doubts. A generous, confident, outgoing independence would understand and engage with the substance of the argument for the Union and it is to that we turn in the next chapter.

5

Understanding the Case against Independence

We went through the factors that bind in the UK. We came up with a list that help us think and behave as a Union:

- The Queen
- The Armed Forces
- The welfare state/National Health Service
- Economic stability
- The BBC
- The UK passport
- The Olympic Games (every four years)

Potent though these factors are, we need more – considerably more. The Union is no longer a fixed map in the collective UK mind; no longer an automatic pilot guiding shared consciousness. I wish it were. I profoundly hope it can be once more.

Peter Hennessy, *The Kingdom to Come: Thoughts on the Union Before and After the Scottish Referendum*, 2015

The debate on independence, and winning the public discussion, necessitates that people understand the logic and rationale of opposing views to their own. This is true of both sides; and particularly true of the independence side as only through understanding the case for the Union can it win over converts to achieve victory in any future vote.

Understanding your opponents can also lead to a better quality of political debate, where there is a degree of mutual comprehension and shared ground. US Secretary of Defense Robert McNamara served under Presidents John F. Kennedy and Lyndon B. Johnson, and in his film *The Fog of War* about a life in public service he reflected upon the Cuban missile crisis between the US and Soviets in 1962, and American involvement in Vietnam. Looking back on the first, McNamara felt that having people in JFK's team who could understand Soviet leader Nikita Khrushchev possibly made the difference about whether the world faced a nuclear war. On the escalating US military involvement in the Vietnam War in the 1960s, he assessed that the US never came to understand the North Vietnamese, drawing from this the lesson that you should always 'empathise with your enemy' and always, even in war, not dehumanise them to better follow what their motivations and calculations are.[1]

We are not yet living in as high-octane an environment as the two McNamara outlined (although the Russian invasion of Ukraine in March 2022 has brought new tensions and the prospect of a new Cold War). And for all the occasional hyperbole, the SNP are not similar to a Vietcong liberation army or the British state to the Americans, despite an official in Boris Johnson's Downing Street talking in 2021 comparing the SNP to 'the Viet Cong'.[2] But this insight assists us in recognising that this debate is firstly aided by mutual respect, secondly that there is a case for the Union which should be understood, so that its logic and appeal can be better debated and challenged, and voters aided by better quality public conversations.

The argument for the Union has several different aspects. There is one strand based on a defence of the UK and notion of the Union as 'a partnership for good'.[3] Another is predicated on the argument that Scotland gets 'the best of both worlds' by being in the Union and having within it a degree of autonomy. A further line of argument emphasises the risk and uncertainty inherent in today's world and the shock absorbers that are supposedly more resilient due to the economic size of the UK. And a more pragmatic perspective concedes that in principle in an ideal world independence could be a good thing, but in the real world would all that upheaval and disruption be worth it?

Seven arguments for the Union

The case for the Union should then be better understood by those who are pro-independence. And the opposite case is equally valid: the case for independence should be more fully comprehended by those pro-Union. Below are seven main arguments to maintain the Union and Scotland's role within it from the pro-Union perspective:

- *Financial issues*

Scotland is better off financially in the Union, it is asserted. The UK government via the Barnett Formula engages in fiscal transfers to Scotland, alongside Wales and Northern Ireland. This would clearly stop in the event of independence, leaving Scotland with a difficult period of fiscal transition, and in the eyes of pro-Union opinion, an unsustainable financial deficit that would have to be rectified by massive cuts of 'shock therapy' proportions.

- *Borders*

A hard border between Scotland and England would be divisive, disruptive and costly, it is claimed. The notion of an independent Scotland would, post-Brexit, see the issue of the border, border controls and custom checks raised as threats. Scotland post-independence, if it joins the EU, could have a hard border with the rest of the UK, restricting movement of goods and even people, it would be claimed. This could make the Scottish–English border potentially the subject of political friction and controversy in a manner similar to the Northern Irish–Britain border down the Irish Sea after Brexit.

- *Money*

Money matters – that brings us to the currency question. What currency would an independent Scotland use? This taps into concerns about transition, uncertainty and costs including how an independent currency would be underwritten, and how strong it would be on global markets. Related to this is the subject of eventual euro membership (or not). There are also related concerns about mortgages and pensions, taken out in UK sterling and/or via UK financial institutions, and how these would be affected. All of which poses the spectre of financial instability versus the supposed 'stability' of the UK.

- *Europe*

Where would an independent Scotland sit in relation to Europe? The details of membership of EU re-entry, timing and ultimate membership conditions post-Brexit are another set of variables. This brings up the subject of the border, currency issues and also the prospect of invoking an isolated independent Scotland on the island of Britain with major barriers between it and its English neighbour.

- *Identity*

Independence is not like devolution. It is an existential debate and choice. It throws up questions about who people are, how they see themselves, who they identify as, and deep issues of belonging. Thus, the argument goes, this is not just about democracy, governance and legal citizenship, but about how people see themselves, feelings and emotions, and a deeper social sense of community and citizenship. Independence for some is an attack on their sense of self, while seeing British identity as much as an emotional identity as well as a legal entity and identity.

- *Solidarity*

Solidarity, co-operation and coming together are positive virtues. This is the politics of class above nation in the pro-Union argument, that at times in the past has been put with conviction by the labour movement and trade unions. This point stresses that a worker in Coatbridge has more in common with a worker in Coventry than a Scottish worker does with a landowner living in the same country. A secondary argument states that workers do not need extra divisions put in the way of how they organise and co-operate. A politics of solidarity is not about dividing but uniting the working classes across the UK and not breaking up existing labour and trade union organisations.

- *Risk*

Greater risk is inherent to the independent project, pro-Union voices claim. An independent Scotland might be conceded by some pro-Union views to be theoretically an attractive proposition. But the reality is of risk and uncertainty which cannot be quantified or calculated this side of independence, but it is stressed is inherent to the project. An added dimension is the context of the world filled with threats, shocks and unpredictability. In this train of thinking, why launch an independent

Scotland out of the supposedly settled UK in a global environment filled with instability, agents of disinformation and disrupters? Independence in this argument is an idea for a different time which of course is never now, but is seen as particularly unsuited to the current age of global crisis and chaos.

The UK on the international stage

As well as the above strands there is the argument that the UK is 'a force for good' in today's world of threats and instability and a major player in the world's leading forms and institutions, able to make its voice heard in the UN Security Council, NATO and in its close military and security relationship with the USA. An independent Scotland would arguably not have the gravitas, respect, history or experience to assume a similar role – for the foreseeable future at least.

This stresses that Britain's standing in the world draws on its values, history and tradition to champion democracy and oppose forces trying to undermine our way of life; and Scotland gains greater influence and weight through that influence. Yet this version of talking up Britain's role has been fundamentally weakened by disastrous UK foreign policy decisions of recent years, including the Iraq war and 20-year Afghanistan military operation, alongside Brexit which has completely undermined the UK's long-term alliance with its European neighbours, and weakened its global influence.

A related argument to this sees the continuation of the UK as positive in a world of increasing instability, threats, both conventional and non-conventional, and the need for Western co-operation and unity. This can stress the virtues of the UK as an international force and the flipside, that some of the main enemies of the West and democracy such as Russia could potentially gain from the break-up of the UK, an argument with some salience in times of major global disruption and crisis.[4]

Another major dimension for the Union is to emphasise the positive stories of the UK and Britain of the past. These include shared collective endeavours experienced by the UK population such as the mass mobilisation of the Second World War and the defeat of Nazism and fascism. This was the precursor to the subsequent creation of the welfare state and NHS by the post-war Labour government. For a long time, these offered a shared prospectus across the political spectrum which invoked pride and support, but this has become less so as UK politics has shifted rightwards in recent times and the once-relied upon institutions are much less the safety nets and cradle-to-grave services they were intended to be.

The journalist Alan Cochrane noted in relation to Scottishness the influence of Britishness in what is a two-way process: 'there is no recognition among most Nats that Scots are as much the authors of Britishness as are the English...'[5] His argument was that some independence supporters were positing a completely separate idea of Scottishness, morally superior and wiped clean of all the bits of history people disapproved of, allowing Scots to claim all the good parts (the welfare state, NHS, etc.) and hence deeply ahistorical.

It has been claimed that independence has a 'pick 'n' mix' approach to what it likes and does not like in the present-day UK and that in 2014 it was 'guilty of attempting to have their cake and eat it, by implying that an independent Scotland could preserve certain aspects of being part of the UK... even a sense of "Britishness".'[6]

As the 'good news' account of Britishness has retreated into the past and become more threadbare, so one pro-Union perspective has become more pronounced – emphasising the supposed financial Armageddon of independence which would reduce Scotland it seems to a modern wasteland. This interpretation stresses that there is a financial 'Union dividend' for Scotland in being part of the UK, and that this is an intrinsic part of the 'pooling and sharing' of resources and risk that makes up the UK.[7] This is a defence of the Union based on transactional relations and seems to predicate a pro-Union defence on the grounds of the maintenance of the Barnett Formula or the equivalent from Westminster. This is a very narrow front line on which to pitch the case for the Union – one which is not only defensive, conditional on the largesse of Barnett and future actions of UK governments, and represents an argument which is in retreat. Its thin line can be seen in the other major pro-Union position still to the fore: demanding of independence that it answer every variable about the nature of a future self-governing Scotland in the here and now.

Thus, this perspective declares, what will be Scotland's future currency, borders, EU terms and membership, fiscal policies and defence policy, to name but the most obvious. This has become part of the last line of defence of the Union, demanding certainty and assurances from a future independence, and taking succour in the answers not being forthcoming and not fulsome enough when they are. Pro-Union sentiment tends to ignore that this is not a positive case for the Union, but positioning the main body of your argument on entirely negative terrain.

The pro-Union case may be able to hold on to these positions for a period, holding out as a besieged defensive line against the parries and thrusts of the independence case but in so doing facing attrition and exhaustion. It is an incredibly high-risk strategy, and offers little prospect of remaking and redefining the debate in the long run. This is an unsustainable position, and the best that can be said is that it is hoping that by playing for time something will come up. This could be in the positive, in that somehow the UK government address some of the fundamentals of this debate by actions such as reforming the political centre or genuinely 'levelling up' across the UK; or in the negative such as the SNP imploding or becoming exhausted by its years in office and running out of steam. The former does seem less than likely for the foreseeable future.

Kevin Hague who set up the pro-Union organisation These Islands has spent much time on the finances of Scotland and independence, but he does not think this is the main terrain of the debate. He states that this is about more important things:

> My opposition to breaking up the UK is not based on purely transactional economics. There are more fundamental issues relating to solidarity with people across these islands – the bonds of a common citizenship built through centuries of shared endeavour, made real in the form of our welfare state – that mean I struggle to imagine choosing to abandon the UK.[8]

John Lloyd, author of *Should Auld Acquaintance Be Forgot: The Great Mistake of Scottish Independence*, takes a wider interpretation of why independence is a bad idea:

> There are many reasons why I am against Scottish independence, but the most important can be summed up by 'impoverishment' – impoverishment of Scotland, at least into the medium-term future; impoverishment of the United Kingdom, which is enriched by Scotland's membership; and the cultural impoverishment inherent in nationalism's sour view of England, the UK, unionism and attempts at objective journalism, which the SNP has spread and popularised.[9]

The pro-Union case's lack of understanding of Scottish independence

Pro-Union thought does seem to be bereft of significant strategic insight and lacking in a political intelligence which is now running at all-time low. One example of this latter feature is the propensity of too many pro-Union supporters to believe in a complete caricature of Scottish independence to the extent that they are wilfully refusing to understand the main tenets of its case.

A visible strand of criticising independence has been to pose it as motivated by romantic, sentimental notions looking backward and obsessed with flags, symbols and ancient shibboleths. Ben Jackson of Oxford University, author of a study of the evolution of independence thinking, believes: 'People who are opposed to Scottish independence think it is a nativist, ephemeral, emotional creed.'[10]

Former Scottish Labour leader Johann Lamont in 2014 posed the choice as between two competing visions of society – one open and the other insular:

The debate is not Scotland versus England or Scotland versus the Tories. It is an argument among Scots, a choice of two visions – one insular and turning away, the other open, embracing the interdependency of our world.[11]

Former UK Prime Minister Gordon Brown has characterised the argument of independence as: 'the SNP want to force us to choose between being Scottish and British'. In the 2014 referendum, Brown observed that the debate was narrowed to a choice where being 'pro-Scottish was to be for independence' and to be against it was to be 'anti-Scottish'.[12]

Brown does get some things right. While trying too hard to present Brexit nationalism as the same as Scottish and Welsh nationalism, beholden to an 'absolutist-us-versus-them view of the world', he does comprehend the one-dimensional nature of what is on offer from the UK government, commenting that: 'Boris Johnson's "muscular unionism" simply plays into the hands of Nicola Sturgeon... He wants to badge new roads and bridges as British, as if hoisting more Union Jacks will make people decide they are only British, and not also Scottish or Welsh.'[13]

These two Brown interventions, like many, have elicited a fascinating array of responses. His stereotyping of Scottish independence was welcomed by some passionate believers in the cause who felt that he was correct in posing this simple binary choice. Comments such as: 'Well done Gordon Brown, you finally got it!'; 'He'll be absolutely right! It won't be the hardest decision of my life!' and 'Once so proud to be British, it's all gone, Scottish it is.'[14] Underlining that, while Brown misrepresented and misread the debate at its fringes, there was an unlikely common ground between Union voices trying to do down independence and its more fervent supporters impatient for change.

Brown's more substantial *New Statesman* piece brought forth a litany of responses including from former Labour MP, MSP and Scottish minister John Home Robertson who said: 'Brexit Britain is itself a disruptive nationalist entity' and that 'Brown's critique of "narrow nationalists" who "do not want to co-operate with their closest neighbours" is in fact a disturbing critique of what Britain has become.'[15]

There is also the claim of a moral dimension to the case for the UK that celebrates the country's history of standing up for democracy, the rule of law, due process and the UK's role in the Second World War and Cold War standing against tyranny and military aggression: none of which dwells on the negative side of the history of the UK. The main defenders of the UK along these lines without apology have been, not surprisingly, Tories, but Gordon Brown has also tried to make the case for progressive Britishness and a country based on 'a golden thread which runs through British history' – which does sound a bit like the Whig interpretation of Britain's past told by the liberal British establishment.[16] In 2014 Brown explicitly laid claim to a moral argument about the benefits of the Union having: 'a fundamental moral purpose – that no matter where you reside and what your background is, every citizen enjoys the dignity of not just equal civil and political rights, but the same social and economic rights too'.[17] This thread draws upon a British exceptionalism, a selective understanding of the UK's past, and even in Brown's account, misrepresenting the present, talking about 'the same social and economic rights', when 20 years into the Scottish Parliament that is no longer true across 'the four nations' of the UK.

One final argument made against Scottish independence is the allegation that it is grounded on deep-seated anti-English prejudice. There are numerous examples of this charge. Former Scottish Liberal Democrat leader Willie Rennie, in the aftermath of the Euro 2020 football tournament (played in 2021) and England's success, talked of 'growing anti-English sentiment in Scotland' and people moving from England to Scotland being 'made to feel like strangers in their own home'.[18] In his aforementioned book, John Lloyd in an attempt to critique independence brought forth anti-Englishness in Scottish politics and culture, citing Hugh MacDiarmid, Tom Nairn and James Kelman, on the latter two providing thin examples, stating: 'The anti-English sentiment is the expression of a political wound... now allowed release as nationalist feeling rises and becomes socially legitimised, the more because it is aimed only at upper-class snobs, ever fair game.'[19]

Despite this strategic weakness in unionism, its deliberate refusal to understand Scottish independence, and its rationale and confidence being at a historic low, there is still a case for the Union which has popular support and a logic – and which has to be understood and not misrepresented by the forces of independence. The forces of self-government cannot fall into the trap that the unionist case has about it – and nor can they afford complacency and the belief that the argument for change can win by default.

Taking all of this into account, it is still salutary to note that the British establishment may not now be what it once was, and does not have the sense of self-assuredness and elan that it had in previous times. Yet, even in decline it still has significant resources of intelligence and insight to draw upon. Some of these have at least some small grasp of the multiple crises of the UK – both domestic and geo-political. In this milieu, it is just possible to imagine that elements of British elite opinion may have the wherewithal to attempt to make one last serious attempt to 'save' the UK and undertake a final grand gesture to remake the Union and a version of it which keeps Scotland in it.

This above scenario may seem unlikely to many – who have grown weary of Labour mood music on federalism without any convincing detail. But what it does underline is that the debate on Scotland's future, its relationship with the rest of the UK and how the UK evolves, is not static. Rather, it is influenced by a variety of factors, including the Welsh and Northern Irish dimensions, what happens to England, and the nature of the UK post-Brexit.

There is no comforting option of clinging to the status quo, and no safe journey back to the Britain of the past pre-Thatcher or the high point of Labour Britain circa 1945–65. This sometimes seems to be the political outlook underpinning the Labour leadership: of just wishing they could turn back the clock on recent decades to some supposed 'golden era'. It is an approach which hinders understanding the scale of the task of reforming and democratising the British state.

This is a political debate shaped by fluidity, change and continual shocks and surprises. This can assist the case for independence if it is open-minded, generous and serious about the challenges ahead. But it could just assist the forces of the

Union if it comprehends the state it is in and crises it faces. That would require it recognising that the Scottish discussion is part of a wider one about the nature of the UK which so far it has been unwilling to do and act seriously and systematically upon. We now move to explore the main policy, intellectual and substantive points which inform the push for Scottish independence and the multiple crises of the UK.

PART III

Scotland's Choices and the Divided Kingdom

6

Empire State Britain

Labour leaders have never made clear to their followers the extent to which British prosperity depends on the exploitation of the coloured peoples. It has always been tacitly pretended that we could 'set India free' and raise our own wages simultaneously. The first task of the Labour Government is to make people realise that Britain is not self-contained, but is part of a worldwide network. Even the problem of introducing socialism is secondary to that. For Britain cannot become a genuinely socialist country while continuing to plunder Asia and Africa; while on the other hand no amount of nationalisation, no cutting-out of profits and destruction of privilege, could keep up our standard of living if we lost all our markets and our sources of raw materials at one blow.

George Orwell, *The British General Election*,
Commentary, November 1945

I am not going to pretend that this country is something we are not. Every day I go into an office so vast that you could comfortably fit two squash courts and so dripping with gilt bling that it looks like something from the Kardashians and as I sit at the desk of George Nathaniel Curzon I sometimes reflect that this was once the nerve centre of an Empire that was seven times the size of the Roman Empire at its greatest extent under Trajan and when I go into the Map Room of Palmerston I cannot help remembering that this country over the last two hundred years has directed the invasion or conquest of 178 countries – that is most of the members of the UN...

Boris Johnson, UK Foreign Secretary, Speech to
Conservative Party Conference, 2 October 2016

The UK is increasingly characterised and shaped by being a divided kingdom – economically, socially and politically. This is not an accident or a product of some random factors. Nor is it just a product of Conservative and Labour governments which have failed to tackle many of the fundamentals. And nor is this state of division and inequality something that can be mostly blamed on Thatcherism and New Labour, as if the UK before them was immune to such factors and that we can yearn to return to this past of Britain pre-1979.

Rather the scale and depth of inequality which so disfigures and distorts life in the UK is the direct result of the unreformed centralising British state and the incontrovertible fact that the UK is at its core not a fully-fledged political democracy. This, alongside the historic nature of British capitalism, are the two main drivers in underpinning and widening the grotesque degrees of inequality of income and wealth which have come to overshadow British life.

Key to this are the central characteristics of the British state which is at its core still an Empire State. This is an entity defined by a culture and practice of systems of domination, militarism and a lack of recognition and support for a culture of citizenship and nurturing of the well-being of the people of the UK.

Empire State Britain affects the UK not just externally in how the UK is seen and acts globally. It affects nearly every part of the UK domestically with a culture and mindset of Empire at home which exists to this day. This analysis of the

UK used to just be held by the left and anti-racist campaigners, but has now become more widespread.

Forty years ago Labour left-winger Tony Benn could state that 'Britain is a colony' in terms of Empire and that Labour's role was to offer 'leadership in that liberation struggle and end our colonial status' – which was thought at the time to be dramatically overstating the state of Britain and inaccurate.[1] Black academics and theorists Paul Gilroy and Stuart Hall understood that the legacy of the British Empire had created a UK where migration from the Commonwealth had produced discrimination, white backlash and mainstream politicians such as Margaret Thatcher, and Labour figures such as David Blunkett, willing to play the race card. Gilroy and others wrote about 'the Empire striking back' meaning the reaction on the right of the Tory Party to immigration, multiculturalism and its effects on British society with an analysis which was prescient about the evolution of Thatcherism but also the trajectory of UK politics since under Tory and Labour governments.[2]

Today this is about more than the continuation of racist, discriminatory policies, the 'hostile environment' policy of the UK Home Office, dawn raids and deportations, the dehumanisation of asylum seekers and refugees, and legacy of Windrush, appalling as they all undoubtedly are. Empire State Britain is about something even more far-reaching, going to the core of what the UK is and stands for and how the central organs of government rule and see the people of the entire country.

The Empire State and Britain's global reach and retreat

This Empire State has been shaped and reinforced by numerous factors including the partial process of democratisation more fully explored in the next chapter. The ethos of the Empire State is based on the UK's acquisition – through conquest, administration of and extractive brutal exploitation – of territories across the world which made up the British Empire. The historian Caroline Elkins, who helped expose the brutal violence of British rule in Kenya post-independence, coined the phrase 'legalised lawlessness' to describe the formal basis for how the Empire functioned.[3]

The British addiction to militarism is seen in the fact that British armed forces have been involved in active combat according to one account in every single year since the onset of the First World War in 1914. The writer Ian Cobain commented on this record:

> The British are unique in this respect: the same could not be said of the Americans, the Russians, the French or any other nation. Only the British are perpetually at war.[4]

There is a direct relationship between the kind of state that evolved in the UK and the development of British capitalism. Significant UK military and intelligence operations often involved the protection of British overseas commercial interests. Thus, the 1953 UK-backed coup with the CIA which overthrew the Iranian government of Mohammad Mosaddegh was a direct result of the Iranians nationalising the Anglo-Iranian Oil Company (itself now a part of BP).[5] This restored the company to the private sector and led to the reinstallation of a regime headed up by the Shah, ultimately leading to the Iranian revolution of 1979.

A few years after this coup, the Egyptian leader Gamal Abdel Nasser nationalised the Suez Canal administered by the Anglo-French Canal Company and regarded as vital to British commercial and military interests. This produced in October 1956 the joint UK–French invasion and occupation of the Suez Canal undertaken by Anthony Eden and French Premier Guy Mollet in association with the Israelis who invaded Egypt from the east: the false pretext of the British and French intervention being to separate Egyptian and Israeli forces.[6] What followed in Suez was illustrative of the decline in UK power. The US, having not been consulted or forewarned, publicly refused to support the action and moreover as sterling fell under international pressure US authorities refused to support it, leaving the UK little option but to withdraw militarily. Added to this, Eden had denied in the Commons that this was undertaken with prior agreement with the Israelis and in January 1957 under the pretext of ill-health he resigned with his reputation forever tainted by Suez.

The reality of imperial withdrawal

The UK slow withdrawal from formal Empire is now presented as a great act of British benevolence and wisdom, compared favourably to the French and Belgians. But it wasn't as clear-cut or far-sighted at the time. After the independence of India and Pakistan in 1947 and retreat from Palestine in 1948, the British were slow on decolonisation and particularly in relation to the African continent, wanting to encourage British-created 'federations' where white minority settlers would retain power and hence the UK would still by proxy have influence.

The UK continued post-Suez to believe that it could remain a major global power, the West's second superpower after the USA. Events proved different with popular uprisings in parts of Africa, the idea of federations proving unworkable, and in February 1960 Harold Macmillan gave his 'winds of change' speech to an unreceptive Cape Town Parliament in apartheid South Africa. Six weeks later the South African regime showed the world its brutality in Sharpeville massacring 69 people and the following year was expelled from the Commonwealth.

A backdrop to this was France's announcement in 1960 of plans to withdraw from most of its African colonies bar Algeria and the Belgian debacle in the Congo, all against the realpolitik of the Cold War, and the UK and US worrying whether newly independent states would be pro-Western or tilt to the Soviets: which aided the British speeding up decolonisation in the coming decade. Meanwhile the UK, searching for a new international role, belatedly decided to apply to join the European Economic Community (EEC) in 1961 (after it had been set up in 1957), an application vetoed by the French President de Gaulle in 1963.

These strategic problems were inherited by Labour and Harold Wilson when they won office in 1964. From then on, they experienced pressure on the pound from international markets but wished to avoid devaluation with the loss of status and effect on the pound's global role. And despite significant constraints on public spending, they wanted to maintain the UK's worldwide military commitments, all of which limited the potential for domestic change.

Like Macmillan, Wilson believed in Britain's global role, defending the UK's interests in Asia in June 1965 commenting that: 'Britain's frontiers are on the Himalayas' which represented a note of solidarity with India in its stand-off with China as well as British delusions of grandeur.[7] Reality was rather different. The UK wished to remain committed to east of Suez – covering a vast tract of water from East Africa to Australia and New Zealand including the Persian Gulf. But facing the twin pull of economic pressures and the UK's global role, the government announced first it would stay in Malaysia and Singapore, then withdraw in two stages, all against the backdrop of the final exit from Aden in November 1967 after a four-year British operation against a local insurgency.

Worse struck when on 18 November 1967 the government had to bow to the inevitable and devalue the pound. Wilson declared on TV that it 'does not mean that the pound here in Britain, in your pocket or purse or in your bank, has been devalued' and faced national ridicule while his government was never viewed in the same light.[8] Two months later on 16 January 1968 Wilson speeded up the east of Suez withdrawal bringing it forward to three years hence. This was the end of an era: of the British investment in the Pacific region which had taken them to the disasters of Singapore (1942) and Suez (1956). Labour minister Richard Crossman wrote in his diaries that 'the status barrier' which shaped how Britain projected itself in the world had finally been broken.[9]

Wilson tried to get the UK into the EEC in 1967 and faced a second French veto, but after de Gaulle resigned that road was at least clear. Ted Heath's Tory government negotiated Britain's terms of membership, and on 1 January 1973 the UK (with Ireland and Denmark) joined. The UK even had its first national referendum on remaining in the EEC in June 1975 that was won 67:33 and that seemed the conclusion. But elements of the Tory right and Labour left were never reconciled to the UK being part of the European project, and in June 2016 another referendum voted 52:48 for the UK to leave which it did on 31 January 2020. The UK had joined without much fanfare and left with even less.

Remnants of Empire

Remnants of Empire have caused the UK problems as imperial retreat got under way. The breakaway of Rhodesia under a minority white settler rule by Iain Smith from 1965 to 1979 was a running embarrassment as it underlined UK impotence while incurring the wrath of newly independent African states; it eventually became formally independent as Zimbabwe in 1980 under majority rule.

In two other territories major challenges were faced. The Falkland Islands were invaded in April 1982 by Argentina after several years of failed discussions between the UK and Argentina on some kind of compromise settlement. This led to the UK sending a naval task force thousands of miles to the South Atlantic and retaking the islands in a hazardous operation. There was significant loss of British life (258 dead), controversy in the sinking of the *Belgrano*, and major assistance to the UK via US military intelligence. At the time this debacle was presented by Thatcher as a revival of national pride, and a rolling back of decline and humiliation seen at Suez. It however gave Thatcher the self-confidence to begin the imperial period of her premiership in style and domestic politics, with phrases such as 'we put the Great back into Great Britain' and played some part in her 1983 landslide victory and hence her dominance of British politics in the 1980s.

Finally, in terms of the last problematic relics of Empire there is also the example of Hong Kong which saw the UK recognise realpolitik in that its 150-year lease on the territory expired in 1997, resulting in a UK–Chinese agreement on British withdrawal, the handing back of sovereignty to the Chinese, and a 50-year transitional period, supposedly under the understanding of 'one nation, two systems' to maintain the economic powerhouse that Hong Kong had become and its importance to the Chinese economy.

The British had few if any levers to influence the Chinese, reaching agreement on handover in 1984. The last British Governor Chris Patten in typical colonial style then engaged in a last-minute exercise to encourage a degree of democracy in the province, followed by the transfer to China in 1997 with full British pomp and circumstance, replete with HMS *Britannia* and Prince Charles. Subsequently, the Chinese government slowly reasserted their control, limiting freedoms and corroding the rule of law, to the worry of the Hong Kong population and British impotence.

The day Empire formally died

Britain's remnants of Empire do not end there. Beyond the direct constitutional governance of the UK sit three Crown Dependencies and fourteen British Overseas Territories (of which the Falkland Islands are one). One significant and little-known historical fact in the legal retreat of Empire is that the concept of the British Empire was only fairly recently abolished.

This occurred when the term 'colony' was taken out of UK law. The British Empire was abolished by the British Nationality Act 1981 and passed out of existence on 1 January 1983 – an act of the Thatcher government months after the Falklands War.

The term 'colony' was replaced by British Dependent Territories which became the current British Overseas Territories. The end of Empire occurred with no fanfare, announcement or recognition: a historic change uncommented upon by Thatcher then, which in her memoirs is reduced to two short mentions about how the act was seen in India and Hong Kong. Thatcher defended it to Indian Premier Indira Gandhi in April 1981 as 'a part of our proposals to limit future large-scale immigration to Britain'.[10]

The Nationality Act could even be seen as an act of decolonising Britishness saying goodbye to the concept of 'imperial citizenship': the pretence that the subjects of the British Empire were somehow equal citizens with the right to move to the UK.[11] The 1948 Nationality Act was the first serious attempt by British government to qualify and dilute this notion, a task completed by the 1981 abolition of the term.

It is a deep contemporary irony in Brexit right-wingers like Nigel Farage who for years berated the EU notion of free movement of people that they invoked a longing and yearning for the days of Britain being a great power and the impact and influence of Empire. They did so without ever really talking about the reality of Empire and imperialism, and without remembering the concept of 'imperial citizenship' which was about a spurious free movement of people in a 'free union' which was an expression of a 'global Britain' of the past. But then nostalgia for Empire has always been based on a deliberate collective amnesia for what it actually stood for.

It is not an accident that the Crown Dependencies and British Overseas Territories contain some of the biggest tax havens in the global economy, places which act as jurisdictions for dodgy money arrangements and act as the equivalent of black holes in the world capitalist system, sucking in monies, shell companies and offering shelter for money laundering and criminal activities.

Politically and constitutionally these entities rarely appear in discussion about the UK, their relationship to the UK, or their connection to UK politics. In this they are unlike French overseas departments such as French Guiana in South America and Reunion Island in the Indian Ocean which are part of France, represented in the French National Assembly and hence the European Union.

The Crown Dependencies and British Overseas Territories are not only not part of the UK, nor represented in the UK Parliament, they were never part of the EU during the UK's 47-year membership of the union (the exception on this last point being Gibraltar because of its land border with Spain). One rare example of thinking about these territories and challenging this constitutional offshoring was the 1973 Kilbrandon Commission on the Constitution. It specifically in its remit included a commitment to look at the Isle of Man and Channel Islands, its report examining the responsibilities of the Crown in relation to the dependencies.[12]

The City of London, Empire and commerce

Another potent legacy of Empire which remains to the present is the City of London, whose origins and global role are a direct descendant of the scale and reach of the British imperial project. Many of the commercial interests which forged the Empire were companies who made their reputation and wealth on the back of British military conquest. These included the Royal African Company, formed in 1660, which received from King Charles II a monopoly of the trade to supply ships to the colonies in the Caribbean; historian David Olusoga described it as 'the most prolific slave trading entity in British history'.[13] Edward Colston, whose statute was toppled in Bristol in June 2020, was a shareholder in the company and its deputy director, a slave trader and MP.

The East India Company, established in 1600, was given a royal charter by Queen Elizabeth I of England and a monopoly on English trade with all territories east of the Cape of Good Hope and west of the Straits of Magellan, for a period of 15 years. The company became in effect the imperial ruler of large parts of India from 1757 to 1858, during which period it exercised military power and ran local administration; after the Indian Rebellion of 1857, the Government of India Act in effect nationalised the company's activities leading to the UK taking direct control of India and beginning the era of direct rule under the moniker 'the British Raj'.

The Hudson's Bay Company, formed in 1670, via royal charter granted by King Charles II gave the company a monopoly over all the rivers and streams flowing from the Hudson Bay region, covering one-third of present-day Canada, with the company facing historic allegations of exploitation of native populations for animal skins and even spreading diseases amongst aboriginal communities; these practices came to light in the 1920s. Today the company trades as HBC, headquartered in Canada and is a worldwide company.

Numerous military battles and wars fought during the British Empire were about the extension and protection of British commercial interests. The American War of Independence which began in 1775 was instigated about commerce, trade and the issue of taxation, with the Tea Act of 1773 giving the East India Company a trading monopoly in the Thirteen Colonies of what is today the eastern coast of the USA, leading to opposition which came to be known as 'the Boston Tea Party', which stood for the principle of no taxation without representation, believing they could only be taxed by local representatives not a faraway British Parliament in which they had no representation.

The Opium Wars fought between Britain and China had a similar logic. The first conflict from 1839 to 1842 was about the right of the UK to sell opium to Chinese markets that was causing mass addiction which the Chinese authorities wanted to end. The UK intervened militarily and were victorious, the resulting treaty ceding Hong Kong to the UK for 150 years. A second war between 1856 and 1860 after further Chinese objections, saw them forced to give even more concessions including to the French and Russians.

The entire slave trade degraded human beings reducing them to objects of property to be brutally used and exploited. The British Empire undertook a huge traffic in slaves which amounted to overall eleven million men, women and children, many of whom died in the most unimaginable of conditions. An abolitionist movement grew in Britain, passing the Slave Trade Act 1807 abolishing the slave trade in the British Empire, but it was not until the Slavery Abolition Act 1833 that slavery was abolished in the Empire with this act leading to slaveowners being compensated for their loss of 'property' and income.[14] The amount this cost was £20 million pounds, then the equivalent of 40 per cent of the UK's national budget and the debt incurred took until 2015 to be paid off.[15]

The City of London's Empire origins meant that from the outset it had a semi-detached relationship with the UK economy and domestic businesses. This has been grasped by some mainstream historians and analysts, with *The Economist*'s Bagehot column putting it:

> Imperial trade and investment made London a world financial centre; the City became vital to the British economy, while at the same time, preoccupied as it was with foreign deals, largely separate from the rest of it.[16]

This has bequeathed an anti-industrial ethos that has formed a major strand running through the British establishment, private schools and landed money, and which found expression in nineteenth-century Toryism which represented old money versus the new industrial monies associated with the Liberals. The modern Tory Party with its valorisation of rentier capitalism, hedge funds, speculators and financiers, is a descendant of this earlier Toryism and British capitalism, which to this day has little interest in the real economy and instead is interested in monetising and financialising assets.

Adding to this mindset, the City of London has acted as a bulwark against real economic growth, investment and productivity, with banks and financiers not interested in the returns on investment in actually existing businesses. The dominance of the City has led to the lack of a political economy analysis of the City which understands its detrimental effect on the wider UK economy, and that this springs from the model of finance capitalism it represents.

This is founded upon disinterest in the UK economy and a belief in short-termism, speculation, dividends and shareholder value. Ultimately all of this adds up to a City which occupies such a central place in the UK's economic landscape that it 'overcrowds' the potential of the rest of the economy, over-shadowing the potential to champion other versions of the economy and UK capitalism. The rise of the City – this offshore capitalism part based in the UK – has historically harmed and held back the development of the UK and the wealth and well-being of the people. It has of course provided spectacularly for a very narrow elite and has spun a message of its success and importance which has been completely bought by the main political parties.

Britain as a Warfare State

An additional strand alongside all this is the contribution by the UK's military mindset to what historian David Edgerton has called 'a warfare state'. By this he means that, for example, in the twentieth century many of the leading industrialists, inventers, innovators, engineers, scientists and technicians, along with cutting-edge ideas and technology were consis-tently taken up with working on military projects. Edgerton writes:

> Admitting the existence of a modern and modernising warfare state, in peace or war, would have entailed profound changes in the analysis of the state, and of the place of expertise, science and technology in the life of the state and nation.[17]

In this thesis the notion of Britain as a 'warfare state' both challenges the separation of civilian and military history rein-tegrating them, and post-war accounts on the left and right which posed 'the rise of the welfare state' as the main charac-teristic of the UK after 1945: the former seeing it as positive, the latter negative. Instead, the UK was both a 'warfare state' and a 'welfare state', but the focus on the latter across the political spectrum hid the expansion and endurance of the former.

The 'warfare state' meant that the UK had a 'military-industrial complex' at the heart of government and business, but never described in such terms. But this also meant that this expertise, innovation, R&D and investment was not available for the wider economy's domestic and trade needs. After the Second World War, West Germany and Japan rebuilt after defeat aided by historically low defence spending, as well as the share of R&D and expertise going into the non-defence economy, while benefitting from being able to modernise their economies in a way not open to the UK. Thus, the legacy of Empire and the warfare state contributed to the endurance of an imperial outlook which manifested itself at the centre of national government and found echoes throughout society, all of which validated the Empire State.

An Empire of the mind in the present

At the core of Empire was a British arrogance and standing apart from others, centred on a belief in the moral superiority of Britain and the British way of life. It had a condescending view of most foreigners and saw the colonial peoples of the Empire as inferior, all of which fed into the concept of an ideal British system of government and administration.[18]

It is hard to summarise such an outlook from the present, but well into post-war Britain there was still a sense that the British constitutional arrangements were filled with wisdom and intelligence, and their expertise and adaptability should be utilised around the world, particularly as the UK withdrew from imperial colonies. This was a view even held in the Labour Party, found by an American visitor to the UK in 1953 who heard a leading left-winger opine that the British constitution was 'as nearly perfect as any human institution could be'.[19]

Such an attitude, an Empire of the mind, exists to this day in the Tory Party and the 'Global Britain' pretensions of Brexit and the obsession on the right with revitalising 'the Anglo-sphere' (of English-speaking democracies) and CANZUK (standing for Canada, Australia, New Zealand, UK): an idea for a trade and security alliance of the four supported by the Adam Smith Institute and Henry Jackson Society. It is now more than apparent that this illusionary Britain has little con-nection to the reality of the choices facing the UK, but rather focuses on chasing and reliving the ghosts of past imperial endeavours. However unreal it is, this chimera still has a hold on part of the political classes and the intellectual climate of the UK in the twenty-first century.

Thus, the endurance and survival of the British Empire State up to the present is characterised by the historical development of the state, governments, professional expertise and capitalism. In the day-to-day experiences and lives of people across the UK, it is evident that a belief in militarism and British military intervention and expertise as the solution to problems both internationally and at home continues to endure.

It goes much further than that. The very idea of Britain as it has retreated from 'the rise of the welfare state' thesis has become more saturated, even in the everyday, with the memory and contested accounts of the legacy of Empire. It has become part of the ideological 'cultural wars' and so-called 'woke culture', Frankenstein creations invoked by the right to scare mainstream opinion, but has also become a struggle about public space and how history is celebrated. Thus, we see endless controversies over statues such as the national debate on the toppling of Edward Colston in Bristol and the plaque on Henry Dundas in Edinburgh, and on the names of streets and buildings feting benefactors of the past who supported and created institutions whose money was based upon expropriated wealth, Empire and slavery.

Empire is alive and kicking in today's Britain and these unreconstructed ideas are not just found exclusively on the right. Rather, the failure to abolish this edifice is part the result of the failures of 30 years of post war Labour governments to dismantle the forces of power, privilege and inequality, and what Andrew Gamble called 'the Conservative nation', meaning the Britain and England which gave succour to the values of Toryism beyond the party.

There is more to it than the failure to take on the forces of reaction. There has been to this day a powerful, even dominant strand in Labour which saw the Empire State – with its associated all-powerful centre, absolutism and parliamentary sovereignty – not as a relic of the past and not as an obstacle and enemy, but a force which could be turned into an ally and battering ram to effect political and social change.

Through the likes of the centralising tendencies of the post-war Labour government of Clement Attlee which built the NHS and modern welfare state, the practices and codes of the Empire State were seen as an edifice, even a foundation stone, on which to build democratic socialism, by being able to overcome reactionary resistance, and not only that, but to impose order compared to the anarchy of laissez-faire economics, and to plan out and deliver a vision of tomorrow. This drew from the reification of technical expertise, planners and designers which was a nexus where the 'welfare state' and 'warfare state' met, informed by modernity and Fabianism's belief in the state as a force for good.

This was a view shared collectively across the Labour Party, left and right, parliamentary and trade union wings, and which the party has clung to despite events throwing many of its core assumptions into question. The pursuit of planning, expertise and science did not as had been hoped prove to be powerful and convincing forces in the process of the modernisation of Britain, as the post-war Attlee government and then Harold Wilson's 'New Britain' vision of the 1960s illustrated.

The old order proved remarkably resilient, the forces of government lacked the clarity of vision they thought they had and were divided amongst themselves, while the internal and external constraints on the UK proved too much. The Attlee government's far-reaching and venerated reforms were thrown off course as early as 1950–51 with the onset of the Korean War, escalating defence expenditure and bringing in prescription charges (leading to the resignations of Nye Bevan and Harold Wilson from government). The Wilson administrations of 1964–70 were crippled from the outset by the UK's global exposure, economic frailties, Balance of Payments deficits, and weakness of the pound which saw eventual devaluation after much delay and a military curtailment of the UK's international responsibilities.

The experience of Thatcherism with its authoritarian populism and espousal of a very selective brand of 'freedom' can only really be fully understood against the backdrop of the Empire State. Thatcherism mixed class, race, populism, militarism and a British-English nationalism – the last of which did not translate well in Scotland and Wales. It also could not be seen in isolation in its heyday, but rather as part of the longer story of the failure of Labour to be a transformative party remaking Britain and Britishness, the caution and timidity of the wider centre-left project, and the nature and evolution of British capitalism.

On living in an old country: from the Blitz to Brexit

Similarly, the reinvention of the past as one which has become increasingly filled with pantomime caricature has become one of the dominant cultural representations of the idea of Britain.[20]

This is not just the endless loop of World War II references, but how the UK's European neighbours are portrayed through stereotypes, and about how domestic Britain is shown, with class hierarchy celebrated with upper and lower classes each knowing their place and relying on one another to fulfil their part.

This can be seen in the huge success of Julian Fellowes' *Downton Abbey*, but also in the constant referencing of Winston Churchill who seems to have become the defining figure of British history, whether you regard him as 'the Greatest Briton' of all-time as the BBC found in a public poll, or 'a white supremacist mass murderer' as Green MSP Ross Greer does.[21] This veneration of the critical period in British history in the Second World War of 1940–41, now repacked as 'their finest hour', meaning collectively the people of Britain and of Churchill's single-minded determination, was much more complex. It was also one of UK strategic weakness, of global retreat and defeat at the hands of the Germans and then Japanese, a set of humiliations which profoundly weakened the self-confidence of the British imperial project and noted across the Empire by liberation movements in the likes of India and Egypt.

The continual referencing of a narrow period of the Second World War pointed to some uncomfortable truths about present-day Britain. It underlined that 1940–41 and a mythical version of it had become the sole foundational story of modern Britain, a story which could be passed down the generations with pride and shared history and memories, no matter how simplified. Even more, it points to a country seemingly unwilling to look to the future and new challenges, but instead content to find its best stories for today and tomorrow in the past. Conspicuous by its absence in Britain are collective stories of the future which can enthuse, mobilise and bring people together; the nearest we have contemporaneously has been the minority interests of the right-wing fantasy Britain project and the brief popularity of the Corbynistas in the 2017 UK election.

All of this amounts to, in the evocative phrase of Patrick Wright, the trials and tribulations of 'living in an old country' by which the dead and the past are used to sustain a deeply unequal, unjust economic, social and political order, but also to offer cover for what is in many respects a restoration of class and privilege to legitimise the state of the country.

Wright points out that the English left had a major ambivalence about how they talked about the country, avoiding invoking 'the nation' and 'the national imagination' addressing England and Britain.[22] Instead they took shelter in the words of Neal Ascherson with 'this notion of "a people", free of British national mythology...'[23] It has proven to be a fatal mistake – one with which we are all living with the consequences – for a people without a nation and national imagination are like a boat which has been stranded after the seas have gone out.

Not even content with this mistake, the English left has not only gifted the notion of 'the nation' to the Tories and the right, it has left abandoned the terrain of 'England' to the same forces. This lamentable decision has led to the increasingly toxic, intolerant politics of English nationalism on the right, and was a major factor in the 2016 Brexit debate, vote and subsequent developments. All of which Labour and the centre-left continue to show little understanding as they cling to their self-denying ordinance on this defining landscape.

The hard truth is that without fundamental change and disruption to the British state the Empire State will continue entrenched and fortified representing the economic, social and ideological interests it serves – characterising a version of the 'Global Britain' and the global class who continually present their self-interests as a worldview and seek to impose it on the UK.

The twilight of the British state has long been predicted by such long-term observers as Tom Nairn, and the continuation of the British state as a rebuff of this thesis.[24] But the present threadbare defence of the British state, the venal nature of the establishment, the speculative, exploitative nature of British capitalism, all point to dramatic change coming. And how ever change comes, Scottish self-government is a blow to the pride and prestige of the Empire State and an opportunity for a different England to arise which is not patronised and humiliated but dares to speak as a modern democratic country. All of this requires dismantling the undemocratic scaffolding which supports the British state and Britain at its core, and it is to how that impacts on Scotland that we now focus.

7

Scotland's Democratic Argument

We are like a house that hasn't been lived in for a long time. You go in, and you can see familiar things, but nothing really works, and you know the water needs sorting out and switched on again, and there is a lot of dust around.

Andy Wightman, former MSP and campaigner on land reform and democracy, interview, December 2011

The undemocratic nature of the British state: FPTP voting system, only one elected pillar of state, an unelected Upper House, the monarchy, the proliferation of quangos and public bodies, the outsourced state, the City of London, the Crown Dependencies and Overseas Territories, many of them major tax havens, the security state of NATO, Trident and the military-industrial UK/US alliance, engaging in mass citizen surveillance, all unelected, all democratically unaccountable, have served to entrench a version of the UK centred on power, privilege, money and its related institutions. This is now a culture of neo-liberalism as an all-pervasive social order, which prioritises the individual as competitive, self-defining and, under the guise of choice, as consumer.

Kathy Galloway, activist and campaigner, personal communication, February 2022

Scotland's democracy is restricted in numerous ways by its continued membership of the UK as it is currently constituted; it is also restricted by the narrow bandwidth of much of present-day Scottish politics and public life. The present state of the UK damages Scotland in a number of ways. For example, it restricts Scotland from having conversations about the health of Scottish society and the limits of our own home-grown democracy and institutions.

This is done by the perception and reality that formal political power lies outside Scotland and is critically beyond our collective reach. This is not just a matter of geography but about political dynamics, cultures and codes, and the political centre and the British state's understanding of the UK. And all of this can aid in places a feeling that Scotland's main disadvantages and problems are all external – Westminster, Tories, the nature of the British economy and capitalism – limiting the prospect to discuss the nature of Scottish society, values and priorities. Scotland's membership of the UK has been impacted by the rightward drift of UK politics over the past 40 years. This reduces Scotland's political influence in the Union from being one of an equal partnership to being a bystander in someone else's story.

Who governs Scotland?

Who governs Scotland is not some abstract principle, and can be seen in the dynamic and facts of post-war British politics. The UK Tory governments of Churchill, Eden and Macmillan elected in 1951, 1955 and 1959 all had a popular mandate in Scotland.[1] In each of these elections the Tories won more votes in Scotland than Labour; although it is also true that Scotland began to turn away from the overall UK trend in 1959, swinging towards Labour particularly in seats. The critical point here is that this was during a period not only when British politics seemed very British, but that Scotland and every part of the UK seemed to move to the same political beat – an assumption so ingrained that the shift in 1959 was not fully picked up and appreciated at the time.

This meant that the 1970 UK election and the return of Ted Heath's Conservatives was the first post-war occasion when a Tory administration was elected without any kind of Scottish mandate, winning a minority vote (38.0 per cent) significantly behind Labour (44.5 per cent) and 23 out of 71 Scottish seats compared to Labour's 44 seats. The 1970 contest was also significant for one other reason in Scotland. It witnessed the first ever UK general election where the SNP returned an MP to Westminster – Donald Stewart from the Western Isles – as the party won 11.4 per cent across Scotland. This was at that point its highest ever vote, although itself a major comedown from the highs of Winnie Ewing winning Govan three years previously.

It is not an accident that this was a period where constitutional politics began to come to the fore, aided by multiple challenges to government across the UK from the 'who governs?' question, to the miners' strike, Northern Ireland, and economic uncertainty caused by rising inflation and the OPEC price shock.

It is a cliché and also a truism that Scottish politics were never the same after the SNP victory in Hamilton and that, combined with the discovery of North Sea oil, gave a new energy and vibrancy to the Scottish debate and the self-government debate. Post-1970 the Heath government struggled to find an approach to Scotland, not aided by the popularity of the Upper Clyde Shipbuilders (UCS) work-in during 1971–72. And as questions rose about Westminster government, the STUC brought the phrase 'the democratic deficit' – referring to how Scotland was governed in the Union – into political debate.[2] Little noticed at the time, its influence was to grow in the next decade to become one of the defining terms of the 1980s.

Therefore, the predicament of Scotland being governed by Tory governments it did not vote for (which are in a minority, often declining position) and with Scotland giving a clear mandate to another party – Labour first, then SNP – is a relatively recent historical development. And it is not really comparable to any situation that England could realistically find itself in within the Union, as we will see below.

Take the years 1970–2024 – assuming the current UK Parliament runs to five years. Scotland and the UK will by then have had 36 years of Tory led governments (31 Tory, five Tory–Liberal Democrat) out of 54 years, in other words 67 per cent or two-thirds of the last half century plus.

Examining the period 1979–2024, this pattern becomes even more pronounced: 32 out of 45 years of Tory-led governments Scotland did not vote for – 71 per cent across these years. Eight out of eleven UK elections produced Conservative administrations with a minority of votes which were defeated in the popular vote by another party (five times Labour, three SNP).

There is also the issue of the long-term declining fortunes of the Scottish Conservatives even when elected to UK government. As we saw, when Ted Heath won in 1970 the Tories gained 38.0 per cent of the Scottish vote and 23 seats out of 71; they also saw an uplift in their vote across Scotland of a mere 0.4 per cent and three seats compared to the previous election. In 1979 when Margaret Thatcher won a UK majority of 43 seats (compared to Heath's 30) her party won 31.4 per cent of the Scottish vote and 22 of 71 seats (although they did increase their vote by 6.7 per cent and gained six seats due to the SNP's collapse).[3]

By Thatcher's third term in 1987, the Tory Scottish vote had fallen to 24.0 per cent, translating to ten seats out of 72 – down 4.4 per cent and a loss of eleven seats. The election of David

Cameron in 2010 and entry in coalition with the Liberal Democrats saw the Tories win a mere 16.7 per cent of the vote and a single seat – unprecedented lows for a governing party.

It is true that subsequently the Scottish Tories had a mini-revival under Ruth Davidson's period of leadership, reaching 28.6 per cent of the vote and 13 seats in 2017 – a rise of 13.7 per cent nearly doubling their vote and a gain of twelve seats. But this increase has to be seen in the context of longer-term decline and is a relatively weak recovery, with Scottish Tories now judging as a success vote shares regarded as a humiliation in the 1980s. And none of this so far threatens to change any of the fundamentals.

Now the counter-claim can be made by some: what happens when England has to put up with a Labour government it does not vote for? It is a good question but the reality of politics and numbers are very different, led by England's predominance in population and seats – 533 out of the 650-member House of Commons (82 per cent) returned at the 2019 UK election. Thus, only a very close UK and English result in votes and seats, where the Conservatives are marginally ahead of Labour in seats, can practically produce a situation whereby Scotland and Wales with their historic anti-Tory traditions push the UK over the line and in a further anti-Conservative direction. In post-war times, this happened in the 1964 and February 1974 elections (the English dimension of which is explored more fully in Chapter 15).

It takes incredibly close elections across the UK and England to make Scotland matter. The electoral predominance of England makes it next to impossible for it to face a situation similar to Scotland and Wales. And as a further point, while Scotland has experienced decades of Tory governments with a mandate which can be called into question, the above two Parliaments produced the sum total of just under two years (one year and 334 days to be precise) – with elections called quickly which produced more decisive results.

The regular and repeated experience of this predicament – of Scotland getting Tory governments it did not vote for, elected on a long-term declining vote and imposing policies on the people of Scotland that it did not support or want, and in many cases actively opposed – is unsustainable. It produces bad government, weakens democracy and accountability, and elects politicians who do not understand the people they are governing and where accountability is weak to non-existent.

It is true that large parts of England – the North West, North East and Yorkshire – experience similar misgovernance, disrespect and the imposition of policies and politics from Westminster which they do not support or want. The malaise and rot of Westminster and the British state is not exclusive to Scotland; it is experienced across the UK – and indeed beyond the UK – in terms of the calamitous geo-political decisions the country has taken.

However, it does matter that the North West and other areas are regions of England. None of these places have their own legal and education systems, or structures of local government and other governance. Scotland is a nation, with some of the attributes of a nation, and is also a political, communicative and social space and a community. And being a nation in a Union of nations that is the UK should give it a sense of status and rights which are recognised; and to an extent is, via factors like the endurance of a separate Scottish legal system post-1707 and the establishment of the Scottish Parliament in 1999, to take but two examples.

Some of the above could be addressed by systematic UK-wide democratisation and far-reaching reform. To take one possible change, the introduction of proportional representation at Westminster would drastically reduce the prospect of a majority Tory government being elected on a minority of the vote – and hence governing Scotland with the sort of vote it has. Yet such a measure appears so far beyond the political insight of the Conservative and Labour Parties for the basic reason that they are both believers in and beneficiaries from the First Past the Post (FPTP) electoral system. They are committed to FPTP not because it produces better government or is good for democracy, but purely out of naked self-interest and their desire to have monopoly political power at the centre and to not share it with others. All of which is reinforced by their attachment to the totems of Westminster ritual – the obsession with parliamentary sovereignty and clinging to absolutism.

The difficulty of UK-wide democratisation

UK-wide constitutional and democratic reform is regularly talked about, but while change can happen it is always limited (Scottish Parliament, Welsh Assembly), rarely involved in remaking the political centre, and never entails reworking the hard wiring of the British state.

There were three major UK-wide moments of constitutional debate and change in the twentieth century: the Speaker's Conference of 1919–20 which looked at the constitutional order of the three nations of Great Britain; the Kilbrandon Royal Commission on the Constitution announced in 1968 (under Lord Crowther) which reported in 1973 proposing devolution for Scotland and Wales; and Labour government reforms of 1997–99 which established the Scottish, Welsh and Northern Irish devolved institutions.[4]

Two of the three instances led to no reform; the second (Kilbrandon) contributed to the debate which led to the Scotland and Wales Acts of 1978 which failed to bring about devolved assemblies. The third (1997–99) instituted devolution as we know it and created a climate of major constitutional change. However, even in this case (and despite political headwinds behind them) the reforms did not alter the fundamental principles and dynamics of the British constitution. Instead, what occurred was ad hoc change, no clear set of principles or objectives were established, and at best the old order was weakened without a new settlement being enunciated. Critically, it did not attempt to remake the political centre of the UK, nor to codify UK constitutional rights.

This brings us to a central issue – the fact that the UK is not and never has been a fully-fledged political democracy. There are numerous ways which contribute to this situation. The upper house at Westminster – the House of Lords – is completely unelected and a mixture of feudal entitlement (92 hereditary peers) and Prime Ministerial patronage. It is ever-expanding, and of an unjustifiable size (after a cull in numbers in 1999), comprising at the start of 2022, 769 members.[5] This makes it the second largest legislative chamber in the world only behind (the equally undemocratic) Chinese National People's Congress that has responsibility for a population of 1.4 billion people. The Lords is also the only upper chamber in any unicameral legislature anywhere in the world larger than the lower house.

One defence of the House of Lords is that it is, like that many things which are part of the British constitutional landscape, an oddity – and not where you would start from if you were starting out today. All of this leads to arguments for convention, tradition and just muddling through, and believing that somehow this all works, is satisfactory, and is a unique British institution.

The Crown is not an apolitical institution

This same argument is put forward to defend many British institutions that are relics from a past age that have somehow survived. The Crown is one of the principal bodies that the case is made for, stressing stability, continuity, apolitical character, while even sometimes having a nod to the ridiculous nature of it all in the cold light of day.[6] These qualities are presented as contributing to Britain's unique brand and appeal across the world, selling ourselves, attracting tourists and winning TV ratings.

The argument for royalty and the British royal family is a diminishing one. TV property presenter Kirsty Allsopp defended the institution from attack, declaring about the image of Britain it projects, 'What is wrong with Britain being a Disneyland?'[7] This sentiment reduces the people of Britain to playpark attractions. Not only that, it amounts to a Disney-fication of British public life – the commodification of privilege, pomp and hierarchy – which contributes to the UK not being a modern, democratic country and prevents its people from legally and politically being citizens.

If this were not enough the royal family is not apolitical. The clue is in the term 'constitutional monarchy'. Rather it is, as that term reveals, part of the constitutional fabric and part of the British state, and hence profoundly political. Being head of state of the UK and 14 'Commonwealth realms', 14 British Overseas Territories and three Crown Dependencies, is political. Being head of the Commonwealth is inherently political. And lest we forget intervening in the 1970s devolution debate and the last stages of the 2014 independence referendum is nothing but political.

In the former, the Queen said when addressing both Houses of Parliament on the occasion of her Silver Jubilee in 1977 that this was an age of 'progress' and 'the complexities of modern administration' which made many people feel that 'metropolitan government is too remote', and this was 'the background for the continued and keen discussion of proposals for

devolution to Scotland and Wales within the United Kingdom'.
And then she added:

> I cannot forget that I was crowned Queen of the United
> Kingdom of Great Britain and Northern Ireland. Perhaps
> the Jubilee is a time to remind ourselves of the benefits which
> Union has conferred, at home and in our international
> dealings, on the inhabitants of all parts of this United
> Kingdom.[8]

These are carefully crafted deeply political words. They are
the head of state of the UK speaking about the importance of
the continuation and constitutional integrity of the UK. No one
could call these apolitical remarks.

Four days before the 2014 vote – on Sunday 14 September
2014 – outside Crathie Kirk by Balmoral, Aberdeenshire, the
Queen told a member of the public that the people of Scotland
should 'think very carefully about the future', in comments
picked up by media.[9] Then Liberal Democrat minister David
Laws commented that it was 'an extraordinary intervention
from a monarch who has made a career of staying above
politics'.[10] The Queen's words were part of an orchestrated
campaign by Tory Prime Minister David Cameron, who
revealed this five years later when promoting his autobiography *For the Record*. Looking back on the Queen's intervention
he said, they – Downing Street – were 'not asking for anything
that would be in any way improper or constitutional'. Rather
it was something both subtle and which could not be missed:
'just a raising of the eyebrow, even you know a quarter of an
inch we thought would make a difference'.[11]

Buckingham Palace let it be known that they were not happy
with the ex-PM's comments, but Cameron had form, having
weeks after the 2014 vote been caught saying in overheard
remarks to former New York mayor Michael Bloomberg that

the Queen 'purred down the line' when told the result of the independence referendum, adding: 'But it should never have been that close. It wasn't in the end.'[12] Again the Palace indicated its displeasure with Cameron.

It is not very surprising that even detailed analysis of the Queen, the Crown and the institution and networks flowing from it refrain from reviewing the construction and edifice of the constitutional entity, and how it is used to legitimise and aid the maintenance of a political order. Studies such as constitutional authority Vernon Bogdanor's *The Monarchy and the Constitution* offer much on the public controversies that we know about.[13] These include Edward VIII's abdication in 1936; and the fact that until 1963 the Queen chose Tory leaders and hence Prime Ministers when the party was in office. This has meant that at times the monarchy has become implicated in the deepest internal workings of the Tory Party and manoeuvrings for the leadership. These include such watershed moments as May 1940 when Churchill rather than Lord Halifax emerged as Prime Minister, and 1963 when Alec Douglas-Home became leader ahead of Rab Butler despite at the time having a peerage and sitting in the Lords, which he renounced to seek a seat in the Commons (which he won).

There is too much emphasis and faith in 'the official history' in accounts such as this. Bogdanor writes that Britain post-abdication was not 'the end of monarchy' but he says, quoting royal historian Robert Lacey, 'Britain's vote for monarchy', adding: 'A vote for a particular style of monarchy, constitutionally limited and modest, a monarchy of traditional values...'[14] This is attempting to offer legitimacy and protection to the role of monarchy about what was a time of major upheaval and uncertainty in how the institution was seen by the public.

The same is true of the first political biography, *The Queen* written by Ben Pimlott, which portrays an individual representing a country which has gone through epic change. In the edition published for the 2012 Diamond Jubilee, historian Peter Hennessy wrote in a foreword that the Queen 'has never put a court shoe wrong as a constitutional sovereign even though as a country we are entirely without a written highway code for monarchy...'[15] Andrew Marr writing at the same time has continually talked of the Queen's reign as 'a new Elizabethan age', as if people still define the times we live in through the monarch.[16] All this contributes to a certain projection of Britain: that no matter the upheavals some things never ever change and can be relied on even if they are only meant to be symbolic.

Yet we now know even more about the political workings and influence of the monarchy. The Netflix TV drama series *The Crown* may be fictionalised, but has exposed for a significant public audience the degree to which the institution is part of the establishment, sitting at the centre of a set of networks of power – Downing Street, government, civil service, the systems of patronage, preferment, titles and landed monies. And thus within this world it has influence and a degree of power.

The Crown and democracy: compatible or not?

How do the Crown and democracy interact? There is the behaviour of Prince Charles, the heir to the throne, and his years of documented lobbying and 'black spider' letters (so called because of his writing) to numerous government ministers. More serious and systematic has been the revelation of the scale of the use of the Queen's Consent and Prince of Wales' Consent, by which parliamentary legislation which affects the private interests of the monarch or Prince of Wales can be changed and altered to give them a further opt-out from the democratic process. Not only has this happened on numerous occasions at Westminster but also within the Scottish

Parliament, with the latter giving the Queen's estates in Scotland exemption from climate change law on reducing carbon emissions. This was one small example of 67 laws, parts of which the Queen was able to veto from the Scottish Parliament.

The scale of democratic opt-out by the royals at Westminster is on a much larger, industrial scale which is truly astonishing. A study by *The Guardian* found a total of 1,062 parliamentary bills subjected to Queen's Consent over the course of the reign of the Queen; in relation to Prince of Wales' Consent a total of 275 parliamentary bills have been subject to this process over 50 years, from 1970 to 2020. That is an average of 15.6 bills per year via Queen's Consent and 5.5 per year by Prince of Wales' Consent.[17] The pressure group Republic has said on this: 'End the royal veto. Scrap Queen's and Prince's consent, so all laws apply to everyone.'[18]

In effect, the Queen and Prince Charles are able via a secretive mechanism between the executive and the Crown to circumvent democratic and legislative process and put themselves as an institution above and beyond the rest of us in defence of their own private, commercial and financial interests. This is the definition of a political system still shaped by the relics of feudal privilege – which of course is exactly what monarchy is – a principle incompatible with what democracy is meant to represent. This is without getting further into use and abuse of the Crown powers which are used as a cloak to prevent democratic scrutiny of the executive, and used to make far-reaching decisions of life and death such as the UK going to war. In both 1914 and 1939 the UK declared war on Germany not as a result of a parliamentary debate and vote but by the executive's use of Crown powers.[19] Besides this is the Crown Estate, property and holdings belonging to the monarch which are not part of their private estate, including massive property assets (Ascot Racecourse; Regent Street,

London) as well as over half of the UK's foreshore and nearly all its territorial seabed.

The Crown and monarch have a complex relationship with law, the Crown being immune from legal action via common law. The monarch also has the protection of personal immunity from criminal proceedings. Academic Adam Tomkins underlines this position which is ultimately indefensible in a modern democracy: 'the Sovereign cannot be arrested; no arrest can be made within the Sovereign's presence or within the royal palaces; the Sovereign's goods may not be seized; and the Sovereign may not give evidence in her own cause'.[20]

No one should say the Crown and monarchy do not matter. The UK is at its core, in the words of Stephen Haseler, 'a royal state' observing: 'For the British, the Crown is the state: state and monarchy are fused.'[21] It is a central pillar of what Britain is and how power is used, not some inconsequential decoration or tourist attraction.

The UK's hesitant journey to democracy

The argument that none of the above matters poses that the UK, unlike other places, has been in the happy position of enjoying a peaceful evolution to political democracy without violence and revolution. Leaving aside that the former is not accurate (Peterloo, suppression of Chartists, Ireland, to name but a few), the forward march of democracy has been much less straightforward and comprehensive than often presented.

The well-versed Whig history of British democracy poses 1832, 1867 and 1884 – three great reform acts and the 1872 and 1883 acts bringing in the secret ballot and the first limits on campaign spending – all leading up to 1918 and women first gaining the vote followed by 1928 and the establishment of an equal franchise between the sexes.[22] However, none of these changes actually produced a world where the UK practised 'one person, one vote' in elections held. Instead, it left a playing field of various anomalies and bastions of privilege and protected rights for the affluent and influential rooted in the age of pre-democracy when some people actually had more votes and representation than others. That sounds like a bizarre world of blatant, indefensible inequality but was how UK politics and democracy worked until fairly recently.

In mainland Britain (excluding Northern Ireland) 'one person, one vote' was only abolished in 1948 by the then post-war Labour government, when it called time on separate university constituencies whereby graduates had another vote and their own seats; as well as this there was 'plural voting' which gave business interests another vote in their constituency.[23] All these worked in the interests of the Tory Party and its supporters, and abolition was the result of sustained democratic pressure by the labour and trade union movement. Not surprisingly, the Tories fought the abolition of university seats bitterly in Parliament seeing it as an example of 'Socialist Party dictatorship', promising in their 1950 election manifesto to restore them, but when they were returned the following year the debate and democracy had moved on.

The last UK general election with university constituencies and plural voting was 1945 when there were twelve such representatives elected to the House of Commons: a not insubstantial figure that could be important in a close election. The last mainland contest which occurred in such a seat was the November 1946 Combined Scottish Universities by-election (it returning three members in a general election) where the Tory candidate was former Secretary of State Walter Elliot who had lost his constituency seat in the previous year's Labour landslide.[24] He re-entered Parliament winning 68.2 per cent of the vote to Labour's 11.5 per cent and the Liberal Party's 8.0 per cent with 32,494 people voting on a 50.7 per cent turnout.[25]

This though is not quite the end of the story. It took another 20 years for this change to be UK-wide, when in 1968 at the start of the Northern Irish 'troubles' 'one person, one vote' was achieved in the province. The last university constituency in the UK was Queen's University, Belfast which was abolished along with plural voting. Both university seats and plural voting had worked disproportionately in favour of the Protestant community. The Electoral Law (Northern Ireland) Act 1968 came into effect the following year, campaigned for by the civil rights movement who saw such practices as part of the abuses of Stormont one-party rule. James Callaghan as the Home Secretary sent the troops into Northern Ireland in 1969 and in a rare comment on the province's lack of democracy reflected in his autobiography that: 'it was not until 1969 that the Ulster Unionists could bring themselves to concede the elementary right of universal adult suffrage'.[26]

The achievement of the basic principle of 'one person, one vote' is therefore messier than a smooth, linear path from 1832 to 1928, taking until 1948 in mainland Britain and 1968 across the entire UK. This is a very different story to that usually told in accounts of British democracy, including in most radical and left-wing accounts which have swallowed a large amount of the Whig history. Take the campaigning journalist Paul Foot. In a study of the vote and 'how it was won' in the UK he has no room for the tale of the survival of university seats and plural voting,[27] while it is a perspective which has fallen from the labour movement's account of the struggle for democratic rights and understanding its own history and achievements.

Brexit and going back to the old country

On top of all this partial, flawed democracy we have to add Brexit and what 'taking back control' has turned out to be. In short, it has become distorted into the abolition of the constitutional safeguards for liberty and freedom which EU membership provided – a sort of fallback constitutional set of rights for citizens in a state with no tradition of protected, entrenched rights. It has also been interpreted by successive Tory administrations to mean the executive reclaiming and reappropriating powers which once laid with the EU. At the same time, the constitutional furniture of the UK is being shifted, in relation to the devolved territories, reasserting the right of the UK political centre to intervene in devolved areas often without proper consultation with the respective administrations. As well as this, there is an executive which wants to row back on checks on its power, whether judicial review, the Supreme Court or the remit of the Electoral Commission.

Brexit was always going to be a constitutional moment for the UK, which had at least on paper the principle of greater democratisation and dispersal of power. But that was never the aim of the right-wing ideological project of Brexit. In relation to Scotland, Wales and Northern Ireland, two of the three voted decisively to remain in the EU.

The EU (Withdrawal Agreement) Act 2020 saw consent for it withheld by all three devolved legislatures: the Scottish Parliament (by a vote of 92–29 on 8 January 2020), Welsh Senedd and Northern Irish Assembly, but it was still passed by the UK Parliament.[28] The Welsh First Minister Mark Drakeford and former First Minister Carwyn Jones consistently warned of the constitutional and democratic damage being done to the UK by the pursuit of a hard Brexit which took little account of Scottish and Welsh sensitivities. Jones in a speech to the Welsh Senedd in January 2020 attacked the mythology of parliamentary sovereignty and noted it was an English tradition with no pan-British roots:

> Scotland will have imposed on it a form of sovereignty that firstly doesn't exist in Scotland and secondly cuts across the

Treaty of Union of 1707... This is a fundamental attack on the 1707 Treaty of Union in Scotland.[29]

Northern Ireland with all its 'special' status, the Good Friday Agreement and the need to prevent a hard Irish border in the context of a hard Brexit was the subject of much negotiation between the UK and EU, and the creation of the Northern Ireland protocol which kept the province in the EU Customs Union. This latter agreement written and signed by the UK government and its lead negotiator Lord Frost was the subject of endless opprobrium from Tory Brexiteers and the Democratic Unionist Party.

Underlying these tensions is what it says about the state of the Union. The UK is a differentiated Union with different legal territories and arrangements for different UK nations. Despite the constant mythology of the UK as a unitary state it has never been so and instead has been accurately described as a 'union state' and even a 'state of unions'.[30] The tragedy of Brexit and recent decades has been the rise of a dogmatic unionism which has clung to the idea of the UK as an unitary state and seen Brexit in terms of a unitary state politics.[31]

An intelligent, confident unionism would have adapted and even celebrated this Union through a differentiated form of Brexit within the UK, making a positive of the different arrangements and diversity of the UK. Instead, the UK government was dragged to compromise on Northern Ireland showing no insight into the fragile status of the peace process, time and again revealing that Tory Westminster politicians knew and seemed to care little about the province and wider subject of Ireland.

The UK's non-democracy and the challenge to Scotland

The above story of the UK as a partial, flawed democracy is not what political elites and the insider class continually tell us.

The unreformed political system and its increasingly debased culture and norms work to the advantage of those groups. Hence there is little push within the system for fundamental change – and Labour despite four periods of post-war government covering 30 years have shown little inclination and sufficient radicalism to take on and dismantle the *ancien régime*. Whatever the future contours of UK politics, this last observation, about Labour and the dominant politics of the centre-left, looks likely to remain a constant, as they cling to the wreckage of an increasingly discredited UK political order, insisting that 'one more heave' and period of Labour in office can sort things and restore normality.

This unsatisfactory situation has detrimental consequences for Scotland. It affects our politics, democracy and society. It harms the public policy choices made in and for Scotland. It narrows what it is possible to discuss, consider and act upon – whether positively deciding to do something or in relation to Westminster. Critically, it has a psychological dimension: of the dynamics of power and decision-making. The reality that a large part of the decision-making which affects Scotland happen elsewhere – and this state of affairs – diminishes and limits us. The only defence against this is to argue that Westminster is somehow also 'ours', should not be 'othered' and that the challenge to reform it is a project which Scots can have a say in. This might have carried significant weight decades ago, but is increasingly a threadbare argument.

This is not to say that democracy in Scotland is completely healthy. Self-government and public institutions across a range of areas – education, health, law and order, local government – are not exactly in the best of health and in Chapter 9 we will examine the state of Scotland and public services in the area of social justice. Alan Sinclair, founder of the WISE Group, makes the following assessment of the state of Scotland:

The democratic foothills are not in good order in Scotland. Scrutiny and debate in the media is awful. The SNP seems to me to be run by a tight group of people and not in itself very democratic and consistently centralising in how it has restructured public services. The civic/voluntary sector has been co-opted by the Scottish Government   people scared to speak out.[32]

Twenty years plus of devolution have left a public realm and services underfunded, over-centralised and after the experience of the COVID pandemic, exhausted at a human level, and needing nurturing, empathy and understanding at the national and local. Craig Harrow, a Liberal Democrat and public affairs specialist, goes further in his purview which many find uncomfortable:

We should be questioning how Scotland could do better – how our parliament and governments could do better – how our parliament could be reformed, how power can be devolved to communities and communities effectively empowered. After twenty years of devolution many of us are disappointed that the lofty ambitions set out by Donald Dewar in his speech at the first legislative programme have not yet been prioritised and certainly not realised. There has been previous little thinking about how we deliver better public services, reform, modernise and innovate. Most of our institutions are much as they were at the time of the creation of the Scottish Parliament – and yet further powers have been given and not taken up by the Scottish Government![33]

A self-governing Scotland worthy of the name would aspire to be about more than the administration and bureaucratic delivery of services, which is the legacy of how Scotland was governed pre-devolution (in a system which was actually called 'administrative devolution'). It would recognise the need not just to go past the practices which have dominated Scotland prior to and since 1999, but to embrace an understanding of political and institutional change which is not just about independence as statehood.

We will return to this terrain later in the book – exploring political change beyond formal politics. Suffice for now to point out that a formally self-governing Scotland does not on its own shift who has power in society. That requires a second transformation which encourages a wider idea of self-determination dispersing power across society and communities.

The embryonic traditions of Scottish self-government need care and love, attention and repair-work as well as renewal and reappraisal. That will necessitate a degree of honesty and self-reflection from significant sections of Scottish society and Scotland's own political classes and insider groups to recognise that there are limits to how they see the world, and that the view from St Andrews House, Edinburgh, home of the Scottish Government, is like all seats of power, partial.

None of this is aided by a Westminster and UK political system broken beyond repair, that does not serve the vast majority of the people of the UK, and looks for the foreseeable future to be incapable of fundamental reform. The UK is not and never has been a fully-functioning political democracy. Scotland has the chance to be a democracy and to take decisions into our own hands. One of the pressures in recent decades on democracy in the UK and Scotland has been the dominant economic paradigm which has led to huge concentrations of wealth and power as well as insecurity and inequality; and the next chapter outlines this situation and what first steps can be taken to challenge it.

8

Economic Injustice

When historians write the epitaph for neoliberalism, they will have to conclude that it was the form of capitalism that systematically prioritised political imperatives over economic ones. That is: given a choice between a course of action that will make capitalism seem like the only possible economic system, and one that will make capitalism actually be a more viable long-term economic system, neoliberalism has meant always choosing the former.

David Graeber, *The Utopia of Rules: On Technology, Stupidity, and the Secret Joys of Bureaucracy*, 2013

I think the obvious incomplete task is the crushing of myths about Scotland's poverty and insolvency, and a campaign of persuasion among No supporters featuring the sort of information about Scotland's underlying economic strength promoted by Believe In Scotland. Many people remain astonishingly ignorant about the extent of Scotland's basic underlying wealth, and persist in seeing us as a poor relation to England, which is actually the reverse of the truth, in terms of everything that matters. Building up this confidence is more important than having a detailed plan, which can only be guesswork anyway. The point is to convince people we'd be negotiating from a position of strength, and that we have, or easily could have, all that it takes to be a prosperous 21st century country.

Joyce McMillan, personal communication, February 2022

Scotland is a wealthy country. It is not the wealthiest – or close to the absolutely richest – but sits comfortably just off the top group that can be called the wealthiest countries in the world. Scotland is blessed with an abundance of assets, resources and advantages – natural and human, geographic and geo-political – which give it the prospect of a stable, successful and prosperous future that can be enjoyed by the vast majority of people who live in Scotland.

In this chapter we will examine Scotland's economic condition by conventional measurements before looking at alternative ways of thinking about the economy and wealth. And such thinking cannot be done in isolation but has to examine the nature of the UK and its economy, the nature of British capitalism and the wider ideological dynamics which have framed the UK economy and global order in recent decades.

A short history of post-war British capitalism

The Scottish economy exists within the context of the evolution and dynamics of British capitalism, its economy and its patterns of growth. There have been many critiques of British capitalism emphasising its historic lack of support for manufacturing, short-termism, lack of championing innovation and research and development. There has also been a focus on the long-term relative decline of the UK in the global economy – which was the second largest economy in the world until the mid-1960s – followed by bitter debates in the 1960s and 1970s on whether decline was inevitable and the UK's reputation as 'the sick man of Europe'.[1]

From the perspective of the right, there then follows 'the great British miracle' – the reversing of decline and 'putting the great back into Great Britain' under Thatcherism: all of which was explicitly accepted by the New Labour era of Tony Blair and Gordon Brown. The trouble with this interpretation is that it is not true about the era before Thatcher, the Thatcher period or subsequently. Instead, as Table 1 shows, the pre-1979 era saw higher average growth than post-1979, and the entire arc of the UK post-1945 has witnessed a long-term decline in economic growth with the highest growth in the 1950s, 1960s and 1970s and lower growth since. There was (despite all the hype) no Thatcherite 'economic miracle' and no continuation under New Labour.

This means that nearly everything presented in the conventional economic reading of the UK economic history in recent decades is wrong. The ideological spin of Thatcherism and New Labour was a deliberate mirage, aided by North Sea oil, privatisation and debt; with (for all the Thatcher rhetoric of 'household economics') household debt as a share of GDP rising from 37 per cent in 1979 to 73 per cent in 1990.[2] And this framing of the UK economy is based on the promotion of the interests of finance capital and the rise of the rentier class, who want to expand their appropriation and profits until it takes the maximum extraction.[3] This version of capitalism has to be resisted and defeated across the UK, and in Scotland the reluctance to talk about ownership, governance of business and even economic democracy and self-government has to be challenged.

Table 1   Annualised increase in real GDP per capita of post-war governments[4]

Government	Years	Annualised growth rate
Conservative	1951–64	2.82%
Labour	1964–70	2.22%
Conservative	1970–74	2.59%
Labour	1974–79	2.31%
Conservative	1979–97	2.09%
Labour	1997–2010	1.37%
Coalition (Cons/Lib Dem)	2010–15	1.32%
Conservative	2015–19	0.89%

Scotland's recent economic history

Scotland's economic debate takes place against a backdrop of how the economy performed when the UK became the capitalist powerhouse of the global economy, leading to rapid industrialisation and expansion of urban Scotland in the nineteenth century, followed by a long period of relative decline and accelerated deindustrialisation in the 1980s.[5] Post-war debates from the 1950s onward became centred on Scotland's lower economic growth rate than the UK average, levels of unemployment and migration, inward investment and the role of government. Gavin McCrone, chief economist at the Scottish Office for over 20 years, writes now:

> In the 1950s and 1960s, Scotland's GDP per head was one of the lowest in the UK, along with Wales and Northern Ireland. Now, it is exceeded only by London, the South East and the Eastern Region of England. Although Scotland's rate of economic growth has generally been below that of the UK, it has been matched by a lower population growth.[6]

The scale of transformation of the Scottish economy seldom gets enough attention beyond academics and policy-makers, apart from the seismic loss of jobs which occurred in the 1980s. This painful period still carries deep wounds in parts of Scotland that need to be recognised, but we also have to acknowledge longer-term changes which have shaped post-war Scotland which the 1980s are but one part of.

Scotland's economy has shifted from manufacturing, heavy goods and male jobs to service and consumption, less about exports than domestic markets, facilitated by a huge rise in female employment. There are strengths in this new economy and successes, Scottish innovators and leading-edge companies in new tech and energy, and firms which are leading exporters.

But there are weaknesses such as the branch line nature of much of the private sector; exports being concentrated in a few sectors; and the changing nature of finance capitalism in Scotland, the UK and globally.

Taking all this into account Scotland's economy has, relative to the rest of the UK, shifted from one which in the 1950s and 1960s was seen as facing acute challenges of transition and shaped by a declinist narrative to, by the early part of the 21st century, being the most prosperous part of the UK outside London and the South East. This change has to inform the constitutional debate – the strengths and qualities of the economy in Scotland as well as the challenges, both current and future, which it will face.

Scotland's wealth

There are numerous ways to assess and measure Scotland's wealth. First, are the conventional measurements which produce Scottish GDP of £173.6 billion in 2021 (including oil and gas), down from £180.7 billion in 2019 reflecting the impact of COVID and falling oil prices; GDP in 2021 was £164.7 billion for the onshore economy. This produces per capita figures of £31,748 per head (including oil and gas) and £30,113 for the onshore economy.[7]

These figures put Scotland comfortably in the slipstream of other successful, prosperous developed countries, with the economist John McLaren writing:

> Although lying mid-table, Scotland can still be viewed as a relatively prosperous OECD nation. This ranking is likely to apply regardless of whether Scotland is part of the UK or independent.[8]

Second, one part of Scotland's economy that needs special attention is the offshore economy, and what is called 'extra-regio economic activity' which includes North Sea oil and gas. The scale of this activity has been at times as large as 18 per cent of Scottish onshore GDP and while there has been a sharp downturn in recent years, it still stands at around 5 per cent. We will return to the concept of the offshore economy later in this chapter when looking at the Scottish economy in the wider frame of the global economy.

Third, talking of national aggregates of wealth, irrespective of the limits of GDP, are not how people live and experience their lives. Rather, all across Scotland people go about their daily business in communities, cities, towns and regions – places with very different levels of wealth and poverty. While there are issues with GDP measurements at city and local government areas, they are indicative of different levels of wealth. For example, Edinburgh had GDP per capita in 2021 of £45,000 per head and Glasgow £35,000, while East and North Ayrshire had £16,000. This led Alex Massie to observe that while the UK government's 'levelling up' had its limits, such an agenda was missing from much of the Scottish Government's thinking, commenting that 'Edinburgh is now Scotland's economic powerhouse' and that it should be asked 'who speaks for Ayrshire or Dundee?'[9] All of this confirms a consistent picture over decades of the parts of Scotland which have been the most prosperous and those which have been less prosperous; the following chapter explores more in depth different facets of inequality in Scotland.

The Barnett Formula

The UK as a Union engages in fiscal transfers from the centre, and in relation to Scotland, Wales and Northern Ireland, much of this comes under what is called the Barnett Formula. This is named after Joel Barnett, Chief Secretary to the Treasury in the Labour government of 1974–79, who first used this in relation to the Scotland Act 1978 (which was meant to set up a devolved Scottish Assembly, but didn't after the 1979 referendum). Subsequently, it was retained by the Thatcher government and extended to Northern Ireland in 1979 and Wales in 1980.

Barnett has a predecessor, the Goschen Formula, named after George Goschen, UK Chancellor of the Exchequer from 1887 to 1892 who introduced it in 1888.[10] This allocated funding to Scotland and Ireland compared to England and Wales on a much narrower range of areas – a variation of which continued after Irish independence up until 1959 when it was officially abolished but retained informally in an even narrower set of areas. This illustrates that unions made up of different nations and territories usually have a central mechanism for distributing resources; Barnett in this is not exceptional but how it is determined is unusual.

Barnett has contributed to Scottish, Welsh and Northern Irish spending remaining higher than the UK and England averages, although the opposite was intended. It is put forward as one of the main arguments for the Union – a fiscal transfer of resources to Scotland – along with Wales and Northern Ireland. Yet there are problems with Barnett. It is unsustainable and indefensible as it currently exists in the long run; it is not based, as many territorial mechanisms are, on 'need', but on an accumulation of historical spending and current changes. It has, like many key elements of the UK, no legal basis and is merely Treasury policy and thus could be abolished without any legislation. And its inefficient mix of historic composition and ad hoc nature in the present aids the UK political centre, who can make it up as it goes along, deciding what are and are not Barnett consequentials – hardly conducive to a sustainable settlement.

On the latter, this is not some arcane point but has real impact. One example was provided by the experience of the

London Olympics of 2012. The UK government said that spending on this was not relevant to 'Barnett' with the devolved administrations eventually getting £30 million extra – one-tenth of what they had originally claimed. The constitutional observer Alan Trench commented that this 'illustrated the arbitrary nature of the Treasury's power over the Block Grant and formula system, and how it acts as both judge and jury in its own cause'.[11]

The thorny subject of GERS

Much of the question of what Scotland contributes to and gets from UK finances, and the degree to which it benefits, centres around the annual controversies over the Government Expenditure and Revenue Scotland (GERS) figures and publications. These Scottish Government figures attract heat in part because they display the financial imbalances in the UK and, because they are disaggregating UK-wide public spending and territorialising, involve a degree of guesstimates. For example, major tranches of UK 'national' spending such as research and development significantly favour London and the South East, but for obvious reasons the UK government does not want to provide authoritative data on this.

There is an additional argument that a set of figures which explain the constitutional current order do not offer much of a guide to the long-term prospects of Scottish independence – namely to do things differently from the present. But they do, with all these caveats, offer insights into where Scotland currently is in the Union and where an independent Scotland would start from. Craig Dalzell in a review of GERS stated that: 'The argument against Scotland's fiscal sustainability is that the deficit – as highlighted by GERS in recent years – is one of the largest in Europe,' concluding: 'this view says far more about the nature of devolution in the UK and Scotland's place within the Union than it does about Scotland's prospects as an independent nation'.[12] This does offer a starting point and baseline to begin from but says little about future prospects.

Working out public spending and revenue in Scotland is not simple as it involves three sources of spending: money spent in Scotland by the Scottish Government; money spent in Scotland by the UK government; and monies spent elsewhere in the UK or UK-related which can be seen as on behalf of Scotland or its relevant share. GERS figures suggest that Scotland's notional fiscal deficit in 2019–20 was 8.6 per cent of GDP, compared to 2.7 per cent for the UK. All of these figures have been blown out of the water by the experience of the COVID-19 pandemic which has massively increased UK public spending and deficit. The UK deficit has increased in the year 2020–21 to 15.3 per cent of GDP, while overall debt has risen to 103.7 per cent of GDP – a staggering £2,223 billion at the end of March 2021.[13] Scotland's notional fiscal deficit at the same time was calculated to have risen to 22.4 per cent of GDP.

These figures produce a notional deficit per head in 2019–20 of £2,800 – a figure which is higher per head in large parts of the UK – Northern Ireland, Wales, North West, North East and West Midlands. In the year 2020–21, Scotland made a notional contribution of £11,496 per head to the UK compared to an UK average of £11,878 – a difference of £382 per head; the Scottish figure being the highest in the UK outside of London, the South East and Eastern regions. Meanwhile, public spending in 2020–21 is notionally £1,828 higher than the UK average, the highest anywhere in the UK bar Northern Ireland.

Two observations can be made from the above. The first is that the economic imbalance of the UK drives these figures and fiscal transfers from Greater London and the South, as David Heald has pointed out: 'The economic geography of the UK is damaged by the excessive dominance of its capital and its expanding hinterland.'[14] Jim Cuthbert, when examining an Office for National Statistics study in 2019 that explored regional balances across the UK, came to the view that:

> These figures for 2018–19 show that only three of the 12 countries/regions of the UK had a positive net fiscal balance for that year. What dominates the figures is the large positive fiscal balance in London and the South East. In fact, five areas (North East, North West, West Midlands, Wales and Northern Ireland) had larger net fiscal deficits per head than Scotland.[15]

The second is that, on these notional figures, the major difference between Scotland and the UK average is higher public spending per head, and not weaker income tax per head which is the highest outside London.

Many of the reasons for higher public spending in Scotland are historic, aided by geography and need. But it is important to also raise the question of where Scotland chooses to put its public spending and make its choices – and are they the right choices? In the year 2020–21 the big differences between Scotland and the UK per head saw the former prioritise more: housing (+100 per cent), public and common services (+69 per cent), agriculture, forestry and fishing (+69 per cent), recreation and culture (+56 per cent), environmental protection (+49 per cent), transport (+22 per cent).

An independent Scotland would debate whether these were the right choices strategically, and what the distributional and societal consequences of this were. This discussion has been mostly absent from two decades of devolution and the subject of independence. It is also true that Scotland's fiscal debate has to be less fixated about GERS and look at a wider picture, with Dalzell taking the view: 'The Scottish independence debate has been ill served by the focus up till now on GERS alone as an indication and predictor of the finances of an independent Scotland.'[16]

One analysis by Graeme Roy and David Eiser comes to the conclusion:

An independent Scotland would undoubtedly be financially viable, but would likely face a period of challenging fiscal consolidation... in its early years.

They come to the view about Scotland and rUK:

Once these transitionary challenges are overcome, an independent Scotland would have greater autonomy to address the long-term fiscal challenges that both it and the remaining UK will need to tackle over the coming decades.[17]

There is a need to look more creatively at ways of defining economic prosperity, success and wealth. There are numerous well-being and sustainable indices, one of which is the UN Human Development Index (HDI). Across the entire world the highest ranked nation-states for 2020 are: in first place, Norway with a score of 0.957, followed by Ireland and Switzerland in joint second on 0.955, with the UK in 13th place on 0.932.[18] Within the UK not surprisingly there are significant differences, with Scotland moving from a score of 0.777 in 1990 to 0.925 in 2019; while London has consistently rated highest on this index, moving from 0.843 in 1990 to 0.976 in 2019.[19]

Scotland's economy in a global context

Scotland's numerous other advantages and resources need to be taken into account. In 2020 Scotland had 8.4 per cent of the UK population and 17 per cent of the UK natural capital assets,

86.4 per cent of fossil fuels, 79.8 per cent of fish capture, 60.3 per cent of timber and 61.6 per cent of renewable energy.[20]

There is an even more substantive offshore economy than the one dominated by oil and gas. This is the actual wealth of Scotland and its global footprint. The UK economy is well-known for being at the centre of a network of relationships of how global wealth is invested, hidden and placed – including the use of offshore arrangements, tax havens and arcane accounting rules. The World Inequality Database has calculated that the ratio of wealth to income in the UK is 605 per cent in the direction of wealth to income, the highest since 1913 having nearly doubled in the past 40 years, rising from 337 per cent in 1977.[21]

This reflects the scale of investments in the UK in terms of assets, shares, property, offshoring and the cumulative effect of 'the hidden economy'. It is difficult to measure such figures for Scotland, but one estimate of the Scottish income to wealth ratio is, in the words of Oxford University's Danny Dorling, that 'the Scottish figure is likely to be similar to the UK figure, possibly slightly lower', an astronomical amount in billions of pounds.[22]

This is the reality of the global capitalist system and Scotland's place in it. Rather than just concentrate on the things that are easily measurable such as Barnett and GERS, it calls for a more ambitious and far-sighted debate where all opinions look beyond the Scotland that is immediately in front of them and see the wider environment of global capital, assets and wealth that Scotland is situated in and has a relationship with. It would also be beneficial to be able to estimate and monetise this global reach more accurately and perhaps the Scottish Government or an independent institute could consider a comprehensive audit of all of Scotland's wealth.

Scotland is much bigger in its global footprint than the tangibles we see or the land and terrain around us. It reaches out into international, secretive networks and hidden accounts in ways that can challenge the very idea of what Scotland is. In this it has echoes with how the size and reach of Scotland's maritime waters illustrate how much larger Scotland is than its land mass, and the implications and potential flowing from that.

In a similar vein, looking past the conventional fiscal figures which dominate so much of the independence debate, Scotland's economy and society suffers to some degree by being part of the Union. Being within a political entity where decisions are made for you by people not acting directly in your interests has negative consequences.

The retort to this argument would say that in the present Scotland's interests are well represented in key decision-making places at the heart of UK government, and even when it is not, Scotland's interests are always thought of. In the abstract principle, pro-Union supporters are no doubt being sincere when they elucidate the latter point, but increasingly, as the UK has become more unequal, we have witnessed the effective rise of government for London and the South East and the growth hubs of the UK economy.

A historic case can be made that in the past Scotland's union with England enhanced both economies as they both gained security and stability on the island of Britain, the creation of a bigger trading area and the joint project of Empire and British imperialism. But something that was true in the eighteenth and nineteenth centuries is not necessarily true in the interdependent world of the twenty-first century. It is also curiously backward looking in making a central pillar of the Union an argument from 300 years ago, this from a case which likes to regale against Scottish independence continually calling it 'backward looking', 'romantic' and 'a nineteenth-century concept'. All of these charges could be levelled against the current defence of the UK.

Scotland in the Union

The argument that there is a cost to Scotland being in the Union will be controversial to some pro-Union perspectives. This is not to suggest that there are no identifiable benefits of being in the Union, merely to point out that a more nuanced acknowledgement of the benefits and negatives of Scotland's membership of the UK would be helpful to all involved.

Several examples can illustrate the cost of the Union to Scotland. Starting from the premise used of 'the Union dividend', and a per head figure which is stated as to the benefit of every single person living in Scotland, it should be possible to counter this with the actual cost to every single person of being in the Union.

Take the ten years of Tory-led austerity in the decade (2010–20) of the Union pre-COVID. This cut billions from public spending across the UK including Scotland and had a detrimental cost to everyone living in Scotland. Related to this is the cost of a hard Brexit which, according to the Office for Budget Responsibility, has left the UK 4 per cent worse off in terms of GDP over 2020–21, this hard Brexit having a similar detrimental effect on the Scottish economy.[23]

In the recent catastrophe and tragedy of COVID-19, the UK government took a series of calamitous decisions, dithering and delaying at the outset on restrictions and a lockdown to curb the spread of the virus. In two years, over 150,000 UK people died from the virus, making the UK (again) 'the sick man of Europe'. The UK government's chaotic, incoherent and at times corrupt response to the pandemic came at huge human and financial cost. Fiscally, there was the damage done to the UK economy, with the UK the worst affected OECD economy from the pandemic with the sharpest fall in economic output.

All of this had implications for Scotland, which is not to say that the Scottish Government made every call correctly.

However, the effects of the UK government's set of serial missteps and miscalls translate into a direct COVID cost to Scotland and a cost to every single individual living in Scotland.

In retrospect, the cumulative cost of five decades of North Sea oil extraction could have been used to invest long-term in Scotland and the UK in a manner similar to Norway.[24] Over those decades, approximately £400 billion of revenue from oil extraction has come to the UK government (in real terms up to 2014) that would come out at a significant figure over those five decades to every individual in Scotland and the UK, and could have been invested in a long-term fund such as Norway's Sovereign Wealth Fund.[25]

If that were not enough, in terms of Treasury orthodoxy and short-termism is the cost of the privatisation of UK state assets over four decades, which began in earnest under the Thatcher government but continued under governments of all persuasions: Labour, Conservative/Liberal Democrat, and Conservative after Thatcher. The cumulative selling off of state assets amounts to a minimum £70 billion (up to 2014) without adjusting for it in real terms.[26] This has involved billions taken from taxpayers in deliberately selling off assets under their marketable value, and then billions made in profits from natural and semi-monopolies that would have gone into the public purse being expropriated for private gain.

Seldom touched upon is the deeper ideological shift behind privatisation which goes beyond a public–private rebalancing to the expansion of a rentier capitalism and the selling off of natural monopolies such as gas, electricity, and in England and Wales, water, which ultimately involve the capture and selling-off of the public as customers. James Meek in *Private Island: Why Britain Now Belongs to Someone Else* has summed up this shift:

millions of customers who have no choice of supplier, no choice but to take the water, and no choice but to pay for it. Millions of captive monthly payments in perpetuity... a form of buy-to-let scheme, with us, the customers, as the tenants, paying water bills, like rent... [If] we don't like the property, the management and agency or the landlords, or if we think the rent is too high, we don't have any choice. We can't move to a cheaper property, or a better-run one; we're stuck.

The affrontery on this operates on so many levels – and extends beyond water privatisation (which was specific to England and Wales). Privatisation was fundamentally not just about selling off public assets and natural monopolies, it also sold the public as an entity along with our rights. In Meek's words, we were sold as captive 'bill-paying citizens' and our capture and legal obligation to pay for the service gave a guaranteed income stream and value to monopolies and underwrote their sale.[27] Such has been the right-wing rachet of British politics over recent decades that this criticism of privatisation has been seldom mounted by Labour and the centre-left, enthralled as they have been to the Thatcherite remaking of British politics and society.

All of the above shows that there is an ongoing cost – financial and ideological – to Scotland, its economic development, fiscal state and well-being as a society of being in a Union where these collective decisions have been made in our name but not in any real sense by us. The overall logic of these and other decisions has been that, over decades, government decisions have not been made in the best interests of Scotland but for the growth points of the UK. There has been, in the past, a difference between a Tory-led government which in 2015 was returned with a UK majority with a solitary Scottish Tory MP, and past Labour governments which used to return 40–50

Labour MPs. But still the dynamics of the UK economy and capitalism has pushed governments of all persuasions to focus on what 'the Golden Triangle' of London, the City and surrounds.

The distorting, damaging nature of the UK economy and capitalism has to be centre-stage in any serious consideration of Scottish independence. It follows from this that any future Scottish economic development which reproduces the short-comings of the UK economy with its short-termism, promotion of inequality and celebration of the global classes, and triumph of finance capitalism, is an independence in name only, hardly worthy of the effort and disruption. Some on the left who are pro-independence made this criticism of the SNP Growth Commission chaired by former SNP MSP Andrew Wilson.[28] This emphasises the need in Scotland to encourage more economic and alternative thinking that challenges the dominant paradigms of recent decades, which is a big ask but needs to be urgently undertaken.[29]

The UK is one of the most unequal countries in the developed world, a situation which is not an accident but the deliberate consequence of government policy and the evolution of British capitalism. Thus, the rise of finance-dominated capitalism in the UK has come at a cost to real business, industry and commerce, because it has been easier to get a return through speculation or acting as corporate outsources or scavengers, than creating and growing a real business doing real things which have an economic impact.

All of this can be seen in the low levels of investment and research and development in UK business compared to the UK's competitors. This used to be of concern to past post-war governments led by Conservatives like Harold Macmillan and Ted Heath, as well as Labour Prime Ministers such as Harold Wilson, but under the influence of the Thatcher government and its mirage of a 'British economic miracle' and that of the administrations which followed, this has ceased to be a major concern of government and policy makers.

London's dominance of the UK economy, which also holds true culturally and socially, comes at the expense of sustainable growth and prosperity for the rest of the UK. In particular, English regions outside London and the greater South East are disadvantaged by this, which no talk of a 'Northern Powerhouse' or 'levelling up' will address because this is mood music to disguise the concentration of power and resources in the South.

London is only 13 per cent of the UK's population but occupies a much bigger footprint, economically, socially and culturally. It has, for example, 40 per cent of the entire creative sector employment in the UK and one-third of all UK businesses in the sector,[30] but more than that, large parts of the UK and in particular England outside London are perceived as 'creative industries cold spots' and dismissed by many of the creative class networks making decisions.[31]

The UK economy and capitalism no longer work for the vast majority of the UK population. In the past decade and a half, we have witnessed several seismic shocks to the system: the 2008 banking crisis, Brexit, the COVID-19 pandemic and the Russian invasion of Ukraine. But none of these so far has produced a real resetting or 'rebalancing' of this hugely unequal, unsustainable kingdom. That is because the main interests and players in the UK's political and economic system have a self-interest in maintaining this state of affairs and will not change unless they are forced to.

Sadly, for everyone who lives in the UK system change – economically, socially, politically – cannot come from within the system which has presided over this state and encouraged and supported it at every instance. The insider classes who make the key decisions in the UK and who frame the parameters of public debate are entrenched in their worldview, how they see capitalism and how they perceive Britain's place and role in this to the detriment of most of us.

The dynamics of UK shareholder capitalism with its emphasis on dividends, share values, takeovers and acquisitions, all the while fixated on short-term horizons is an environment aided by legislation, regulation, corporate governance and culture, and comes at a cost to the UK and Scottish economies. Major Scottish firms have been taken over underlining this problem, including in recent years Scottish Power by Spanish company Iberdrola and Scottish & Newcastle Breweries by Carlsberg and Heineken.

An even bigger story has been that of Scottish banks post-crash – and indeed their role in the crash.[32] The Royal Bank of Scotland Group collapsed under Fred Goodwin's reign after a disastrous series of policy decisions and acquisitions, including the suicidal decision to proceed with a takeover of the Dutch bank ABN AMRO at an inflated price three months after the credit crisis had commenced. Bank of Scotland ended up being taken over by Yorkshire-based Halifax in September 2001 to become the uber-reckless HBOS; post-crash, Bank of Scotland has become a trading name of its rescuer Lloyds Banking Group. Clydesdale Bank ceased being Scottish-owned in the 1920s but in 2018 its shareholders bought the UK operation of Virgin Money and in 2021 changed the names of both the group and operating business to Virgin Money. TSB was part of Lloyds from 1995 to 2013, when it was spun out. Its shares were listed on the London Stock Exchange in 2014 a year before being swallowed up by the Spanish bank Sabadell.

Whatever the appearances, in terms of residual 'brass plaques' and legacy offices north of the border, what remains of both RBS and HBOS is overseen from London. The Scottish banking sector, once domestically run, is now controlled from elsewhere. This is bad for Scotland's economy, as key decisions are no longer made locally, and the banks' knowledge and understanding of the needs of Scottish customers is at risk of atrophy.

It is a big change from the 'big four' banks of commercial life, and provokes concerns for the future in relation to the Scottish business and financial community, as well as the viability of Edinburgh as a financial centre, even though some areas of finance, including fund management and fintech, remain in reasonably good health. There could be future possibilities post-independence for rUK finance businesses setting up in Scotland, an established English-speaking financial centre with a skills base that are a match for Dublin's, as a location from which to gain 'passporting' rights to market financial products across the EU – but that is predicated on EU membership.

This leaves Scotland in a position where independence (that is not without risk, unknowns and uncertainties) can allow Scotland to chart a different path from that of the UK and its elites in recent decades and chart to a degree our own direction and priorities. Small and significant steps have been undertaken such as the creation of a Scottish National Investment Bank in November 2020, although the balance of its remit between strategic economic and commercial decisions has yet to be clear (as well as its first Chief Executive resigning in February 2022[33]). And a commitment to establish a Scottish National Energy Company by the SNP made in 2017 by Nicola Sturgeon seems to have been quietly shelved when the case for such an intervention has never been greater.[34]

A cornerstone of any alternative economic policy in Scotland will build on the work of the Just Transition Partnership set up in 2016 by the STUC and Friends of the Earth Scotland.[35] But while the Scottish Government and Parliament have passed motions declaring a climate crisis and committed to ambitious future net zero targets, this does not seem to impact on the conventional economic policies and mindset of the government.[36] This is evident from their most recent economic strategy, the lack of official backing for Just Transition, the potential of a Green New Deal in Scotland, or exploring how government intervention during COVID lockdown such as the furlough scheme decoupled formal work and income. A large part of the Scottish Government economic agenda merely mimics discredited policies of the UK and globally over recent decades and does not prepare Scotland for the economics and challenges of the future.

Undertaking a new economic path will have many challenges and require a much deeper economic literacy than at present, a greater depth of analysis, along with research and understanding of Scotland's position in the global order and potential choices that we have as a society to embark on that journey. Scotland starts with many advantages, and is not in as weak a position as some like to make out. The broken model of the UK and finance capital-led development and growth is in front of us, but making a successful departure from that requires a medium- to long-term strategy that Scotland has barely begun to think about. Also relevant to this is the social division and dislocation caused by such an approach and the next chapter addresses social inequalities in Scotland.

9

A Socially Just Scotland

One in four Scottish children before they reach school are way behind their age-appropriate social and cognitive milestones. School does not make this any the better. 'Real men' talk budgets and constitutions. Or run services like health or the police who mop up problems where they break out – not where they originate.

Alan Sinclair, founder of WISE Group, interview, March 2021

I think the most important work that is needed is an understanding of just how similar to England Scotland is. How Edinburgh is a city just as divided by inequality as London. How, if Scotland were to become independent, it would immediately become the most economically divided Nordic state – a country in which people had grown up living parallel lives.

Danny Dorling, academic, personal communication, February 2022

Scotland is a wealthy country but is also one of the most unequal countries in the developed world, a reality that ill sits with Scotland's prevalent view of itself. Twenty years of devolution, and mapping inequality in Scotland across Great Britain via the Gini co-efficient which measures income inequality, show that Scotland has consistently been more equal than Great Britain, but that there has been no real progress

towards becoming more equal, and that once London is taken
out of the equation, the two territories are broadly comparable.[1]
Thus Scotland has been subject to the same economic and
social forces and many of the same political choices due to the
UK government as Great Britain and the UK overall in the past
two decades.

Comparing Scotland and the UK with the Nordic countries
by the Gini co-efficient – with 0 representing zero inequality
and 100 total inequality – puts Denmark and Norway on 26,
Finland on 27 and the UK on 37 in 2019 – significantly more
unequal than the Nordics.[2] Figures for the Scottish Government
for the period 2016–19 produce a Scottish figure of 32 and a
UK figure of 35 – a much smaller difference (with the Scottish
and UK figures becoming more unequal when housing costs
are added to 36 and 40 respectively).[3]

Wealth in Scotland is even more unequally distributed than
income with one recent study emphasising:

In 2016–2018, a typical household in the top 10% of the
wealth distribution held £1.6 million in financial, physical,
property and pension wealth, whereas a typical household in
the bottom 10% held only £7,500.[4]

The themes of social justice and inequality are vast and this
chapter can only offer a brief overview in addressing a number
of key areas – poverty, drug deaths, education, the ultra-
wealthy and land ownership. It addresses the relationship
between social justice and independence, before examining the
legacy of authority, power and powerlessness and how it still
impacts on the present.

Scotland has across a range of social indicators a damning
record of entrenched inequalities far from the often portrayed
picture of an egalitarian country. Life expectancy in Scotland
on average is 76.8 years for males and 81.0 for females in

2018–20, but within these figures there are huge differences. One set of figures from Save the Children Fund showed that a child born in 2013 living in Lenzie on the outskirts of Glasgow would live a staggering 28 years longer than a child born in Calton in the East End of Glasgow.[5] The geographic difference of seven miles produces a seismic difference of four years life expectancy per mile.

Scotland's staggering record of drug deaths are the highest in Western Europe. This reached a high of 1,339 deaths in 2020, a rise from 527 in 2013, representing an increase of 137 per cent in seven years.[6] First Minister Nicola Sturgeon has called Scotland's death rate, representing 252 fatalities per 100,000 population, three and a half times the level of the rest of the UK, 'shameful'.

This tragic pattern is not equally spread across the country but impacts disadvantaged communities more. Hence, the three areas with the highest death rates between 2016 and 2020 were Dundee (43.1 per 100,000), Glasgow (39.8) and Inverclyde (36.7) which includes Greenock and Port Glasgow; East Renfrewshire (8.8), Aberdeenshire (9.3) and East Dunbartonshire (9.5) had the lowest.[7] Dundee has the largest increase in drug-related deaths, up from 5.9 per 100,000 in 2000–04 to 43.1 in 2016–20, followed by Inverclyde (up from 11.3 to 36.7) and Glasgow (14.5 to 39.8).[8]

Alan Sinclair, who set up the pioneering WISE Group in Glasgow working with the long-term unemployed, thinks we need a reality check about modern Scotland:

Take a single yardstick – deaths from misery and despair (alcohol and drug deaths plus suicide) has been steadily increasing. Have our housing schemes improved? Has attainment in education improved? Has the climate for open discussion and respect for people we disagree with improved?

Have the civil service and local authorities upped their game in the last couple of decades?[9]

Education, opportunity and inequality

Investment in good education and early years intervention has become a mantra of government to reduce inequalities and enhance life opportunities. Yet Scotland's educational inequalities are as stark and wide as they have ever been, and have of late been increasing on a number of criteria. The nationwide picture has been in the past couple of years less clear due to COVID and the Scottish Government stopping the Scottish Survey of Literacy and Numeracy, its final report being published in 2017.

The Scottish Survey found that in 2016 a quarter of Primary 4 pupils said they 'hardly ever or never' had someone read to them at home. In 2019 the Achievement of Curriculum for Excellence painted a detailed picture of educational inequalities. This included that in the wealthiest parts of Scotland nearly 40 per cent of all Higher Grade awards were A grades, whereas for poorer parts of Scotland the figure was just 16 per cent. The education writer James McEnaney sums this up: 'This new data makes the link between affluence and attainment brutally clear.'[10]

If that were not enough, young pupils who live in the poorest areas of the country are educationally disadvantaged several times over. They are likely to study fewer subjects; less likely to pass their courses; less likely to gain A grades; and have fewer choices open to them as they go through the school system. This last disadvantage has been reinforced by the narrowing of the school curriculum which has hit pupils from poorer areas more. Scotland's education system has been literally failing these young people and entrenching inequalities.

Educational inequalities are though not just about those who are poor. It is also about privilege. And here the picture is equally stark and damning. Take the network of private education in Scotland and the access it gives to getting to university and then getting the chance of a well-remunerated career.

Edinburgh as a city is characterised by educational apartheid with, in recent years, 24.7 per cent of secondary school children attending private schools. This translates into university places: 40 per cent of St Andrews University students in 2017–18 were privately educated, the highest of any UK university bar Durham; as were 34 per cent of Edinburgh University students. A St Andrews University spokesperson said of this: 'We don't recruit on the basis of schooling but look for academic potential. Using that approach, this year 49% of our Scottish students had access markers – background in care, a low progression school, or living in an area of multiple deprivation.'[11]

Not all of these are privately educated in Scotland. Many will be from private schools in England given the intake of these bodies. The effect will still be to crowd out state pupils and also to alter the culture and values of these universities over time. It is no accident that St Andrews, along with Durham University, is referred to as 'Oxbridge for Oxbridge rejects'.

St Andrews University is where Prince William and Kate Middleton met while studying; and it is no accident that there is *The Tatler Guide to the University of St Andrews*.[12] Former First Minister Henry McLeish, when reflecting on growing up in Fife Labour politics, said to me: 'One of the disadvantages I had was that, unlike Glasgow or Edinburgh, Fife did not have a university with the political networks to draw upon', a revealing observation about St Andrews University that most definitely is in Fife.[13]

The public marketing of privilege and elitism is something with wider consequences than any one particular institution. It normalises social values and norms, creating cultures of entitlement and exclusion. It creates a mindset among those privately educated and from the most affluent areas that getting the university place and job they want is their right, while for too many bright working-class young people the opposite is true.

Take the example of the Glasgow School of Art, famous for its Charles Rennie Macintosh connections and now sadly renowned for its two fires of 2014 and 2018 which burned down the Macintosh Building. Glasgow School of Art used to pride itself on its democratic and egalitarian credentials which gave opportunity to a host of challenging, creative voices, many who came from a working-class background. Such is the ongoing marketisation and pressures on higher education that this is now increasingly a world of the past. In 2013–14, first-year entrants to Glasgow School of Art included only seven students from a working-class background.[14] This figure is against the backdrop of the school being situated in a city which is predominantly working class and the efforts of a significant access and participation programme and staff.

These figures are not a one-off. The same year the figures for St Andrews University showed that it had a mere 19 students from a working-class background in its first-year intake. When I made public these figures in 2014, I was privately contacted by Universities Scotland, the body overseeing the sector, and told I had got things wrong, not on the substance of the facts but because they had changed the criteria for what counted and did not count as a working-class background.

Scotland's inequalities in education extend through all aspects of institutions including the pay and conditions of those in the top jobs. These have become engaged in an arms race of salaries and add-ons, while students in Scotland face record levels of debt (admittedly not of the astronomical levels students in England face). The burgeoning world of university principal pay is another world. The highest paid is Professor Jim McDonald, Principal of Strathclyde University, who in 2018 was reportedly on £366,000 per year and also had a £1,180,000 five-floor townhouse purchased in Park Circus, Glasgow for his use with a further £300,000 spent refurbishing it.[15] When his salary was increased to the above figure, because it only amounted to a £6,000 annual increase *The Times* ran the sympathetic headline: 'Strathclyde University chief receives lowest pay rise in five years.'[16]

Scotland's 'super rich' and land ownership

All of this baulks in comparison to the world of 'the super rich', an elite group venerated in large sections of the media, politics and culture, and every year showcased in *The Sunday Times* 'Rich List'. The richest person in Scotland is Danish-born Anders Povlsen, worth in 2021 £6 billion – up £1.27 billion in one year – who has acquired Topshop, Topman and Miss Selfridge in the past year.[17] He owns more land in the UK than the Queen and Church of Scotland combined, with more than a dozen estates across the country including 221,000 acres of land in Scotland. In second place is Glenn Gordon and his family, owners of the William Grant & Sons whisky firm worth £3.6 billion, up £409 million in the past year. Following them is John Shaw from Glasgow and wife Kiran Mazumbar-Shaw, owners of the India-based pharmaceutical business, Biocon, who are worth £2.942 billion, an increase of £1.134 billion in one year; Ian Wood of the Wood Group is worth £1.819 billion, up £119 million in the past year. All of this is the context of the ultra-rich increasing their fortunes to the backdrop of COVID in Scotland and the UK, 'The Rich List' identifying ten Scottish based billionaires and a record high of 171 billionaires in the UK, a rise of 24 on 2020, to the highest ever and the highest ever year-on-year increase. Mike Danson and Francis Stuart take the view:

> Using *Sunday Times* 'Rich List' data for 2021, the combined wealth of Scotland's top ten 'Rich Listers' increased by 12% from £19.8 billion to £22.4 billion. Scotland's two richest families now have as much wealth as the poorest 20% of the population, whilst Scotland's 14 richest families are wealthier than the bottom 30% of the population combined.[18]

Land ownership is one of the oldest sources of wealth, and a situation with Scottish and international ramifications. The campaigning group Global Justice Now undertook research which found that a number of significant landowners in Scotland were guilty of significant global human rights abuses. They named these individuals as Anders Povlsen (from the 'Rich List') whose fashion chains have been reported to violate some of the most basic working conditions. Others included the Vestey family; the de Spoelberch family; Majid Jafar and Lovat Investments Ltd; their activities included unregulated fracking, land grabs, privatisation of national parks in Africa and large-scale union busting.[19]

Land in Scotland and the UK is just another commodity, another tradeable asset that can be bought and sold, put on a balance sheet, used as a tax write-off and utilised for carbon offsetting. Scottish landowners get very defensive in the face of any criticism and the mildest reforms being suggested and are very quick to verbally fight back. Lord William Astor, David Cameron's father-in-law, talked of land reform in hyperbolic terms, describing it as a 'Mugabe-style land grab' where estates could be 'nationalised'. He then went further in his indignation, asking of the criticisms he and his landowning class have faced: 'Is it because we don't sound Scottish?' And reasoned: 'We should not all have to speak like Rob Roy.'[20]

A host of land reform acts and initiatives, particularly in the early days of the Scottish Parliament, have not yet made a significant shift in Scotland's massive concentration and legacy of private land ownership, including the issue of foreign and absentee ownership.

To effect fundamental change on a scale which could begin to address and break up that concentration of ownership would require a political will and intent currently absent, and a popular coalition that would together create the conditions to take on vested interests. This would introduce restrictions on foreign and absentee ownership and strengthen mechanisms to give a greater say to local communities and buy-outs. Such an agenda has to be linked not just to social justice and fairness, but to issues of community empowerment and economic development.

This picture of a Scotland of inequality and entrenched privilege does not sit easily with the account we like to tell ourselves and present to the modern world. It also does not fit well with the official story of devolution of the past two decades and its account that we as a society are incrementally progressing towards a fairer, more equal country, the mantras of first Labour and now the SNP in office and the mindset of the professional policy class.

This matters to the Scottish independence debate if it is to move beyond abstract principles. Rather it has to connect to and address the realities of a divided, unequal nation and offer concrete solutions which are about policy, but also about understanding power and the legacy of years of powerlessness.

What has any of this got to do with independence?

One argument put forward in this debate is: 'What has this got to do with independence?' There are two versions of this: pro-independence and anti-independence takes. The former can be wary of the quicksand of this terrain and of being sucked into a debate which at first looks alluring but is actually dangerous and full of traps. Rather than challenging power dynamics, it would focus on the broad brush and principle of winning back the sovereignty of the Scottish people. Everything else flows from that, this perspective stresses.

The latter makes the case that many of the changes talked about – on poverty, inequality, education, land and more – can actually happen under devolution and it is a misnomer to confuse the debate by linking them to independence. A version of this argument was evident in the 2014 referendum in challenging many of the social benefits outlined in the Scottish Government White Paper, countering that many did not need to wait for independence.

There is a common ground in both the above that reinforces conservative interpretations of independence that wishes to stick to a narrow constitutional agenda leaving other issues to be discussed elsewhere. Both would protest otherwise, but by such interpretations and saying where and when you can appropriately discuss radical ideas and effectively making some areas 'idea free', they are each in different ways discouraging radical change and reinforcing the status quo. Neither should be offered any encouragement. Independence has to be about issues of social justice and power in the here and now, or it will have less chance of connection with large sections of the public.

Putting a social justice agenda at the heart of independence has to have an answer to the above and to have specifics. First, some of the legislation and policies needed to enact far-reaching change sits with Westminster, and are thus beyond the current remit of the Scottish Parliament. A whole host of policies on the economy, welfare, employment, public spending and more are not fully in control of the Scottish Parliament but reserved to Westminster.

Second, the Scottish Parliament's current balance of responsibilities in relation to Westminster and the political dynamic between them has meant that the former has had to spend significant time and resources attempting to mitigate some of the worst examples of the latter such as the bedroom tax. And on another level, extensive public debates about such measures as the efficacy and harm of the rape clause deflect from a more constructive discussion about how best to target resources and support people in need.

Third, the shadow of Westminster along with the narrowness of much of the Scottish debate, defined often by a defensive and reactive mindset trying to mitigate the impact of what are usually Tory-led governments, does not aid candid and in-depth conversation about the scale of inequalities and injustice in modern Scotland.

Fourth, the above impacts on those campaigning and wanting change with some radical voices thinking that the only real obstacles to change are all external: Westminster, the British state and Tory governments, and removing these will automatically produce the conditions for change. This misses the need to build popular support for change, redistribution and understanding the need to make choices and trade-offs about what to prioritise with spending and legislation.

The legacy of Scottish authoritarianism and the good authority

A final observation from the above. Social justice is not just about legislation and resources, it is also about cultural values and norms and there is no doubt that Westminster and the British political system has a detrimental impact on Scotland. There is also a home-grown element to this.

Scotland has a legacy and, even in places, an enduring tradition of punitive authority which saw its moral right and code to be policing and punishing people regarded as less worthy – often those poorer but also those who stepped out of line and were deemed troublemakers. For example, Scotland's Poor Laws were in places more brutal than those in England; the discriminatory ways that waves of Irish Catholic immigrants were treated, or the brutal tradition of corporal punishment in schools which only ended in 1986.

This damaging tradition of Scottish authority and authoritarianism is often shied away from in recent times. There is a tendency to think we have left the Scotland of the dark ages in the past, and entered a new age of liberal enlightenment. Yet, the shadow of centuries of brutalism, punitiveness and oppression does not just vanish, and some of these liberal changes only happened in recent times: think of Scotland's record on homosexuality, only decriminalised in 1980, 13 years after England and Wales; and the controversy over abolishing Margaret Thatcher's Section 28 in 1999–2000.[21]

All of this leaves a feeling of damage, distrust and foreboding: of a lingering, understandable distrust in authority within certain communities; fractured public relationships where there should be trust; and a kind of collective wound and residual hurt carried in the psyche of some of those who come from communities that have historically been done wrong to. The writer Deborah Orr reflecting on growing up in Motherwell in the 1960s and 1970s, in sentiments that could be used to describe vast acres of Scotland wrote: 'Conformity was absolutely everything... Difference was criticism, criticism was unwelcome, so difference was unwelcome.'[22]

This is a difficult terrain to open up but if we are to make the idea of good authority in Scotland, we have to bring out the harm and hurt caused previously in order to try to heal that. And if that sounds too vague, just think of the cumulative damage done to generations of Irish Catholic immigrants, lesbians, gays and bisexuals, gypsies and travellers, and what were regarded by significant sections of the state as 'the undeserving poor', which affected the allocation of council homes, education and health service provision and more.

This means that social justice and advancing a fairer, more egalitarian Scotland requires a much richer, deeper and more challenging public conversation than what we have had so far. We really need to be able to go beyond politics. We also need to be able to go past the simplicities on offer from some on the left and the right – offering prospectuses which are solely about structural issues in the former, and exclusively focusing on the individual in the latter. This is a terrain which the writer Darren McGarvey has bravely explored: trying to find a sense of agency which deals with personal responsibility and the need for collective action.[23]

This requires hard thinking which will challenge many in Scotland. The traditional definition of social justice in our political discourse has not offered any meaningful philosophical sense of what it is, what it stands for, or defined its values. This has meant it has travelled light as a fairly pragmatic concept across the entirety of post-war Scotland from the era of Labour dominance to the rise of the SNP, true of the pre-devolution era and of the past two decades of the Scottish Parliament.

We have to ask who has benefited from not defining social justice? Not those without voice, power or needing support to live a fuller life. Rather it has worked for the professional interest groups who have traditionally run Scotland. It has allowed them to portray themselves as the champions of the people, as egalitarian and progressive, while zealously making sure that they define what is 'social justice' and 'fairness' and that it concords with their own self-interest and maintaining their position: a version of what McGarvey calls 'poverty safari'.[24] That seems to be a negation of everything social justice should be about, which has to put the idea of power and who holds it centre-stage.

Therefore, not only do we need to critique the inadequacies of the social justice offered so far from official and professional Scotland but most of the political classes; we have to come up with a meaningful concept for early twenty-first-century Scotland. Any such version would not just be about those disadvantaged but also those with privilege, and would recognise the crucial roles of agency, self-organisation and self-determination, and power and voice. And in doing so it would draw from radical notions of social justice the world over from environmental campaigners, feminists, land reformers, DIY local activists and disrupters and many more.

Our notion of social justice needs to be reinvigorated, renewed and remade in light of the multiple challenges we face. A holistic, all-encompassing version linking Scotland to wider campaigns for justice would be aided through being progressed in an independent Scotland, where we see ourselves taking responsibility domestically and directly seeing ourselves as part of something bigger on a global stage.

Breaking free of Westminster and the British state would allow Scotland to look honestly at who we are, what we do and what we don't do, what can happen in our country including in our own name by institutions claiming they represent us. That would be cathartic, liberating and intimidating at times but would be a profoundly enabling opportunity.

We would have the chance to decide who we want to be, and to be prepared to confront some home truths if we really want to live in a Scotland more equal and fairer, less scarred by poverty and the dead hand of entitlement and privilege. We would have the chance to honour the hopes and dreams of past generations of radical campaigners; to break the devolution mindset which works for those most connected to the system; to make independence about real change, and not forget the scandals of inequality which blight our prosperous country. Far-reaching change requires more than just politicians and party politics, and the next chapter looks at the wider tapestry of cultural change which has become more and more critical in the modern world.

10

Cultural Change and Self-Determination

Freud can help here. He reminds us that what the psyche cannot handle, the mind represses. In a world where one does not exist, being ignored and, at the same time, being the subject of daily acts of violence, is difficult if not impossible. The mind, or rather the psyche, represses the reality of what is happening in order to survive. Furthermore, one's psyche may also repress the truth that one is working-class in order to survive.

Cynthia Cruz, *The Melancholia of Class:*
A Manifesto for the Working Class, 2021

Everyone kept everyone else in line, using phrases developed for such a purpose: 'If she was ice cream, she'd eat hersel'; 'She'd buy tickets to her ain show'; 'She's so sharp she'll cut hersel'; 'She thinks she's somebody'; and the one I hated most of all: 'Whit's fir ye ah'll no go by ye', which translates as 'Don't embarrass us all by striving for something different. See what you get and be content with it.'

Deborah Orr, *Motherwell: A Childhood*, 2020

The dominant version of independence for the past two decades, if not longer, has emphasised an institutional and formal focus stressing political parties, politicians and the centrality of mainstream political change above consideration of other interpretations that could sit alongside and complement these.

This can be seen in many facets, one of which is the SNP stress on party and party politics to the exclusion of a wider cultural approach and the repeated emphasis of a political civic nationalism, to the marginalisation of cultural nationalism and cultural change.

Part of this has arisen due to the mainstreaming of the SNP, and the cost of success becoming a conventional electoral political party whose modus operandi is winning elections and power and retaining power. Drawing a distinct line between where the nationalist project is now and where it has been in the past, as the SNP has done, is another factor.

In the 1920s and 1930s, for example, an array of Scottish writers emphasised the power of cultural nationalism and how it could reshape Scotland.[1] Similarly, in the 1940s there was a debate on the role of a wider cross-party movement for home rule – the Scottish Covenant – independent of any political party. Indeed, the debate between party and movement in the constitutional debate could still be seen in the 1960s and 1970s and the first wave of an electorally successful SNP.[2]

Thus, the stress on the party has been a way for the SNP to distance itself from its own past, normalising and modernising itself and its appeal. But this has also come with wider consequences which need to be understood in relation to independence, social change and power.

One of the fundamental cornerstones of this approach has been to stress that independence is centred on 'full powers of the Scottish Parliament'. The rationale is very easy to understand – it normalises, makes understandable and institutionalises the concept of independence. It attempts to make it real and connected to the Scotland of the present that people see before them.

Such a version of independence minimises the notion of disruption, rupture, risk and fear of destabilising change. It attempts to make independence an understandable process – an extension of the Scotland that we live in – and, because the notion of an existing independent Scotland is in the past, invites the public to imagine a modern version that is an expanded idea of the present.

An extreme version of this was put to me by a senior SNP Scottish Government minister prior to the 2011 election: 'Independence is straightforward and simple: all it would take is to expand the Scotland Act 1998 to cover all aspects of domestic policy and everything else until eventually we become independent.'[3] This is independence without any 'Big Bang' and without an explicit public discussion and mandate; and an approach which has been overtaken by the 2014 vote and its aftermath.

What this dominant version of independence does besides the above is to minimise the prospect of change, to emphasise continuity and limit independence to a process not just led by, but focusing on, the Scottish Parliament and politicians, and hence excluding the vast majority of the population.

Given that in any realistic scenario only a tiny portion of Scotland will ever be elected to the Scottish Parliament, or involved in some capacity, this has an impact. Thus, this version of independence centres change around a narrow political class of politicians, civil servants, advisers and administrators. This is a version of independence remarkably constraining and top-down, and in many respects a direct continuation of the elite Scotland we have seen in the past, such as the Scotland of the 1940s and 1950 where experts, planners and professionals were the key drivers and shapers in creating and building the new post-war Scotland (which as we will see later on while being top-down left a beneficial legacy with lessons for now).

Remaking the cultural landscape of Scotland

The terrain of cultural policy, cultural change and self-determination should be a key area of the independence question and beyond. If we take the arena of cultural policy first, there have been numerous initiatives since the establishment of the Scottish Parliament in 1999 and the coming to power of the SNP in 2007.

The Scottish Broadcasting Commission was set up within months of the SNP winning the 2007 election, reported in September 2008, and one of its central recommendations – a designated Scottish TV channel – led to BBC Scotland beginning broadcasting on 24 February 2019.

Then there was the establishment of Creative Scotland created from the merger of the old Scottish Arts Council and Screen Scotland, that formally came into existence in July 2010. Since then, there have been major announcements on Scottish film studio sites in Leith in 2018 and in December 2021 a £11.9 million TV studio to be built in Glasgow's Kelvin Hall and operated by the BBC.[4] *A Culture Strategy for Scotland* was launched in February 2020, prior to the COVID lockdown, and contains much to admire, but Scotland does seem to be filled with ambitious strategies which sit on the shelf unconnected to delivery.[5]

These have been the cultural highlights of 15 years of the SNP Scottish Government; a period in which the Culture Secretary for twelve of those years was Fiona Hyslop (2009–21). In this period, the world of arts and culture funding were significantly curtailed by constraints of 'Tory austerity' from Westminster, and local government cutbacks in Scotland shaped by Holyrood spending decisions. Thus, the prevailing ethos of Hyslop's tenure became increasingly about trying to maintain arts and culture spending, the ecology of the sector and existing organisations, rather than have the headroom to think anew and innovatively.

Yet even allowing for this, there has been a paucity of strategic government thinking and action in the area of cultural policy. This is even more stark when it is remembered that Creative Scotland was not originally a SNP idea but from the last days of Labour in office and promoted by First Minister Jack McConnell and culture ministers Mike Watson and Frank McAveety. They in turn were drawing upon then fashionable ideas about the 'creative class' and 'creative industries' that the New Labour Westminster government had promoted in part to give support to 'Cool Britannia' and 'New Britain'.[6]

The Scottish Government's relative lack of intervention and activity over cultural policy has grown more pronounced the longer the SNP has been in office and since that initial flurry. There also seems to be a decrease in dynamism in the shift from Alex Salmond's administration to that of Nicola Sturgeon. At the outset of the SNP being in office, there was a desire and intent to embrace the new in the cultural realm, addressing broadcasting and the public sphere, and challenging the contours of the devolution settlement while attempting to expand the arena of cultural autonomy and representation.

Post-2014 the Nicola Sturgeon administration has paradox-ically presided over an environment where the intent and intelligence on this has mostly retreated, and even on occasion fallen silent. The terrain of cultural practice and thinking about the role of government, public agencies and other actors in con-tributing to a more dynamic cultural canvas has overall fallen out of the priorities of the Scottish Government and SNP. And this is to the loss of both, independence and Scotland itself.

This has direct real-life consequences. Is it any easier, and are there more supports or opportunities, to be an artist, cultural practitioner or cultural producer in today's Scotland? Have agencies such as Creative Scotland effectively championed our own distinct ethos and values, or have many artists merely bought into a managerial, bureaucratic mindset? And given concerns across the UK of the 'toffication' of the arts and culture with middle-class voices of privilege, is enough being done to aid diversity and those who are being pushed out?[7] Scotland's cultural landscape needs to address these issues along with the role of publicly supported culture alongside the commercial scene in an increasingly globalised digital world.

The role of the Scottish Government and other agencies are key in how the nation, its cultures and creativities can be best nurtured in the age of Amazon and Netflix. Philip Schlesinger of the Centre for Cultural Policy Research states that:

> The main consequence is that there's no coherent view of Scotland as a cultural player as we enter further into the digital age. No debate. I don't think that has to depend on whether or not we're independent as so much of the cultural space is autonomous. It affects representation.[8]

A corollary, and more positive take, is provided by Stuart Cosgrove who observes that 'the push for much greater film and TV production has been transformative. I suspect there has been a trickle-down strategy led by cities, Glasgow's conversion of Kelvin Hall into a busy TV studio and Dundee's championing of the V&A.'[9]

There is a mismatch here at the level of the personal, infrastructure and bigger canvas, with movement in the first two. To take one example, First Minister Nicola Sturgeon has made it a personal mission and credo to champion Scottish and Nordic fiction, books and writing, consistently promoting them at book festivals and from her home.

Secondly, there have been significant infrastructure developments, including those identified by Stuart Cosgrove. But the question remains: what kind of Scotland in cultural policy and representation is this trying to contribute to? In what way does cultural policy link to investment and economic growth and the kind of economy which underpins this? On all this there is mostly silence, and at best no coherent set of perspectives of even a sketch of a future cultural Scotland.

Surfing the future already here

The next area that needs to be reclaimed and championed is cultural change. This is because the SNP have, due to their tenure of office, slowly transformed into a mainstream political party which has narrowed the bandwidth of what it considers political and which, in many respects, has become more like other political parties in how it operates and does politics.

Understanding and embracing cultural change is not an add-on or luxury to any modern politics: it is a vital, essential component. This works on many levels as the cultural and societal trends and directing of a country has profound consequences for politics. More transformational politics go with the grain of the emerging cultural and social trends and attempt to capture and define them, working with these long-term factors to map out a future landscape.

Several examples close to home underline this. For example, the post-war Labour government which reshaped the UK after 1945, building the NHS and welfare state and instituting full employment as government policy, did not emerge from nowhere. Rather the collective experience of mobilising and planning during the Second World War made people see the power of the state and collective action; and they counterposed this to the failures of the 1930s from appeasement to mass unemployment and laissez-faire economics.[10]

Take the more contentious and still bitterly argued over legacy of the Thatcher administrations. The evolution of the Thatcher era of 1979–90 was not set in stone to begin with, but adapted, changed and morphed into a more confident ideological project over the eleven years while containing at its core from the outset the wish to assault the barricades and values of post-war British institutions.

Critically, the Thatcher project emerged as a critique of the failures of the post-war consensus and in particular the Ted Heath Tory government of 1970–74 and Labour government of 1974–79, a period seeing rising unemployment and inflation along with political instability. This – combined with a debate on trade union influence, concerns over the size of the state and public spending, and an increasing culture of individualism, self-expression and autonomy which was not just about consumerism – gave impetus to what became Thatcherism.

The slow death of the 1974–79 Labour administration gave added ammunition to this emerging right-wing insurrection. The 1976 IMF crisis saw Labour preside over major public spending cuts, and Prime Minister Jim Callaghan abandon the goal of full employment as government policy and explicitly embrace monetarism – then intellectually part of the Thatcher agenda. And following this came the 1979 'winter of discontent' where trade union members rebelled against the government's income policies with a wave of strike action. In the 1979 election campaign, sensing this shift, Callaghan said: 'You know there are times; perhaps once every thirty years, when there is a sea-change in politics… I suspect there is now such a sea change and it is for Mrs Thatcher.'[11]

None of the above excuses Thatcherism or argues that it was inevitable. It is rather to locate and understand it, to challenge the notion that it happened in a vacuum and that Britain was in a good state until 1979 when it turned upside down. Instead, there was a contentious political debate then about the future direction of the UK with different political projects – Thatcherism, the new left of the Labour Party and the centrist Social Democrats – all offering alternative paths of renewal and change which broke with the past, and in which in the 1980s the right emerged to shape the political agenda.[12]

All of the above has major lessons for the future of Scottish politics. How Scotland has evolved in cultural and social trends in recent decades, and how the SNP has risen to become the dominant electoral force, has been about changes and forces beyond party politics.

The emergence of the SNP as an effective electoral force did not happen suddenly. First there was the nationwide impact and breakthrough in the 1960s and 1970s, followed by a shallow period in the 1980s and a sustained building of support from 1999 and the arrival of the Scottish Parliament. All of this mirrored and drew from deep shifts in Scotland including a rise in Scottish identity, culture and distinctiveness across a number of areas of life; a decline in faith in Britain and a deference to authority; and a withering of the institutions in Scotland and the UK which transmuted British values like the military, Empire, religion. This shift was, in the words of historian Tom Devine, something which happened so widely that it was in effect 'Scotland's velvet revolution' to use the language of the Czech/Slovak divorce of 1993.[13]

With echoes to far-reaching change across the UK, the collectivism of 'Labour Scotland' began to fissure and crack from the 1960s onward, but was given a new impetus (or at least the appearance of it) by Thatcherism and majority Scottish opposition.[14] Yet underneath, currents were slowly undermining and eroding 'Labour Scotland', desirous of a politics that was more emphatically Scottish in its identity and interests, that was pro-autonomy and championing the national question and issue of self-government; and doing this from a centre-left position. The rise of the SNP, while not inevitable in a determinist sense, like other examples, draws from an interplay of powerful long-term factors which go beyond party and even politics.

The referendum did not just happen because the SNP won in 2011. That was rather the issue of timing, not the principle. The bigger picture was the long-term decline of the traditional unionist establishment and authority which facilitated debate about the kind of governing authority we want, and hence the kind of country we want to live in. This in effect became a 'big bang' – a release of energy, hope and enthusiasm, which for a period remade the contours of public life. Its effects will be long-lasting but in many respects, beyond normalising of the idea of independence, it is still too early to tell.

Cultural thinking in the age of hyper-capitalism

The above should not be contentious, but many want to ignore the wider terrain in which politics sits and is partly shaped. However, this has attracted the interest of many left-wing thinkers and academics, and more mainstream writers and commentators. Steve Richards has commented on 'the rise of the outsiders' and revolt against the mainstream across the West, a set of trends which includes the rise of the SNP and independence.[15]

Contemporary thinkers like Jeremy Gilbert and the late Mark Fisher attempt to understand the cultural terrain and its connection to politics in contemporary capitalism as part of their core intellectual work.[16] This is an environment where traditional tropes of left and right are no longer convincing; yet we still live in a world which is clearly unsustainable and unequal, for which politics fails to provide convincing remedies. Mark Fisher invoked the idea of 'hauntology' to explore how versions of the past were continually remade to maintain a nostalgia industry, and more cynically to transfix and envelop us. To Fisher this was about denying humanity the collective agency to create different futures, writing:

At a time of political reaction and restoration, when cultural innovation has stalled and even gone backwards, when 'power... operates predictively as much as retrospectively', one function of hauntology is to keep insisting that there are futures beyond postmodernity's terminal time. When the present has given up on the future, we must listen for the relics of the future in the unactivated potentials of the past.[17]

Two recent texts have addressed cultural change in Scotland. The first is Carol Craig's *The Scots' Crisis of Confidence*.[18] This argued that Scottish political debate had a propensity to talk about external and structural issues to the detriment of the more immediate and home-grown. The book cited examples of the over-attention given to the relationship with England and its detrimental impact on Scotland alongside the scale of poverty and inequality. Craig argued that these issues were framed to reinforce a lack of power – and what the psychologist Martin Seligman called 'learned helplessness' – while also marginalising the prospect of focusing on other areas.[19] Putting too much investment in an abstract idea of change did not ultimately help bring about lasting change, the argument went.

The other book, *The Glass Half-Full: Moving Beyond Scottish Miserablism* by Eleanor Yule and David Manderson, addressed the cultural representation of Scotland, particularly through the genre of 'cultural miserablism' associated with films of Peter Mullan and others.[20] This genre was generally characterised by a sense of bleakness, from the weather to the language, nature of relationships, lack of hope and overarching worthlessness. There was often a feeling that a 'superior' power had the upper hand, whether a gang, an addiction taking hold, a figure of authority, or another nation and culture (namely England). Fundamentally, in this account, according to Yule and Manderson: 'there is no escape and no matter how hard a Scottish miserablist hero tries he is doomed to failure'.[21]

These two perspectives are unusual and have had an impact on the self-government debate, both carrying an innate sense of the importance of cultural self-determination. Yet, the reach of Carol Craig's thesis led her in the 2014 referendum to publicly declare that although she felt much pull towards the Yes side, in the end she could not do it. Craig wrote one week before the vote: 'If the No side is Project Fear then, for the most part, Yes is Project Pollyanna', too relentless in its pursuit of positivity and optimism when there are dangers in overdoing each. She concluded: 'My own view is that no matter who governs Scotland post-independence the country will become harsher and more right-wing' and that while Yes were over-optimistic they were selectively 'pessimistic when it comes to anything to do with the UK' such as 'Labour's prospects for regaining power, the rise of UKIP, exit from the EU, Boris Johnson ousting David Cameron' – in all of which the pessimistic case of the UK put by Yes turned out to be accurate.[22] This led commentator Iain Macwhirter to summarise Craig's view of the Yes campaign in 2014 as 'the wrong kind of confidence'.[23]

The above shows the complexity of bringing cultural ideas into politics, let alone the independence debate that demands from its most passionate supporters on either side certainty, and where a binary choice debate forces people to take sides. The critique of 'cultural miserablism' was not appropriated in the 2014 referendum, but it did seem, as Eleanor Yule noted, that the experience of 2014 aided Scotland to move away to an extent from the draw of such grim, predictable stories.

That did not mean telling selective stories pretending everything in the country was fine; rather it meant allowing a different palette and range of accounts, some of which were celebratory, fun, irrelevant, emphasising the joy, wonder and love in Scotland. Yule observed that: 'Scotland is transitioning from a narrative of miserablism and dependence to one of

inclusion, diversity and hope. No longer a nation of Trainspotters... Scotland has boarded the train, but the destination is
something that the nation, the people and its leaders still need
to choose.'[24]

The uneasy relationship of cultural
and political nationalisms

There has been less explicit debate in the past two decades
concerning cultural self-determination but this was not always
the case. Previously there have been periods where this concept
has attracted interest and has even been central to debates about
Scotland. This includes the Scottish literary debate of the 1920s
and 1930s (usually now truncated in retrospect to one
dominated by Hugh MacDiarmid) but which involved other
figures such as Edwin Muir and Lewis Grassic Gibbon, authors
of respectively *Scott and Scotland* and the legendary *A Scots
Quair*.

Another period of illuminating debate occurred in the 1950s
and 1960s associated with the folk music revival, which
paralleled the emergence of CND and the first electoral
stirrings of the modern SNP. Post-1979, when the political
home rule movement seemed to have reached an impasse, there
was also an explosion of the Scottish cultural scene – from the
literary word to theatre, film, the visual arts and popular music
– that produced a flowering of creativity connected to cultural
conversations about self-determination, autonomy and politics.

The influence of this can be exaggerated, and has been
rightly challenged by some such as Scott Hames, but it did
undoubtedly play a part in the mood music of a generation who
grew up in opposition to Thatcherism.[25] Faced with the choice
of being inspired by a group of not very charismatic mostly
male politicians leading the Labour Party or SNP, or going to
a challenging play about some past or present historic injustice

by 7:84 or Communicado Theatre, or being enthralled by the contemporary folk songs on the first Proclaimers' album, for many of us at that time, it was an easy choice.

That is not to deny any ambiguity or uncertainty about the relationship between the cultural and political, but there undoubtedly was a relationship between the two. Opposition to Thatcherism in the 1980s was aided by events run by the STUC and others, and by small-scale publications such as *Radical Scotland* and *Cencrastus* – the former creating the idea of 'the Doomsday scenario' which described Scotland voting for Labour and pro-home rule parties and getting a Conservative government it had not voted for.[26]

Yet the rise of political nationalism and its expression through the SNP has contributed to the marginalisation of this cultural strand, and this is undoubtedly a loss and narrowing. For not only did this disparate force come up with events, cultural productions and ideas, they contributed to a public landscape which allowed for the germination of various political ideas some of which had practical consequences. The idea of a 'Doomsday Scenario', connected to 'the democratic deficit' felt in Scotland, contributed to the palpable sense after the 1987 UK election that saw a Tory third term while the Scottish Tories lost more than half their seats. This was the impetus which led to the publication of *A Claim of Right for Scotland* in 1988 underlining the case for self-government, and which led to the cross-party Scottish Constitutional Convention being set up the following year which produced a detailed plan for a Parliament.[27]

However, while the influence of these ideas and individual figures has been ruminated on, less reflected upon has been the narrowing of public debate evident since the 1980s (with the exception of the long campaign of 2011–14). Over the past 30 or so years – the period since the end of high Thatcherism – Scottish politics and culture has drawn repeatedly from the well of the 1980s, while seeing the narrowing of the cultural terrain of politics and the falling away of cultural nationalism.

The 1980s experience has operated as a watershed decade and framing reference point, both for those defined by it at the time and subsequent generations. But rather than relive the supposed heady days of the past, a more fitting tribute to the ideas and voices of that period would be to reclaim some of the core ideas and explore their relevance now such as self-determination, autonomy, questioning the role of authority, and creating new spaces and platforms for art, culture and ideas which connect to the political.[28]

The relevance of cultural self-determination

It still remains true that the potential of cultural self-determination is relevant and offers a rich tapestry in today's Scotland. The agenda of self-determination has in the past addressed issues of power, the nature of the self and identity, agency and capacity, and what it means to be both individual and part of different collectives in an age of interconnectedness. Articulating some of this has not been easy, and in the future involves the need to think creatively about how to champion and nurture such ideas. Importantly, it also highlights the need to think about how to break in to what has become the equivalent of a closed shop in how mainstream politics is undertaken.

A politics of cultural self-determination has to start from recognising the limits of political nationalism and a perspective predominantly fixated on the powers of the Parliament and role of politicians – the mindset which this chapter laid out the limitations of at the start.

Advancing this requires the creation and encouragement of supportive spaces and platforms, many of which will be embryonic, experimental and speculative (particularly at first); rooted in DIY culture and alternative ideas; and containing notions of self-governing, autonomous culture, of which some will become permanent platforms with institutional connections and/or viable sustainable income streams.

This might seem unrealistic to some but in living memory has happened on at least two occasions. In the post-1979 world a host of publications emerged: the aforementioned *Radical Scotland* and *Cencrastus* and others such as *Chapman* which had an impact. Fast forward to the 2014 referendum campaign, to when a host of platforms gave voice to what I called 'the third Scotland', the Scotland that did not see itself as signed up to either the old establishment (Labour) or the emerging new establishment (the SNP).[29]

This was evident in a host of groups and initiatives such as Radical Independence Campaign, National Collective, Women for Independence, Common Weal, and *Bella Caledonia*, to name the most obvious. This now seems a long time ago but demonstrated a host of profound shifts. For starters, there was a generational shift in how political and cultural production was being done and was being created, with a host of fluid networks and ad hoc pop-ups created which found an audience and had a public constituency.

These examples have to be remembered, utilised and drawn from to identify sustainable models of how to create such resources. This is in the context not just of the crisis of mainstream politics, but the limitations of mainstream media, the pressures of commodified consumer culture and the problems of advanced capitalism. All of this raises questions about how people connect and come together in an age of high-tech and in the aftermath of two years of global COVID accelerating issues of mental health, isolation and anomie.

The overall picture which should be taken from this is not one of pessimism, but of potential and opportunity. For all the challenges and overhang of the influence of a conservative mindset, Scotland in the post-war era has renumerated and reimagined itself as a political community, cultural territory, communicative and social space.

We now have the task to reinvigorate and redefine these notions, and to democratise and energise them in an age of monopoly capitalism, of grotesque concentrations of power and a broken UK political system increasingly distorted and dysfunctional, and shaped by dark monies and interests including foreign oligarchs and investment.[30]

Scotland can draw from past examples, radicals and successful cases of change, as well as embracing the new and emerging. The words of the writer, feminist and campaigner for self-government Naomi Mitchison are as valid now as when she wrote to Roland Muirhead in April 1953:

> It seems to me that you are bound to assume that a self-governing Scotland is going to be immediately morally better, and I don't see it unless there has also been a revolution. I can't see how the people who are likely to govern Scotland under any democratic system are going to be any different from the undoubted Scots who are in positions of local power.[31]

Scotland still needs those two fundamental transformations, indeed revolutions – self-determination as a nation and as a society. The political and the cultural have always been inter-linked, and to make both more effective and far-reaching they need to be explicitly recoupled, aiding a more open, generous and pluralist set of conversations about the future potential of Scotland. The next chapter investigates some of the key challenges and opportunities that an independent Scotland will face on the international stage.

11

Scotland International

EU Membership is not just about reversing Brexit, far more than that. It is about growing our economy and opening up opportunities for all so that we can tackle inequality, cooperate to be effective actors in seizing the challenges and opportunities of the Climate Emergency and ultimately be an outward looking and responsible global citizen committed to making the lives of our citizens and others in the world better.

Stephen Gethins, academic and former SNP MP,
personal communication, February 2022

Proponents of independence should offer credible proposals on EU membership, foreign policy and defence policy based on honesty and detail. They should account for Scotland's post-Brexit circumstances and be sufficiently robust to be able to convince anyone who has not already decided to support independence. Such seriousness requires leaving behind the notions that Scotland would waltz into the EU without profound transformation and that it would effort-lessly achieve great influence in the world. Optimism without substance would not count for much if Scotland actually became an independent state. If a future referendum returned a majority for independence, the realities of inter-national relations would come crashing in whether Scotland was ready for them or not.

Anthony Salamone, European Merchants,
personal communication, February 2022

Scotland is on the move – internationally. This is not as unusual a statement as it first sounds. Nations continually shift and reposition themselves down through the ages, sometimes democratically and by domestic forces, sometimes at the behest of external forces.

Sometimes this can be dramatic and of historic importance. For example, the European focus of the Baltic nation-states – Estonia, Latvia and Lithuania, along with Ukraine – has been pronounced over the past 30 years post-Soviet Union, and in light of a long record of Russian aggression and their recent invasion of Ukraine. And Turkey, after years of wishing to be seen as a European country and considered for EU membership, has become more assertive in seeing itself as a Middle East regional power.

Scotland's geo-political repositioning may not compare to some of the above – such as the exodus from the former Soviet Union – but it is profound and far-reaching, and has already begun. Sometimes history doesn't wait for formal declarations, it just happens and begins to move under our feet.

Scotland's international profile has to be seen against a number of intersecting circles of which there are at least four critical ones: the Union/post-Union UK; the European dimension with a particular emphasis on Northern Europe and the Nordics; Anglo-America; and the Commonwealth.

These can be seen as Scottish variants, informed by how the UK has seen itself historically and in particular by Winston Churchill's famous dictum of viewing Britain through three worlds of Empire and Commonwealth, the English-speaking world and Europe.[1] This came to define much of post-war UK foreign policy, a set of priorities blown apart by the twin disasters of the Iraq war and Brexit.[2]

The Scottish independence debate entails at its core the reappearance of Scotland as a self-governing nation-state on the international stage. It involves the need for Scotland to navigate and negotiate a new set of global relationships; to refine skills and networks of diplomacy; to set up new international connections and alliances, and to draw from Scotland's global reputation and undoubted soft power.

One factor that will play a part in this is the growing European and international awareness of a distinctive, self-governing Scotland which has stood in contrast to the UK state – in particular in relation to Brexit, but also in how it views its nearby neighbours and the role of international agreements and the rule of law. This chapter aims to explore four key areas in relation to Scotland's international profile, namely Brexit, defence, foreign policy and the question of nuclear weapons.

An independent Scotland would be faced with a rUK, raising the prospect because of the UK government's hard Brexit of a hard border between Scotland and England, the spectre of which would be used prior to any future independence vote by those opposed to independence.

The accession process to EU membership would in all likelihood be relatively swift for Scotland, given the nation was part of the EU for 47 years. Hence, Scotland could expect a process of applying, being given candidate status, and then a fairly rapid process to membership. Graham Avery, former member of the UK–EU negotiating team and EU expert has said that an independent Scotland would easily be able to rejoin the EU, stating: 'It would be the best qualified applicant the EU has ever had... It's obvious that Scotland could meet these criteria' and this would take approximately three to four years.[3] Taking all of this into account, there would still be significant challenges for an independent Scotland in relation to the terms of EU membership.

Scotland and the EU

First, the evolution of Scotland from its current position to EU membership involves several stages – a transition out of the

UK, independent statehood and then negotiation of the terms of EU membership. This will involve several agents – Scotland, rUK and the EU – and the nature of the emerging relationship between Scotland and rUK. This will hopefully be one of co-operation and working together but will not be without difficulties and obstacles particularly in the early years. Harmonious relations between Scotland and rUK will impact on the nature of the Scottish–English border that could represent an EU external border with echoes of the controversies over the Irish/Northern Irish border and Brexit.

Second, is the pan-UK issue of whether the Common Travel Area established in 1923 can continue in light of Scottish independence across the present territory it covers. Related to this is the role of any transitional arrangements connected to the current UK and EU Trade and Co-operation Agreement. The nature of the Common Travel Area could offer the prospect of Scotland sitting in the EU and in a common trade area with rUK and the Republic of Ireland, something which could be portrayed as 'the best of both worlds'.

A major point of negotiation would be any opt-outs and special arrangements for Scotland with the EU, and especially whether it could opt-out of the Schengen agreement and EU border free zone, something which the UK and Republic of Ireland did when it was introduced in 1995. If Scotland could get such an opt-out then, along with remaining in the Common Travel Area, an independent Scotland could avoid passport controls between Scotland and rUK, and retain freedom of movement of people, something requiring rUK as well as EU consent.

Third, is the issue of currency. Immediately post-independence, Scotland could stick with the UK pound even for a limited period; a new Scottish currency or agreeing to join the euro in principle at some future date. An independent Scotland within the EU with the currency of another independent state (rUK) would be unprecedented and would in all likelihood be a temporary arrangement. Retaining the pound in the judgement of Paul Mason is not a viable option, as 'A Scotland whose currency is backed by the Bank of England won't just be a monetary colony but a fiscal colony as well.'[4]

The debate about euro membership brings up the thorny subject of whether an independent Scotland declares or agrees to join the euro at a future date.[5] This will be influenced by the reality that Scotland will realistically in the first years of independence not be in a position to meet the criteria of formally joining the euro and hence any decision can be delayed. One choice would be 'the Swedish option'. Sweden formally agreed to join the euro when it finalised its Accession Treaty and joined the EU in 1995, but more than 20 years after the 1999 introduction of the euro it has no current intention to do so, with 56 per cent of Swedes voting against euro membership in a 2003 referendum. There is not an existing EU mechanism to force Sweden into giving up the krona. Another option – although probably less likely – is to negotiate a formal opt-out, as Denmark negotiated along with the UK in the run-up to the euro's establishment in 1999. As a new EU member state, Scotland would have much less leeway to take such a position, when it would be in its interests to show its pro-EU credentials (unlike the UK over the period of its membership).

At the moment, 19 out of 27 EU member states are currently in the euro. This means that a variety of currency arrangements exist across the EU and are likely to continue for the foreseeable future, which is respectful to the rights of small nation-states in the EU. The euro is used unilaterally by Montenegro and Kosovo and four European micro-states – Andorra, Monaco, San Marino and the Vatican City. Eight EU member states do not currently use the euro – Bulgaria, Croatia, the Czech Republic, Denmark, Hungary, Poland, Sweden and Romania.

Fourth, Scottish independence supporters must start thinking seriously now about this debate and the strategic choices involved. Post-Brexit, various options are open to Scotland including EU and European Economic Area (EEA) membership. The latter includes the EU's 27 members and three of the four European Free Trade Association (EFTA) members – Norway, Iceland and Liechtenstein, the one exception being Switzerland – which entitles members to access to the European single market, while not being members of the EU Customs Union, Common Agricultural Policy and Common Fisheries Policy.

EU membership relates to wider questions about Scotland's international role, and evolution of a formal foreign policy. A nascent network of expertise and diplomacy across the world with Scottish Government hubs in Brussels, Berlin, Dublin and Paris have been established, the latter in the last few years, within British embassies in the capitals of the respective countries. This is part of a concerted para-diplomacy internationally which could be the harbinger of a global set of future Scottish embassies around the world.

For some such as Kenny Farquharson of *The Times*, the European dimension involves numerous challenges which have so far not been addressed by independence:

I believe a small, modern European nation has to share sovereignty with its neighbours. Especially its most immediate neighbours with whom we have the deepest ties, economically, culturally and socially. There may be a form of independence where the complexity of this relationship is acknowledged in a detailed blueprint that takes into account shared interests across these islands and the continuing need for pan-British political accountability, but I haven't seen any sign of it yet. Nothing. Nada. Nowt. So I am left exploring these relationships within the context of the UK.[6]

Scotland's foreign policy and the myth
of the UK 'punching above its weight'

The *Scotland's Future* White Paper differentiated between the principles which would shape foreign policy and the instruments through which policy would be progressed. A significant part of Scotland's international profile would be the nurturing and encouragement of soft power – bringing together the country's reach, reputation, skills, culture – as opposed to the projection of 'hard power' of the military or relying on the country's economic capacity.

An independent Scotland would not be an isolationist country. It would not be 'going it alone' or 'cutting itself off'; in that sense it would not be 'separatist'. It would be a fully-paid up member of the international community from the United Nations to the IMF, World Bank, NATO and potentially the EU.

One challenge of independence will be to the continued mirage of 'Great British Powerism', and the belief that the UK punches above its weight in comparison to its size via its history, tradition, profile, resources and expertise. This mantra has increasingly come to the fore as leading UK politicians have felt a need post-Thatcher to mix British exceptionalism, triumphalism and anxiety about the UK's relative position in the world. This assertion was there in Tony Blair's time as PM and was a factor in the Iraq disaster, combined with the fixation on the UK being 'uniquely placed to bridge the transatlantic divide' between the US and Europe.[7] And 'punching above our weight' remained a significant strand in David Cameron's attempts to articulate UK influence pre-Brexit and find a way to project the UK's global role.[8]

It is one way in which the political establishment describe the UK and even though some of the bombast and self-importance it contains has been blown apart by Iraq and Brexit, it still remains as a prop. It is also used by UK allies to legitimise the UK's geo-political support for the US, including the current Biden administration's take. The US National Intelligence Council made the following assessment of the UK in 2021:

> The United Kingdom is likely to continue to punch above its weight internationally given its strong military and financial sector and its global focus. The United Kingdom's nuclear capabilities and permanent UN Security Council membership add to its global influence. Managing the economic and political challenges posed by its departure from the EU will be the country's key challenge; failure could lead to a splintering of the United Kingdom and leave it struggling to maintain its global power.[9]

This claim can even be found in how Scottish pro-Union perspectives justify Scotland's role in the UK's international profile to domestic audiences, as a Liberal Democrat commission headed up by David Steel stated, as one example:

> The Union enabled Scotland to punch above its weight on the world stage and allowed Britain to become more than its parts... the UK as a whole has a greater punch internationally than any of its constituent parts separately...[10]

One variant of this presents Scotland as gaining from the mindset of the UK as a player in global institutions, and stresses that because of this it has a disproportionate influence compared to its size, that of course might well be jeopardised by independence. This view was articulated in the run-up to the UN Climate Change Conference COP 26 in Glasgow in November 2021 with the UK government stating:

Scotland combines its resources and influence with the rest of the UK to play a leading role in tackling global issues like climate change, poverty, conflict and wildlife crime... Scotland plays an important role in delivering a Global Britain...[11]

A Scottish foreign policy would involve understanding the impact of small-sized states in an increasingly interdependent world, and their potential as forces for good and co-operation. In an obvious sense, small democratic states have a built-in interest in supporting a rules-based order, where multi-lateral and multi-national negotiation is encouraged, more than the resort to hard and military power.

An independent Scotland would need to take time, effort and resources to build up a Scottish diplomatic service to maximise the networks and alliances it could utilise. Such a Scotland would not become the equivalent of a successful small state such as Norway, Sweden or New Zealand overnight, but the potential is there. Nicola McEwen of Edinburgh University states that: 'small states invest heavily in networking, and using soft power to persuade, to generate new ideas' and continues that: 'Scotland's brand is far in excess of what most other sub-state actors have'.[12] Academic Daniel Kenealy notes 'with a willingness to prioritise – alongside some patience and a lot of hard work – an independent Scotland could develop a successful and distinctive role in international affairs'.[13]

North by north-west Scotland

Scotland's defence and security policy brings forth all sorts of concerns in the British establishment about the lessening of UK-wide capacity and its global role. What is undoubtedly true is that Scotland's geo-political position sitting in the north-west corner of Europe at a critical and vital point in terms of maritime power and projection has major significance far beyond Scotland and the UK.

Scotland is in a pivotal place in relation to 'the GIUK Gap', an acronym which stands for the 'Greenland Iceland United Kingdom Gap'. This gap is composed of the sea channels which sit between Greenland and Iceland and the north-west coast of Scotland, and has been, in the words of Tim Marshall, 'a choke point in the world's sea lanes'.[14] The GIUK Gap was of major importance in the Second World War when who controlled these vital waters was a factor in the outcome of the Battle of the Atlantic. This was played out in such epic engagements as the sinking of HMS *Hood* and the Nazi battleship *Bismarck* in the north Atlantic in May 1941. Similarly, this was a key arena in the Cold War between NATO and the Warsaw Pact, and subsequently as tensions and stand-offs have increased between NATO and Putin's Russia its importance has risen again.

In the Second World War these waters and land in the area were of strategic importance. It led to the British military occupation of Iceland in 1940 and American occupation of Greenland in 1941, both of which were a response to the German invasion of Denmark in April 1940. Related to this, the Royal Navy's main base at Scapa Flow in the Orkney Islands played a significant role both in the north Atlantic and in protecting Allied convoys heading east around the Norwegian coast taking aid to the Soviet Union. Therefore, the GIUK Gap's geo-political importance matters in capitals and governments far away from Edinburgh and London, and the stance of an independent Scotland on relevant areas will have ramifications around the globe. As Tim Marshall writes, in relation to the Gap's importance:

The GIUK Gap is one of the reasons why London flew into a panic in 2014 when, briefly, the vote on Scottish independence looked as if it might result in a Yes. The loss of power in the North Sea and North Atlantic would have been a strategic blow and a massive dent to the prestige of whatever was left of the UK.[15]

The Arctic region is transitioning permanently from being ice-covered to being seasonally ice-free, inducing changes in human and commercial authority. Similarly, this will impact on how governments, international agencies and businesses think of the concept of 'the High North' which covers the European Arctic. This region is going to be a pressure point for all sorts of competing pressures in the twenty-first century: environmental, commercial, military, and the need to protect and preserve as much as is possible of the Arctic, its ice-sheet and ecology, to prevent rising sea levels.

The significance of Scotland's position and its wider implications has significant consequences for the independence question. Thus, questions about the expenditure and viability of a Scottish defence force, issues of defence capacity, infrastructure, logistics and intelligence, and related issues of NATO membership and nuclear weapons, would all need to be considered.

Scotland's defence stance would be influenced by the legacy of UK defence and the arrangements an independent Scotland and rUK made, not just on defence but on wider matters and whether a conducive spirit of co-operation and compromise was present.

UK defence spending has historically been at a higher level of GDP than most NATO members – the USA apart. This gap has declined post-Cold War, but recent UK governments have embraced the 2 per cent benchmark set by NATO and was 2.1 per cent of GDP in 2018–19, having fallen from 2.5 per cent in 2008–09. There is no guarantee that an independent Scotland would want to – faced with many calls on expenditure and resources – meet immediately the 2 per cent NATO figure. The SNP's Growth Commission report committed to a 1.6 per cent figure, noting this was 'significantly ahead of the small country average (1.1%) and the 8th highest in NATO'.[16] This was all prior to the 2022 Russian invasion of Ukraine, something which has fundamentally altered the international landscape and the nature of NATO.

As critical as the debate on the size, composition and capacity of any Scottish defence force is the increasing importance of intelligence and security. Currently, the UK is part of the 'Five Eyes' intelligence network made up of Australia, Canada, New Zealand, the UK and USA, which is much lauded in public discussions, but has to be seen as part of a wider Western co-ordinated response.

The world of disinformation and destabilisation and future threats

The unfortunate reality of the modern world and international relations are the threats to democracy, peace and stability, from cyber-warfare to disinformation campaigns and the use of dark monies via intermediaries through to mainstream institutions who are not fully transparent about their funding.

For all its hyperbole, the British state and government are highly vulnerable to foreign interventions and influence. The Conservative Party is more than happy to receive millions from Russian oligarchs, while the controversy over Russian involvement in the 2016 Brexit campaign has never been fully exposed including issues around the funding of part of the Leave campaign and the issue of Twitter bots and disinformation. As a US Senate minority report in 2018 concluded in relation to the Brexit vote: 'The Russian government has sought to influence democracy in the United Kingdom through disinformation, cyber hacking and corruption.'[17]

The UK Parliament's Intelligence and Security Committee on Russian involvement in the UK was published after numerous delays in July 2020, redacted in places.[18] Yet nearly two years after its publication the UK government had not acted on its main recommendations when Russia invaded Ukraine in February 2022.[19] The report found no evidence of Russian interference in the 2016 Brexit referendum on the grounds that they had not been authorised to investigate this area; they did controversially claim to find some evidence of Russian interference in the 2014 Scottish vote. SNP MP Stewart Hosie, who served on the committee, commented after its publication:

> Shortly after the referendum Russian election observers suggested there were irregularities in the conduct of the vote. This position was being widely pushed by Russian state media. We understand the UK government viewed this is primarily aimed at discrediting the UK in the eyes of a domestic Russian audience, but nevertheless those messages post-referendum were being put out there to discredit the results. That was a warning light.[20]

This experience and the substance behind it, of the seemingly laissez-faire approach of the UK government to the actions of orchestrated state disinformation and destabilisation in the UK including the influence of Russian individuals and monies does seem inexplicable taking into account the documented actions of the Putin regime including the Salisbury attacks on UK soil. But there is a paradox at the heart of the Tory establishment and British capitalism – talking tough and looking patriotic on military and security matters while accepting money from nearly any source and believing anything can be sold.

This attitude manifests in the heart of Britain's elites as a staggering complacency about the security of infrastructure, strategic assets and how the UK power system works. Oliver Letwin (when UK minister with oversight for the Cabinet Office) was responsible for looking at scenario planning and back-ups concerning digital connectivity – as the UK switched to 'one network of networks on which more or less everything else government, business and family life – relies' and making sure there were contingency plans if there was a network failure and all services including emergency ones went down.[21] He found at the heart of government a complete disinterest in this, illustrating that while UK elites talk of themselves as hard-headed, serious players at the same time they take a deeply cavalier (and poorly informed) approach to real issues of security that have the potential to compromise the UK.

Numerous small countries in and out of NATO have shown themselves capable of being nimble and agile in responding to the new world of political disinformation and destabilisation. Notable examples include the Czech Republic and Estonia – both of which broke from the Soviet bloc and in the latter case the Soviet Union – and have been subject to Russian operations. Relevant to Scotland – geographically and in being long-term members of NATO – are Norway, Denmark and the Netherlands that also have examples of practice that Scotland could draw upon which provide the potential for intelligence partnerships and co-operation.

Scotland's defence, intelligence and security stand would be linked to its foreign policy and international alliances. There has been a strategic lack of considering these issues at the level of experts, given the impact that Scotland being part of the UK has had. But these topics now need serious consideration, moving beyond alarmist claims and scare stories, of which there have been too many warning that an independent Scotland could be a threat to the continuation of Western civilisation.

For example, Baron Fraser, former Solicitor General and Lord Advocate for Scotland, made the outlandish claim that an independent Scotland might force rUK to take action due to a military or terrorist threat: 'If that were to happen what alternative would England have but to come and bomb the hell out of Glasgow Airport and Edinburgh Airport?'[22] This is not an isolated episode, with such apocryphal language regularly trundled out by senior British politicians such as UK Defence Secretary Ben Wallace telling the Tory Conference in October 2021 that an independent Scotland would be 'definitely more vulnerable' to terrorist threats through losing access to vital shared intelligence and the UK nuclear deterrent.[23]

As pertinent is the fact that against a multitude of potential threats and uncertainties alongside anxieties about the potential 'breakdowns' of systems there is no fail-safe security, as academic Andrew Neal puts it:

Whereas old fashioned threats were thought to come from external enemies or enemies within, risks may be produced endogenously through breakdowns in technological, social or economic systems, such as power supplies, transport systems, social disorder or financial crisis.[24]

The present devolved Scotland, according to Neal, already has to address some of the above through resilience arrangements which mirror Whitehall national security plans, illustrating even in this sensitive area the blurring of the lines between devolved and reserved matters.

The nuclear option, Scottish independence and rUK

The UK's four nuclear-armed submarines continue to operate out of Faslane at present, with Trident missiles having replaced the earlier Polaris missiles. Trident itself will be replaced when a new range of missiles are active from 2025 and will also operate from Faslane.

There has been a significant ramping up of UK operations at Faslane, with from 2020 all of the UK's submarines being based there. This includes the four Vanguard-class nuclear submarines with nuclear missiles, as well as what will rise to seven Astute-class attack submarines with the Vanguard submarines replaced by four Dreadnought Trident missile carrying submarines. The Royal Navy said about this focus in 2019:

> By putting our boats and training in one place, our subma-
> riners can put down roots in Scotland knowing that they are
> no longer required to commute from one end of the country
> to another.[25]

The 2002 decision to base the seven new Astute-class attack submarines at Faslane, which is nearing full implementation, has narrowed longer-term basing options in England. In 2016, the UK government announced that it would proceed with the manufacture of four Dreadnought Trident missile-carrying submarines, implementing the 2007 decision on renewal, and confirmed that they would be based in Scotland.

Removing the nuclear capacities and military equipment at Faslane and Coulport is a major endeavour involving the iden-tification of other rUK sites; their preparation at a political and logistical level; and the cleaning up, denuclearisation and detoxification of the Scottish sites. This significant programme will entail a significant, long-term programme of work which may involve international oversight, advice and expertise, and could prove costly in finance and complex in concluding.

This brings us to the highly sensitive subject of nuclear weapons and the siting of the UK's nuclear arsenal on Scottish soil and waters. The scale of this has to be underlined to recognise the importance of this for the UK government and independence movement. The backstory of the militarisation and nuclearisation of part of Scotland just 40 miles from Glasgow is critical. The arrival of nuclear weapons on the Clyde goes back to the US request for basing nuclear weapons in the UK in November 1959, with the first deployment at Holy Loch in March 1961 (with the American presence lasting 31 years until June 1992), and the decision on the UK and Polaris confirmed in March 1963, which would ultimately be based at Faslane.[26]

These life-changing decisions and the critical period in the UK and Scotland's nuclear history began before the emergence of the Scottish constitutional debate as we know it became a live political subject connected to electoral politics. Indeed, this period of the end of the 1950s and early 1960s was one of immense change in Scottish politics and its relationship to UK politics, although little understood and commented upon at the time.

All of this occurred as Harold Macmillan led the Conservatives to a third successive election victory in October 1959, when the party won an overall majority of 100 seats as Scotland swung against the UK national trend and against the Tories in votes and seats. Subsequently, the immediate years saw the rise of the anti-nuclear issue and the profile of CND in Scotland. This became intertwined with the first electoral signs of support for the SNP, with a rise in youth membership, better organisation, and decent performances and support in the two Westminster by-elections of Bridgeton in November 1961 and West Lothian in June 1962 where the SNP finished a strong second.[27] Scottish politics were dominated by issues of the economy and the cost of living like elsewhere in the UK, but to younger voters disenchanted with the pro-nuclear stance of the Tories and Labour, the SNP offered a political home.

It is understandable after 60 years of the nuclearisation of the Clyde that many campaigners want to see the nuclear weapons and submarines removed as quickly as possible. A 2012 Scottish CND report laid out a speedy programme of demilitarisation, with the nuclear weapons disabled within seven days of independence and removal and final dismantling of nuclear warheads within four years.[28]

Others have posited a longer and more drawn-out timescale, with a 2014 Royal United Services Institute (RUSI) report stating that the UK government could find alternatives at a lower cost than the UK government suggests, but doing so would involve time – possibly up to 14 years after independence. Within this there is room for manoeuvre they assess, stressing that it is more likely that rUK would find a replacement site for Faslane quicker than Coulport concluding that it is possible:

> Scotland could be offered a phased location plan, in which Faslane is vacated before Coulport. While this would allow Scotland to at least celebrate the end of submarine basing on its territory, these would likely be muted by the continual presence of nuclear weapons at Coulport – and thus need for warhead convoys and other protective measures.[29]

The British state and thinking the unthinkable

Addressing these issues post-independence would necessitate co-operation and ongoing dialogue from both governments, who in their public stances appear far apart, but the RUSI analysis assesses that this 'may understate the potential for a more co-operative post-separation relationship, given the stakes that both sides would have in avoiding deterioration in their wider security relationship' and concludes: 'This tradition of co-operation would be likely to continue if Scotland were to transition to independence.'[30]

There have been some suggestions that a compromise might be reached by the two governments on Trident and nuclear weapons. This is a subject for very different reasons neither the UK government or independence supporters want to publicly explore, particularly prior to any referendum, but is undoubtedly being explored in private. One observer suggested the possibility of tying Trident to acceptance by rUK of a currency union:

> There might be a certain logic in this as a gaming strategy, but the two issues belonged in different arenas, with differing constituencies. So the position of the Treasury and the Bank of England on sharing sterling would not easily be moved by considerations in another area, while the SNP activists for whom Trident was a touchstone issue would not be consoled by being allowed to keep the pound.[31]

This judgement seems to both have some insight about the pressures in any negotiations but at the same time floats a complete red herring in order to dismiss it out of hand – a formal Trident-currency deal. In so doing, it even poses a world with serious players on one side, the Treasury and Bank of England, and on the other 'SNP activists' – rather than the Scottish Government. This aims to emphasise the David and Goliath nature of the dynamic with one fully conversant with power politics, the other driven by idealism and hence ill-equipped for such high-powered talks.

Post-2014 the UK government has, according to some reports, been more inclined to look at least behind closed doors at options available in light of a future independence vote. To take one case which became public, in September 2021 reports emerged of the UK Ministry of Defence having laid out options, including moving the nuclear weapons to Devonport base in Plymouth and the creation of a 'British Overseas Territory' or 'Nuclear Gibraltar' (as it was sensitively called) to address the UK leasing Faslane and Coulport for at least a period of time.[32]

Apart from the hyperbolic rhetoric about making part of Scotland an 'overseas territory' for which there is no legal basis or chance of, any such deal would require Scottish Government consent. There is the unspoken precedent of negotiations between the UK and Irish in the Anglo-Irish Treaty of 1921 which saw the UK gain the use of three treaty ports on the west and southern coast of Ireland – which the Irish got back 16 years later – and numerous other examples of UK withdrawal the world over.[33] This is different because it strikes at the core of what the UK is and projected as by its elites, of which Scotland was always seen as an integral part. But it does indicate that the UK government is beginning to think about what was once unthinkable – deep inside the corridors of the MOD and Whitehall – something they formally resisted in 2014.

One fundamental in all this is the unprecedented nature of the nuclear question. In an independent Scotland we would literally be in uncharted waters, to quote the title of Malcolm Chalmers and William Walker's study of the nuclear weapons issue in Scotland.[34] There is no comparative example from the collapse of the Soviet bloc and dissolution of the Soviet Union – in the removal of nuclear weapons from the Ukraine, Belarus and Kazakhstan – or from South Africa renouncing nuclear weapons after the fall of apartheid.

William Walker observed that:

Trident's continued deployment out of Faslane and Coulport would create a situation without precedent: a nuclear weapon state's basing of its entire nuclear fleet on the territory of a state seeking to become a non-nuclear weapon state under international law and member (probably) of the recently established Treaty on the Prohibition of Nuclear Weapons. Politically and legally, the problems might only be finessed if Faslane and Coulport remained sovereign base areas of rUK after independence, a proposal that would open many cans of worms.

Some form of temporary agreement and transitional period is one likely outcome in such a process, Walker noting:

> Trident would, of course, be a great bargaining chip if the Scottish Government felt able to use it without offending its supporters.[35]

The independence case, as well as being against nuclear weapons, has to think about the transition questions of becoming a non-nuclear state. As well as the length and kind of transition, this includes such issues as the legal status of the bases for any period until closure; the rights of consultation which the Scottish Government would have; and how control and management of the waterways would be undertaken. As Chalmers and Walker point out in a recent intervention:

> Under the Law of the Sea, the Gareloch (Faslane) and Loch Long (Coulport) would become Scotland's internal waters, with stretches of the Firth of Clyde and down the coast becoming its territorial waters.[36]

This raises many questions. How would traffic involving nuclear-armed submarines and other armed craft in these narrow waters be managed, and issues of access navigated? And by whom? And what rights would rUK retain? And could there be some kind of joint control and oversight of the waterways and bases? Chalmers and Walker come to the view that: 'Timing, cost and compliance – and their uncertainties – would haunt the inquiries and negotiations' and their aftermath.[37] There would need to be clear areas of Scottish and rUK control, with mutual understanding and agreement, and at least for some areas some degree of joint oversight over what would be Scottish waterways and any materials carried across Scotland's roads.

The Scottish independence argument needs to address the phasing out of nuclear weapons and facilities on Scottish land and in Scottish waters which will involve reaching agreement on decommissioning, decontamination and dismantling of the entire nuclear infrastructure. And if that were not difficult enough, this will need to be done against a backdrop of political and geopolitical uncertainty, both in Scotland/rUK and internationally, but this complex and critical thinking needs to be done. In 2021 Anthony Salamone launched two publications on Scotland's foreign policy,[38] and told me at the time:

Scotland has the potential to become a successful European small state with influence in the EU and the world, relative to its size and position. However, that outcome will never be guaranteed. The only path to that future is to recognise the challenges Scotland would face, provide innovative solutions and create new opportunities.[39]

The UK now is far away from being a force for benign, liberal Enlightenment values, but this is still a story explicitly pronounced by UK leaders the more divorced it has become from reality. This is true of Labour and Conservative UK governments but the descent post-Brexit under Boris Johnson has been steep, with David Clark, former Foreign Office adviser to Robin Cook, summarising the toxic mix of the present UK government: 'The Conservative formula for staying in power is common to many right-wing populist movements. Manufactured culture wars at home, manufactured disagreements and conflict with others abroad.'[40] This overall mindset will not completely disappear in the near future, and Scottish opinion has to take cognisance of this in debates and decisions about the future.

Scotland's international profile and role post-independence would depend on the nature and kind of independence Scotland decides upon. That is intrinsic to the strategic choices that go to the core of the independence question. 'Scotland's international footprint cannot be wished away nor can it be assumed to be an automatic success', states Stephen Gethins, former SNP MP and academic.[41]

Fundamental to this is embracing the idea of independence as interdependence. A self-governing Scotland should be a good and reliable neighbour, partner and ally to rUK; European colleagues; in organisations like the Commonwealth, and across the globe in a world which for the foreseeable future is defined by uncertainty, instability and threats. There is a vital need for governments, states and citizens to rise to these multiple challenges and to aspire to transcend them, to imagine and create a world of co-operation, solidarity and justice.

PART IV

The Shape of Things to Come

12

How Scotland Gets an Independence Referendum

Scotland's inalienable right to self-determination includes the right to decide how to exercise that right… To deny it would be to say that of all the nations of the world today we had no national right to self-determination.

George Galloway, *Radical Scotland*, April–May 1983

It is perhaps unfortunate that the main battle to persuade Scots of the advantage of remaining in the UK should have to be fought in Scotland's most deprived area.

Vince Cable, former Liberal Democrat leader,
The Red Paper on Scotland, 1975

For many, whatever their position on independence, this is the big question. Never mind what you think of independence or the related prospects of Scotland, the logic goes. One of the fundamental divides is less about those who think independence will happen, and those who think it won't – but rather the question of whether there will or should be another referendum. This chapter will argue that the question of a prospective second vote is more complex and nuanced than such binary takes suggest.

Scotland and the UK have already established the political precedent of holding an independence referendum in recent times – in 2014. This demonstrates that such a vote can take

place, how it can take place, and that UK political considerations often define, and can trump, narrow legal interpretations.
Prior to 2014, one British constitutional position (based on a
literal reading of the legal position of the Scotland Act 1998
and devolution settlement) was that Scotland did not have the
right to, and could not have, an independence referendum.
This was on the basis that the 1998 act defined constitutional
matters as 'reserved' to Westminster. The only escape route
from this to a referendum was to revisit and revise the 1998 act
which this perspective was not advocating or viewed as appropriate. The 2014 precedent showed that this was unsustainable,
and that politics, public will and a popular mandate would find
a way and be accommodated whatever Westminster legislation
said. The impact of this watershed agreement is profound and
long-lasting, and recognised privately as such by Scottish and
UK governments at senior levels.

The 2014 convergence of the Scottish and UK governments
to create the political and legal framework for an independence
vote was a huge moment. After Scotland voted in a SNP
government in 2011 with an overall majority on a mandate to
have a referendum, the two governments entered talks and
reached agreement on 15 October 2012. In this, Westminster
devolved to Scotland the right to hold such a vote over a
time-limited period of just over two years via a Section 30
order of the Scotland Act 1998, through a compact known as
the 'Edinburgh Agreement'.[1] In it, and its final signing, the UK
government tacitly seemed to concede that the two administrations (Scottish and UK) were equals in this, a significant tactical
win for the Scottish Government (being a devolved government
of a sovereign nation-state).[2]

That historic agreement does not mean that any future
events follow the same path but a precedent has been set that
can be interrogated (including the criteria for triggering a
vote), but ultimately the threshold over which any future vote

has to jump has been lowered by the joint agreement of the Scottish and UK governments. The latter may give the impression, particularly post-Brexit, that the UK is a completely unitary state but this is not the case, as reinforced by the 'Edinburgh Agreement' that implicitly accepts this in acknowledging that issues of 'mandate' and 'consent' (and of course, competing mandates) matter. And all of this has consequences for the future.

The need for realism

There is a need for realism in relation to how a future independence referendum arises and the wider political and legal environment. The legal expert and academic Andrew Tickell notes on this:

> There is no magic bullet for the Scottish Government to fire. The best proof of this is the fact that the pro-independence politicians and activists who have most been agitating for the Scottish Government to fire one – when left to their own devices – seem to have misplaced both ammunition and powder.[3]

It is also true that the pessimism of some in this debate does need serious challenge. Some independence supporters believe that the UK government will never allow another vote, a similar (if opposite) position to gung-ho advocates for the Union who declare that there are no grounds for another vote under any circumstances. Strangely, the two opposing parts of the political spectrum – passionate Scottish independence and pro-Union supporters – who are for the most part locked in continual disagreement, on this find themselves in furious agreement. It is worth exploring why.

This pessimism and stand-off plays to the interests of the UK government, but the impatience and lack of realism in part of the independence side – while understandable – does not do it any favours or make much strategic sense. Both the UK and Scottish Governments are playing a longer-time frame – to the next UK election and its aftermath – and to the near-future post-COVID, or more realistically when the virus is more fully under control and manageable.

It is useful to examine the consequences of blocking indefinitely an independence referendum for the UK political centre, the nature of the UK and UK power, as well as how such matters are seen by Scottish public opinion. By taking such an uncompromising stand, the UK government would change fundamentally the character of the Union. It would do so without the process of widespread public debate which had reached a conclusion, and would instigate the diktat of ministerial judgement – not a very solid basis on which to make such a fundamental change. Such a position would undermine the basis of the Union as being based on consent and at its core being a voluntary Union. It would transform it into one defined narrowly by law – and into being a Union of laws – which can in theory be made and unmade by the Westminster Parliament.

The cost of the UK saying No

Ciaran Martin was lead negotiator in the 2014 referendum for the UK government and in the Edinburgh Agreement between the two administrations. In April 2021 he delivered a keynote address at the Oxford Blavatnik School of Government based on a paper, 'Resist, Reform or Re-Run? Short and Long-Term Reflections on Scotland and the Independence Referendums', which explored this terrain and the consequences of the UK government's continuing to refuse Scotland the right to another referendum into the foreseeable future. He summarised the position of the UK government on Scottish independence starkly:

> The formal position of the UK government appears to be that there will be no lawful, democratic path to achieving Scottish independence for an unspecified number of decades.[4]

This had profound consequences for the nature of the Union that is the United Kingdom:

> So could the United Kingdom still be a voluntary partnership, if those who pursue independence for Scotland lawfully, peacefully and reasonably are left with the choice of, in effect, taking it lying down, or setting out to test the law and the political process? It is not hard to see how this could do terrible damage to trust, not just in government but in the Scots' sense of participation in a Union of equal partners — this being the core historic principle of the Union. A Union is not a Union of equal partners if the bigger partner does not allow the smaller one the option to leave.[5]

Martin's analysis was penetrating, persuasive and calm. He made the compelling prognosis that such a stance of outright refusal by the UK government would have major negative consequences for the UK. Martin took the view that if the UK government continued to say no — when there was a democratic mandate in Scotland for such a vote — that this could do irretrievable damage to the UK's domestic and international reputation. Such a UK stand would in the judgement of Martin alter the fundamental basis of the UK:

> Intrinsic to the modern British sense of self is that the Union is voluntary. Resisting a clearly expressed wish to

exercise self-determination within the Union changes the Union from one of consent, to one of law.[6]

Significant consequences would flow from this. The UK government would not only change the Union, it would undermine the democratic credentials and integrity of the UK, and this would contribute to transforming the appeal of independence. Such a stance held over a period would eventually hollow out the legitimacy of the Union in Scotland with potential negative consequences across the entire Union, Wales and Northern Ireland in particular. It could contribute to a game-changer in Scotland by offering the prospect of making independence synonymous with democracy and Scotland's right to decide. That would be a powerful combination, and if the UK dug in and retained that position it would ultimately lead to the UK government's position becoming unsustainable in Scotland, i.e. bringing about the very vote they were trying to prevent in favourable conditions for independence.

The UK has no real strategy and is playing for time

The UK government is playing for time and hoping that something will turn up to dramatically change the parameters of the debate in Scotland. This much is clear because in the over ten years since the 2011 SNP victory the UK authorities have refused to strategically think about the Scottish independence question and the nature of the UK. And this is despite the 2014 vote. Rather they have just hoped it would all go away while coming up with tactical wheezes such as 'the Vow' and 'English votes for English laws'.

They have hoped that, given enough time, cracks and fissures would appear in the independence movement or voters would turn against the SNP after being so long in office and remove them from power. However, for these to change the political environment they would have to be long-lasting and/ or entail the UK government utilising such openings to undertake far-reaching measures to reset the debate.

Theoretically, there is a possibility that the UK authorities could wake up and realise the existential crisis that the Union is in – what with Scotland and Northern Ireland, an unpopular Brexit amplifying tensions and fault lines, and the unwritten British constitution getting more threadbare and put under renewed scrutiny by the day.

One possible move for the UK political centre to make, that would not involve either Conservatives or Labour abandoning their belief in parliamentary sovereignty, would be to embrace electoral reform at Westminster. The introduction of proportional representation for the House of Commons would minimise the chance of a Conservative government being elected with a parliamentary majority on a minority vote across the UK and (relevant to the independence debate) with little popular Scottish support. It would of course minimise the prospect of a Labour government elected upon a minority of the popular vote, too.

It is worth pointing out that every post-war UK government has seen no single party win a majority of the vote; the same being true of every single Labour government ever elected (eleven in total), while the last UK government where one party won a majority of the vote was 1931 – when Labour Premier Ramsay MacDonald had defected to the Tories.

Introducing proportional representation would overnight dilute the acuteness of the democratic deficit that Scotland experiences at the hands of Westminster. It would dramatically change how Westminster politics and the Conservative and Labour parties represented and saw the UK.

There is no sign of this happening for the foreseeable future, let alone more fundamental reform which attempts to change the British state. But it is salutary to note that in parts of the

British establishment there is still some degree of understanding how severe are the multiple crises the UK faces. Flowing from this is, in some places, there is an awareness of the serious nature of the Scottish and Northern Ireland questions and the reality that they cannot be wished away. But such insights do not extend to the dominant sections of the UK Conservatives and Labour – or indeed it seems most of the British establishment. And none of them seem to be so worried about the state of the UK to envisage a wholesale programme of remaking the political centre and British state.

It is a testimony to the political conservatism and blinkered nature of the Conservative and Labour parties that neither is willing to re-examine the basic tenets of how they do political power, and to consider giving up the allure of majoritarian government for the supposedly greater outcome of trying to maintain the Union. And hence, returning to Ciaran Martin's analysis, this means that the nature of the UK remains a flawed, partial democracy (as discussed in Chapter 7), one where it is more than possible, as the political monopolists cling to power at the centre (without embracing any democratising reforms) that instead they go in the opposite direction and decide to retrench towards an even more undemocratic UK and interpretation of the Union.

The worries of independence supporters

The pessimistic part of independence has to be recognised and explored. Some who are pro-independence believe that there has to be a vote as soon as possible, for a variety of reasons. They include having a referendum while there is still some momentum in the independence movement or – in the more alarmist version – while there is still an independence movement; some of the more siren voices already having declared any movement dead and buried.[7] One senior independence campaigner told me in 2019: 'We have to have an independence vote as soon as possible to keep the Yes movement together'; when I gently said: 'You do know that is a terrible argument' they completely agreed but felt they had no other choice.[8]

Another contributory factor in this pessimism is a doubt about the long-term changes that Scotland has experienced in recent decades in how it sees itself and acts. This shift has seen Scotland become more autonomous and self-governing, with the idea of independence becoming part of the mainstream. There is a fear in sections of independence opinion that this wider set of trends could somehow be reversed or are more fragile and contingent than they actually are. In this there is a lack of understanding of the long-term social and political trends which Scotland has experienced over recent decades (which in a number of cases pre-date Thatcherism) that have benefited the ideals of self-government and independence.

A further dimension of this independence pessimism is based on a caricature of the British state. This is not to defend it or excuse its failings, but the British state is not a completely authoritarian or despotic regime; nor even a political system such as post-Franco Spain where the constitution is seen inflexibly and as a means to keep the state together, hence the stand-off between the Spanish central authorities and Catalonia. The UK will not become like Spain and do a Catalonia. Nor will it go down the Canadian route and, after the experience of the Quebec referendums of 1980 and 1995, pass something similar to the Canada Clarity Act 2000 which addressed the nature of the question in any such future referendums which had to meet the approval of the central government. A germane point is that Spain and Canada have written constitutions.

Former Tory MSP Adam Tomkins put the case for an Act of Union which would prohibit another independence referendum.[9] This would not work in the way he intended, is terrible politics and fundamentally alters the Union into being a legal straightjacket which would be a gift to independence. To make matters worse, it also completely forgets Northern Ireland, the Good Friday Agreement and the prospect of a 'border poll' which presumably such legislation would impact upon.

The British state with all its many faults and lack of fully-fledged democracy does have in part elements of historical adaptability and flexibility which it can occasionally call upon when pushed. Two recent moments underline this in relation to Scotland. The first is that Scotland got a Parliament when it was emphatically shown that the vast majority of public opinion wanted one – the difference between the 1979 and 1997 referendums. The second was that when Scotland produced a mandate for an independence referendum with the SNP victory of 2011 which led to the 2014 vote.

The point that flows from the above is to never underestimate your political opponents and their institutions. The British state is many things with many problems – and is at its heart still an Empire State – but is not completely broken or rotten in everything it does and is capable of showing degrees of political intelligence. It is perhaps an overstatement calling the UK, as historian Tom Devine did several times in the aftermath of the 2014 vote, 'a failed state'.[10] The British state with its historical and long-standing traditions of statecraft, administration and self-importance should never be underestimated by anyone, certainly not by Scottish independence supporters.

The big questions about the kind of question

There are big questions about the nature of another independence referendum. The next chapter explores some of the campaigning issues and challenges for the independence movement, while also looking at them for the pro-Union perspective. How such a vote happens and how is it triggered is only held with the Scottish Government's agreement. The idea that Westminster Tories and Downing Street has floated – that they bring the issue to a head at a time of their choice, with their definition of independence – to put Downing Street and the pro-Union case in charge of the agenda is clearly outlandish. *The Spectator*'s James Forsyth described this thus:

> The UK government would negotiate the basis on which Scotland would leave the UK, with the resulting deal put to the electorate. This would transform the debate from being one about whether Scotland should theoretically be independent into one about the hard truths of separation.[11]

After the much closer result in 2014 than David Cameron and George Osborne first thought, no UK government is likely to gamble with the future of the UK in this way. But it does show the pro-Union case at the most senior level trying to find a way to reset this debate, to get off the defensive and put independence on the back foot. The timing of such a vote, how campaigns would be constituted, run and regulated and the length and context of any campaign are significant considerations. It is highly likely that any future contest would have a relatively short official campaign period rather than the long campaign of 2014.

There would be questions about the referendum vote – its funding, designated campaign criteria and the need to reflect on the terrible shadow of the 2016 Brexit referendum where many questionable things occurred and both Leave campaigns (Vote Leave and Leave.EU were subsequently fined) and rather critically (unlike 2014) there was no coherent version or document presenting the Leave offer.[12] What the question would be and how it is decided are key. It is not completely guaranteed that the question would be a simple rerun of 2014. There were signals after the vote that elements in the pro-Union case were dissatisfied with the fact that independence had the Yes option and the Union the No option and that this might, in their judgement, have given an advantage to the independence side: people liking the positivity and affirmation of Yes while No was associated with negativity.

No hard evidence was produced to support these claims, whereas the bigger point about 2014 was that the question and options were comprehensively understood. Any notion post-Brexit of anti-independence campaigners trying to turn the Scottish debate into Remain and Leave options following on from 2016 is not going to get any traction: not only did 2014 provide a mostly successful campaign, this could be said much less categorically about 2016 and Brexit.

There are many other possibilities. It is not completely automatic that any future vote will be a simple binary choice – Yes and No as in 2014. One story of the long campaign of the independence referendum not fully explored was the discussions after the SNP's 2011 victory where Alex Salmond examined the possibility of a multi-option referendum with independence and greater powers on the ballot only to have it closed down by the UK government. Salmond saw this as 'an insurance policy' to position independence as one element in the pro-change majority which, when excluded, 'ensured that the middle option would be the key battleground' to win swing voters to Yes or No.[13] One senior pro-Union campaigner told me that the only way independence could win was if 'Salmond's version of independence was presented as home rule or devolution max'.[14] Their take was that any version of independence had so much heavy lifting to do in terms of detail and voters that this offered the best chance of victory.

There still remain different options. One would be sequential votes on different options – which would still allow a decisive majority to emerge one way or another. A relevant example here is the New Zealand electoral reform referendums of 1992 and 2011. In the first example in September 1992, New Zealand gave 84.7 per cent support to changing the electoral system in principle, and in the second question adopted the mixed member proportional (MMP) system on a 70.5 per cent vote.

There is also the issue of whether the UK government and related institutions can come up with a convincing set of reforms which could be put on the ballot paper. This has to be more than 'devo max' or mood music about 'federalism', but offer detailed, coherent, deliverable plans and proposals. There has been much talk over the past decades of the UK slowly evolving in a 'quasi-federalist' direction but little real evidence or indeed understanding of what UK-wide federalism might look like. Former UK Prime Minister Gordon Brown has made many interventions over the past 20 years, of which the latest has been Labour's UK Constitutional Commission which reports to Labour leader Keir Starmer. Tasked with coming up with proposals for the entire UK, could this be the radical prospectus which formed the basis of serious reform which remade the British state and how it governs and sees the UK? And which within that could be distilled and put to the people of Scotland in a multi-option referendum?

There has to be a debate about what agreement between a future UK government and the Scottish Government on the framework of any future vote might be. The 2014 referendum was agreed because of a number of factors. There was the emphatic nature of the SNP's 2011 victory and mandate, but also a profound naivety on the part of Downing Street and David Cameron and George Osborne who thought they were taking a low-level risk and seriously believed they could 'win big' and 'kill off the issue'. No UK government will make that mistake in the future.

What kind of agreement could be reached if the Conservatives are replaced as the UK government by Labour? What room would Labour have if, as more than likely, they took office as a minority government? What attitude would they exhibit towards the SNP? Would they feel they had to be tough and unbending, inviting the Scottish nationalists either to vote with them or vote them down and face the electoral consequences (with all the echoes of Labour still invoking 1979 and the fall of the Jim Callaghan Labour government after the inconclusive devolution referendum of March of the same year when Scots voted 52:48 for an Assembly[15])?

The independence question is used by the Tories particularly in England. This cost Labour dearly in the 2015 UK election, and Labour already are anxious about any cost to them in a future election campaign. They worry that the perception that post-election they might be inclined to do a 'deal' with the SNP and go 'soft on the separatists' will be used to undermine them in a campaign and aid the Tories winning – as in 2015.

Numerous Westminster commentators take from this that Labour have to adopt a belligerent attitude of 'no compromise' with the SNP but this is to view the political landscape from where it is now: historically favourable to the Tories in England. Instead of accepting this, Labour could begin to start exploring scenarios about dealing with the SNP, and take on the Tories' defence of the Union as a political weapon against Labour. Any Labour caution and reserve on this comes from political weakness, not strength, and a wariness to take on the built-in advantages that the current dispensation of English political culture gives the Tories.

The independence debate is a live issue

The independence question has many layers, nuances and uncertainties, but also some important certainties. First, this is a live, active and ongoing political topic. As such it cannot be ignored or permanently blocked but eventually has to be addressed, brought to a conclusion and a democratic solution attempted.

Nigel Smith, organiser of the 1997 devolution referendum and campaigner for No in 2014, understood this. He observed in 2019 just before his death that: 'At one point it has to be addressed via a referendum, and Scotland becomes independent or remains in the Union.'[16] The academic and pro-Union observer Colin Kidd noted in 2022: 'An ongoing 50:50 division on the most existential of political questions seems unsustainable in the medium to long-term. We need another referendum – a monsoon to clear the air.'[17]

Second, from this more flows. Namely that Scotland will get an independence referendum when Scottish public opinion decisively makes up its mind that it wants one and consistently supports this position for a sustained period of time. There can be a legitimate argument about what level of support counts as decisive and how long a period of time is judged sustainable, but those are not disagreements on principle, but process and judgement.

A number of surveys paint a picture favourable to the principle of Scotland having the right to decide its future. Asked in June 2020 whether the Scottish or UK Parliament should have the right to decide whether there should be a second independence vote, 62 per cent of respondents said the Scottish Parliament and 38 per cent UK Parliament; in January 2020 the same question found 54 per cent saying the Scottish Parliament, 35 per cent UK Parliament and 12 per cent don't know.[18]

A more complex picture emerges when we get into the specifics of the timing of a future vote. When asked do you think there should be another independence referendum within two years which, when asked in 2021 is broadly within the timeframe suggested by Nicola Sturgeon of by the end of 2023, in November 2021 38 per cent agreed and 54 per cent disagreed;

with similar figures in September 2021 of 38 per cent agree, 52 per cent disagree.[19] Asked if you think there should be another independence referendum: in December 2021 Panelbase found 19 per cent said in the next twelve months, 34 per cent the next two to five years and 46 per cent never; asking the same question over the course of 2021 has found broadly similar findings: with a high of 25 per cent for the next twelve months in April 2021, 29 per cent for two to five years and 46 per cent never.[20]

All sides can take something from the above. There is significant support for the principle of the Scottish Parliament taking a decision to decide on a future referendum: a vote and process 'Made in Scotland'. But there is not support currently for that vote being in the next couple of years. One further detail in which independence supporters can take heart is that when ComRes have given a total of six different choices (including never having a vote), they have consistently found a quarter of voters picking this option – 25 per cent in January 2022 – which indicates again sizeable support for Scotland's right to self-determination.[21]

At the moment, Scottish public opinion is not at a place where it is decisively in favour of another independence referendum. That is not to say that this will not change. If that happens, Scotland will have an independence referendum, and that is understood by both the Scottish and UK governments.

Added to these calculations is the reality of a society and people who have suffered over two years of the COVID pandemic, with thousands dead in Scotland. The human scale of this went far beyond the actual numbers of recorded deaths, with loss, bereavement, grief and trauma felt by many more. One immediate priority for government has to be supporting people and exhausted public services, aiding a culture of healing and comprehending what has just happened to all of us. On any level of emotional intelligence, politicians and public leaders have to put this immediate task ahead of launching another independence referendum. To do otherwise would be judged questionable by many voters. Championing compassion, consideration and solidarity is surely what we expect of politicians in times of crisis and trouble.

The longer any impasse between the Scottish and UK governments goes on, people who are pro-independence may worry that somehow the issue might go off the boil or go away. In a different way, pro-Union supporters worry that the demographics are slowly moving against them and that the independence case is being made every day by the SNP and others.

It is much more fundamental than that. Any narrow legal interpretation by the UK authorities that Scotland cannot have a referendum is a political judgement and one with significant political consequences. Andrew Tickell notes:

This legal impasse represents a real predicament for supporters of Scottish independence, but it is also a critical moment of choice for the UK government. For decades, the notion the Scottish people have a right to self-determination has been recognised by the UK's political institutions.

He assesses that a dogmatic, inflexible unionist stance is one which has high stakes which are unlikely to end well for the Union:

By adopting a 'no, not now, never' policy, the UK government must be conscious that it is at risk of increasing – rather than decreasing – the internal pressure pushing at the UK's territorial seams. Stopping up every constitutional relief valve will not release the internal pressure which has built around Scotland's constitutional future.[22]

Even that voice of unionism, Margaret Thatcher, recognised that Scotland has an inherent right to self-determination:

> As a nation, they have an undoubted right to national self-determination, thus far they have exercised that right by joining and remaining in the Union. Should they determine on independence no English party or politician would stand in their way, however much we might regret their departure.[23]

If Margaret Thatcher could grasp this fundamental principle, then so should all of us today. Of course, it is easier to enunciate an abstract principle than work out what it actually means. Former UK Prime Minister Gordon Brown signed the historic *A Claim of Right for Scotland* declaration in March 1989 affirming 'the sovereign right of the Scottish people', but this principle never informed his subsequent politics.[24] All this underlines that the principle of self-determination in relation to Scotland and the UK is a political, and not a legal, one.

The longer story of Scotland as a nation and political community needs to be remembered in this. If Scottish public opinion wants another independence referendum, we will get one – a vote which will be confirmed by Scottish and UK authorities. There is no political strategy open to the UK government which in perpetuity blocks Scotland's right to decide its own future. The longer they attempt to delay and put obstacles in the way, the more they undermine the nature of the Union as one of 'consent' and 'partnership' and discredit the case for the Union, while making explicit the link between democracy, self-determination and independence. We now turn to the contours of what a future independence referendum will look like for Yes and No, and wider questions.

13
The Next Campaign

The single most important reason for my emphasis on stories not technical arguments for independence is listening to campaigners who now dread the return to the doorsteps because they feel they have to be Masterminds on every aspect of setting up a new country.

Lesley Riddoch, author and campaigner,
personal communication, February 2022

I fear that an over emphasis on providing a pragmatic programme for an independent Scotland, as demanded by unionist detractors, will end up being a complete waste of time and energy. Successful independence campaigns are not won on the fine details of currency and pensions but on the promise that people will feel more secure, more able to influence decisions and better governed. The campaign will have to show that they want to hear from those who disagree and that their voices will be welcome as we build a new nation.

Laura Moodie, Green Party and community activist,
personal communication, March 2022

Some of the defining themes as already seen in the previous chapter for any future independence referendum campaign will be how it comes about, timing and context. But also critical will be the tone, political intelligence, messaging and strategy. This is true of the independence campaign but also the pro-Union side.

In 2014 both sides had to put together campaigns and strategies at relatively short notice after the SNP's surprise 2011 victory.[1] Next time would be very different. There will be the example of 2014 to draw upon; there will be no element of surprise; and on many levels the next independence campaign has already begun and just needs to be formalised. This chapter explores some of the political contours, factors and challenges in a future vote, particularly addressed towards the pro-independence side, while also looking at the pro-Union side and wider terrain including floating voters and non-voters.

Do you remember the first time?

Assessing the state of the independence side has to, at the outset, have a shared understanding for the reasons why Yes lost in 2014 and the lessons which flow from this for any future offer.

It is germane to note two points. The first is that there has been post-2014 no official or formal post-mortem into why Yes lost – where the data has been analysed, strategies and tactics revisited and the messaging and positioning of independence re-examined. This is a conspicuous absence on the independence side and has been explained by the SNP on the grounds that in the aftermath of the 2014 vote there was a quick succession of electoral contests – the 2015 Westminster contest, 2016 Scottish elections and Brexit.

This, on first appearance, if you are in a very generous mind, looks a convincing explanation. There are after all only so many hours in a day and so many things any human being can do. On reflection it does not tell the full truth because part of being a successful politician or a success in any senior role is the ability to prioritise and multi-task.

The missed opportunity of a 2014 post-mortem into the reasons Yes lost the biggest democratic exercise in Scotland's entire history is both telling and has consequences for the present and thinking on the future. Learning from defeat is one of the most important activities in democratic politics. It leads to reassessing the fundamentals of your cause, the language and priorities used, and how you come over to those you still need to convince. This involves listening to external influences beyond your base and the world of true believers. It entails looking at the wider electoral environment, rather than looking internally and believing in the self-regarding superiority and self-evident justice of your cause.

This is what nearly all successful political parties and tribes do. It was what the Labour Party did when it lost big in 1983 and 1987, building the foundations for winning in 1997. It was what the Conservatives did after losing for a third time in 2005 to return to office in 2010. And closer to home, it was what the SNP did after losing the Scottish Parliament elections in 1999 and 2003, then learning how to think and talk beyond its base to win in 2007 and 2011.

The reasons that Yes lost were many and complex. What they were not about is clear: they were not solely due to 'the Vow', Gordon Brown's late intervention or the role of the BBC – all of which are often cited. We know this about the role of 'the Vow' because most voters indicated that they had a scepticism that it would ever be implemented.

In the hectic final month of the 2014 vote, the promise of further powers to Scotland was met with widespread public scepticism. When asked in the event of a No vote if Westminster would transfer substantially more powers to the Scottish Parliament this was thought very or fairly likely by 36 per cent of respondents in the first week of the final month and 40 per cent in week four. Looking at undecided voters in that same period, 26 per cent thought the transfer very or fairly likely in week one and 27 per cent in week four. This leads academic Rob Johns to conclude:

> It was in the interests of those who supported independence to argue that the Vow had been decisive and that Scotland would have voted Yes but for what they claimed was a confidence trick, rather than to focus on their failure to convince enough voters of the case – especially the economic case – for independence.[2]

Rather Yes lost for a variety of reasons. One fundamental factor was what Johns called the 'It's the economy, stupid' – ranging from the finances and public spending, to debt and the over-reliance on North Sea oil and the currency question. Alongside this were anxieties about borders and EU membership, with Better Together famously tweeting that the best guarantee of Scotland remaining a member of the EU was voting No declaring in September 2014: 'What is process for removing our EU citizenship? Voting Yes.'[3]

Adding to this was a sense that Yes never publicly recognised any downsides or major risks in independence, instead giving off a Panglossian air of certainty. There is evidence from focus groups of floating and undecided voters that many did not like this denial of risk. More so, significant numbers thought all this meant something deeper – that Yes knew there were risks inherent in independence but had decided not to admit them because they were big and potentially damaging. That is not a good place for any political campaign to deliberately put itself.

Another topic for some voters was Alex Salmond who was very popular with some and not with others; he had much less appeal for women voters. These factors together contributed to Yes not being able to put together a majority coalition – specific policy concerns, the issue of risk, and personalities.

The post-referendum survey by the Centre for Constitutional Change confirms that while national identity and party political issues were prominent in the reasons given for voting No, over a quarter of respondents cited 'unanswered questions'.

Table 2   Single most important reason for voting No 2014[1]

Because there were too many unanswered questions	26%
Because independence would have made Scotland worse off economically	19%
Because I feel British and believe in the Union	17%
Because being part of the UK is a way of sharing risk and resources	12%
Because I don't want to live in an independent Scotland ruled by the SNP	11%
Because I don't trust Alex Salmond	7%
Because Scotland is going to get the powers I want anyway	3%
Because I wanted to vote Yes but in the end it seemed a bit too risky	1%
Because it would make Britain a more equal society	1%
Something else/Don't know/NA	3%

Source: Centre on Constitutional Change Post-referendum Survey.

A second factor is understanding the appeal of the No case and why it won a majority of voters. This was not because of duplicity, disinformation from the likes of the BBC and other outlets, or false promises. Nor was it entirely based on negative reasons because of the failings of the Yes camp and offer, and to think the latter is to misunderstand the nature of the appeal of No and why it won, which is key to any future contest.

In post-referendum polling by Lord Ashcroft, 47 per cent of No voters said that their main reason for voting No centred on the risks of independence; leaving a majority stressing other reasons: 27 per cent saying a strong attachment to the UK, its shared history, culture and traditions, and 25 per cent saying Scotland had the best of both worlds with a Scottish Parliament.[5]

The enduring appeal of the UK and Scotland having 'the best of both worlds' has to be understood and respected as a message and not just instantly dismissed with disrespect. Both of these latter two points may turn out to be in decline and weakening but still have traction particularly with older voters. An additional factor is the issue of risk, instability and the fear of the unknown and taking 'a leap into the dark'. This will always to an extent be the case with a fundamental change such as independence, and in the age of Brexit and COVID many voters will be sympathetic to the argument that there has been enough uncertainty, upheaval and instability in their lives and that of wider society.

At the same time independence has become normalised and the disastrous effect of Brexit and the chaotic UK government response on COVID has provided the opportunity for people to see the UK state and its continued misgovernance of Scotland (and the UK) as a major and real risk.

Identity politics and looking beyond the labels of Scottish nationalism and unionism

Gordon Brown has made the case against Scottish independence post-2014 using the same language he and many others have used for Brexit. In the *New Statesman* essay in 2021 previously quoted he compared the UK Tory government of Boris Johnson and the case for Scottish independence when writing:

At a time when every country's independence is now constrained by their interdependence, muscular unionism harks back to an unrealistic view of an indivisible, unlimited sovereignty accountable to no one but itself.

He continued in the same vein:

It is a mirror image of the Scottish nationalist playbook, for they also have a one-dimensional and absolutist us-versus-them view of the world. You have to make a choice: Scottish or British – you cannot be both.[6]

This flawed argument is trying to use the mess, intolerances and ideological straightjacket of Brexit to taint and tarnish Scottish independence. The Scottish question has over the years elicited various discussions about multiple identities, the meaning of citizenship, the role of Britishness in an independent Scotland, and debate about the nature of sovereignty in an interdependent world.[7] And it is also true that the main drivers of Scottish independence have never been identity and certainly not any kind of monocultural identity, but rather issues of democracy, governance and values. Yet it is true that a small section of independence supporters, as discussed previously, welcome this framing and the exclusive focus on identity seeing it as a reinforcement for a rigid, essentialist black-and-white politics – not one which most people can see themselves in and find a voice.

However, the pitfall in this argument is that it falls into a caricature of Scottish independence articulated by its opponents which is never a good position. Making the debate an existential choice between Scottish and British identities raises the barrier for people who see themselves as having some form of British identity, which remember is still a majority of the population in Scotland, against voting Yes.

There is a need to not see voters entirely through the prism of unionism versus nationalism because it is restrictive and most voters do not see themselves in these terms. One example is the tendency of many on the independence side to portray the Union case as being entirely 'unionist' – a mirror image of Gordon Brown's caricature above. Sometimes this happens by a sleight of hand but often is a deliberate attempt to label and put in a box pro-Union sentiment.

Trying to understand the diversity of reasons and logics which have brought people to supporting the Union is important in the challenge of changing the minds of voters. People supported the Union in 2014 and do so in the present for a similar spectrum of reasons as many who supported independence then and do now. The political landscape cannot simply be reduced to labelling Yes supporters as 'nationalists' and No supporters as 'unionists'. The academic Colin Kidd, looking to the future and the No campaign which might emerge, observes:

> Scotland's reluctant, reactive and intuitive unionists are far from being the Brit Nats derided by their opponents; at a conscious level many of them are not even 'unionists'. These indysceptics are not so much for something as against – to a degree apolitically against – something else. Sensibly enough, they don't want politics intruding on more important things, whether family, sports, hobbies, volunteering...[8]

Pro-independence supporters should learn from 2014 and address weaknesses and omissions, but this is true of the pro-Union side as well. Kidd observed that the 'economic prospectus' of Yes and No in 2014 arguing that 'independence would jeopardise EU membership' turned out 'spectacularly wrong'. Kidd concludes: 'Both sides should apologise for misleading claims made in the previous referendum campaign.'[9]

This argument impacts now and in the future. It matters when official campaigns fall short of standards expected in public life, and damages and corrodes political discourse and belief in the values of democracy. Look at the damage that the lies and deceptions told by the Leave side in the 2016 Brexit referendum have had on British public life – the £350 million for the NHS on the bus, the claim Turkey was going to join the EU any day soon. All this and more has toxified and turbo-charged the political debate, leading to public figures being called 'traitors' and 'enemies of the people'. We have to be very careful and cannot afford to have any complacency in Scotland.

The former SNP MSP and minister Marco Biagi states:

> The Yes campaign needs to realise the risk that people may yet go into the polling station won over by the merits of both the democratic case for independence and an economic case for the Union.[10]

The prevalence of the 'missing Scotland'

Another critical dimension in a future campaign will be the 'missing Scotland' and 'missing million'. This is a term I coined in the 2014 vote to describe the generation of Scots who had not voted in a generation who critically would have voted if turnout had remained at the level of UK elections over the 20 previous years.

In the run-up to the 2014 vote, working with the Electoral Commission Scotland, I put an exact number on these terms. This produced two figures – 989,540 voters who would have turned out if Holyrood election turnout had not fallen to approximately 50 per cent of the electorate, and 446,954 voters who would have turned out if Westminster voting participation had not steeply declined.[11] The first figure was the more dramatic and the figure which the alliteration 'missing million' fitted. It also brought with it the charge that for the first four Scottish Parliament elections all the main parties had been content to contest a politics based on a mere half of the electorate voting, because politics was about getting the biggest share of a small pie. Now that Scotland had an independence referendum the faulty nature of this logic and the politics which flowed from it was now exposed. And that meant that Yes and No would have to dramatically change their politics.

The 'missing Scotland' are found all across Scotland and are disproportionately younger and poorer, but it is vital not to caricature such people exclusively in these terms. Instead, this politically disconnected constituency of Scotland represents a strand of society which was not that long ago engaged and connected. This 'missing Scotland' is literally all around us – in every street, neighbourhood, community; is it there in our friends, families and networks; it is part of everyone in Scotland's lives as each of us will know people who are part of it, or who on occasion are part of it, switching out and in of non-voting and voting.

In the 2014 referendum three focus groups of non-voters were organised by the pollster Ipsos MORI Scotland – two in Glasgow and one in Dundee between December 2013 and January 2014. Among the many findings was that most non-voters are not apolitical and apathetic in the way commonly assumed and portrayed. Rather they are deeply cynical and dismissive of party politics, politicians and 'the noise' that surrounds mainstream politics.

A dominant theme from the groups was a tendency to see the politics that mattered to them as more personal and focused upon family, community and immediate, tangible things such as individual employment prospects, the homes that they lived in, and the quality of local public services.

It was in this context that people viewed the 2014 referendum differently, and saw it as not about party politics and politicians. In spite of these groups being made up entirely of non-voters at elections, nearly every participant indicated that they would vote in the referendum. The individuals offered comments such as:

This is the biggest decision of our lives and I'm taking part. (Dundee)

Once it is done there's no going back. (Glasgow)

This is very important. It's a big deal. There's no back-up plan with this one. (Dundee)

All politicians are crap, but this is different. (Glasgow)[12]

These voices of the 'missing Scotland' indicate that they were not completely detached and disengaged from politics and participating in the democratic process, as proven by the 2014 result and 84.6 per cent turnout, the highest participation rate since the introduction of the mass franchise in any nationwide contest ever in Scotland.[13]

The 'missing Scotland' has increased in number over the past 20 years as society has become more individualist and fragmented. Politics here as well as elsewhere across the West has become more consumerist and concerned with 'branding', 'marketing' and 'offers' – all concepts about selling something to voters. All of which makes our public culture not about us as informed citizens but about us as customers who assess politics and make choices in a way similar to how we decide about products. Added to this the notion of 'a political class' as apart from the rest of us and not drawn from us and like us, has become the normal way of seeing politicians with all the corrosive connotations that flow from it. It is true that this is less pronounced in Scotland but that should not leave any grounds for thinking we are immune to these trends.

The 'missing Scotland' are still with us

The 'missing million' and more turned out to vote in the independence referendum. This cause for celebration about the vitality of civic engagement led many on the Yes and No sides to take a short-term and complacent view which took the view that 'the missing Scotland' had been addressed, re-engaged and re-energised and the problem was now effectively over as they had been motivated to vote once.

This is a damning attitude to take about something as important as the strength and vibrancy of democratic culture, and has to be examined and resisted. For one, a single vote does not permanently re-engage voters who have nearly permanently given up on party politics and politicians. Instead, the political system and culture has to learn to listen, adapt and recognise what it has got wrong. The closed order of too much politics in Scotland as well as elsewhere does not show enough serious signs of wanting or willing to change.

Secondly, if anyone thinks that too hard a judgement then they should look around at the state of Scottish politics in the years after 2014. It is true that turnout went up marginally in the 2015 Westminster elections and subsequent 2016 and 2021 Scottish elections. But not dramatically. More fundamentally, the explosion of activism, energy and dynamism which reshaped politics and public life in the 2014 campaign was just left to wilt, unsupported, unnurtured, with no mainstream organisations permanently changed. Rather it was in too many places back to business as usual and politics as a protected minority interest.

Thirdly, there is the issue of the damage to politics of the cumulative effect of years of prior disengagement and narrow bandwidth politics. UK and Scottish politics pre-2014 was increasingly dominated by voters who were growing more and more unrepresentative of the actual electorate. This at its most extenuated becomes what is known as 'the truncated electorate'; seen in its advanced stages in the US but evident in the UK where those who vote are more middle-class, affluent and older.[14] All of this feeds a political environment focused on the needs of those who vote and ignoring those who don't, which accentuates the political divide and non-engagement.

Finally, the idea of the 'missing Scotland' was interpreted in a narrow way by Yes and No about the act of voting on one historic day. They also saw the notion as just about voting when it is clearly about more. The 'missing Scotland' is about a society which is deeply divided and unequal by any measurement — socio-economic, cultural, geographic, generational, gender, ethnicity and more.[15] The unfortunate truth that the dominant stories of Scottish politics from all sides have chosen not to recognise and act upon this over decades is telling in terms of the limited ambition of that politics and the thin nature of the progressive values repeatedly espoused.

There are also the voters who do not see themselves in the certainties and label of Yes and No. Gordon Brown called this 'middle Scotland' which does hark back to classic New Labour's 'middle England' in its heyday. He offers the following explanation of this group:

> Middle Scotland has not written a British dimension out of their lives. They don't want to be forced to make a choice between being Scottish and British. They are best described as patriots who love our country, but not nationalists who see life in terms of a never-ending struggle between 'us', the Scots, and 'them', the rest of the UK.[16]

This is to put it mildly a fairly prescriptive interpretation filled with partisan judgement and strengthening the politics of labelling and division. The floating and undecided voters do need to be heard and given space, and an understanding of the political landscape advanced that is not just about two semi-static closed tribes. And yet it does contain some level of insight even if it might be a simplification. Many voters do feel they are being forced to choose between part of their identity, a part they don't want to give up, and any framing of the debate based on a forced choice between Scottish and British identities as polar opposites is not going to be a healthy one.

The secret and soft No voters

As critical are the 'secret Nos' of 2014 and subsequently. These are the voters who were drawn to Yes in their heart and who in the quiet and deliberation of the polling station voted No and kept quiet about it, telling few if any people about their decision.

There were and are lots of 'secret Nos', voters who feel pulled in both directions by different calculations and motivations. There are many of these voters who like the appeal and logic of independence, making our own decisions, and taking democracy back home. Such voters are also cumulatively appalled at the gathering storm that is the cesspit of Westminster and the British state in recent decades which has culminated in Brexit and the low of Boris Johnson as UK Prime Minister.

This brings them to be well disposed to the idea and offer of independence but they still need something more which has been until now mostly missing. This is reassurance but more: a bit of detail, acknowledgement of the risks inherent in any major change, a greater embracing of democracy now and in the future, and an embracing of pluralism, diversity and the need to hold power to account. The last thread is one which in particular cuts across significant sections of Scotland which are soft Nos and Yeses – the awareness that in contemporary Scotland and through large periods of history Scottish society has not been very good at holding institutional power to account aided by the collective groupthink which down the ages defined public life.

Take an example of a 'secret No' voter in 2014: Kirsty, in her early 50s at the time of the referendum, lives in Glasgow, works in the creative sector and has two teenage children. In the week after the 2014 vote she told me:

> I voted Yes but with great reservations and uncertainty. I didn't think we were ready for it.

Then a couple of hours later she without any prompting from myself opened up:

> I am daft. I don't know why I said that, I actually voted No.

In the month after 18 September 2014 she told all her Yes friends that she had voted Yes and all her No friends that she voted No. The only people who knew how she really voted and the contortions she had gone through were her partner, two children and myself. Kirsty's deliberations and predicaments are not that different from a large constituency in modern Scotland: feeling the push and pull both ways and not sure which way to jump. I asked her how divided she was between Yes and No in 2014 and she said:

> Basically 50:50. I wanted to vote Yes, but I don't think we were ready. I was also put off by the tone of Yes: the certainty, the superiority, being endlessly lectured by lifelong friends.[17]

My friend Kirsty is now with her partner firmly of the Yes persuasion. Here is what she said six years after the vote, reflecting back on 2014 as part of her political education and reawakening:

I got into not raising my head above the parapet in life. I am still in the process of finding my voice. I want to know where and how I can have my say. I put my foot in the water — found my voice and I now want to find out more, get involved and not be patronised by anyone.

She says she still wants to hear more about independence:

I want to hear how Scotland becomes an independent country and about the difference independence is going to make. And I want to know the kind of Scotland my children are going to grow up and become adults in.

There were also appropriate words of warning with regard to Brexit and the use of high-profile financial figures to define and dominate a debate:

The £350 million figure on the red bus worked with Brexit. In a future Scottish vote the No side will have their equivalent: you will lose x thousands if you vote for independence. The independence side have to have simple, clear, understandable figures to counter that or it will cost them.[18]

Other unsure voters I spoke to still wanted reassurance from independence. Aileen from Clydebank, in her 60s and retired was an unsure No in 2014 but now open to Yes:

The independence movement needs to be more realistic and understanding why their fellow Scots are not as confident as they are. Bluntly, I suppose the movement needs to grow up. In an age of huge change, having a sense of doubt or uncertainty about seismic change is understandable and not a bad thing.[19]

Andy, 48, who lives in Greenock and works in the voluntary sector, reluctantly voted No:

Scotland really need a generous, confident and honest vision of independence. One which contrasts uncertain risks which come with independence with the certain risks of staying in the Union.[20]

Aileen judges that independence has to have 'a healthy dose of pragmatic realism'. Even more she finds the tone of a significant section of Yes does not sit well with her and others she knows: 'The Yes movement seems prey at times to fanciful utopianism. We need to take Scotland as it is, and work with the Scotland we have.'[21]

Matthew, 62, from North Berwick, who worked in the computer industry, did not hear the answers and attitude from Yes in 2014 he had been hoping for:

The currency issue in 2014 was a very simple to understand example of the lack of a plan. It was emotive and could be exposed. But it really wasn't just about a currency. And that needs work – not just about the technical question of a currency.[22]

Elizabeth, in her late 60s, lives in Stirlingshire, worked in media and gives her reasons for being a reluctant No:

Primarily for economic reasons as well as the over positivity of the case for Yes. If they had come out and said it was going to be really tough, but that it is going to be worth it for solidarity or other things that we could do with independence – I could have voted Yes.[23]

A final observation from Andy from Greenock on the future debate and the need to avoid pseudo-discussions where participants use pre-prepared points and scripts at each other in a dialogue of the deaf. There was a lot of that in 2014 as well as many good things:

We need to hear more diverse voices, more surprising voices. People who do not sound like they have been put on platforms or scripted by political parties. I want to hear from new voices widening the public conversation.[24]

There is a belief in parts of the Yes constituency that the only significant movement pre- and post-2014 is from No to Yes, ignoring the complex churn of political change and volatility.

The writer Christopher Silver was one of many articulate, thoughtful Yes voices in 2014, but eight years later he is firmly in the agnostic camp:

I no longer view Scottish independence as particularly relevant or central to my politics. I cannot recall the last time a prominent pro-independence figure seriously linked the prospect of Scottish statehood, or the current governance of Scotland, to the multiple crises that are eroding the conditions for life everywhere. Beyond asserting the basic facts of nationality and expressing embarrassment at post-imperial Britain, I no longer have a coherent sense of what the point of Scottish independence might be.

Silver offers the following critique of the conventional critique of independence:

Whatever I do hear seems to offer a promise of continuity that jars on a fundamental level with the experience of my own class (precarious workers with no inherited wealth) and generation. For these reasons I'm not sure that the work required is particularly obvious, which bodes ill. However, I would suggest that a starting point for any renewed independence project must be to ditch the coded mantra that has seeped into all aspects of the prospectus: 'for things to remain the same, everything must change'.[25]

Some pro-independence supporters will want to dismiss such views as an isolated example, but they are a warning not to believe in a one-dimensional view of politics and not to fall for the hyperbole of your own side. There is a significant generational and class dimension to Silver's analysis: that the concerns of the growing numbers of young people who find themselves in the precariat and changing nature of the working class, cannot be assumed to just be a banker for the independence side. That lazy assumption – that such voters have nowhere else to go – when they can shift to abstention, become less enthused and mobilised, and ultimately even adopt an anti-independence position, needs urgent recognition.

One powerful observation which aids insight on all of the above was said by the pro-independence campaigner 'SouthsideGrrl' when in a conversation covering some of the above terrain she declared: 'There is no such thing as No voters, only people who voted No.'[26] It is a brilliant, penetrating comment which goes straight to the heart of refusing to see a binary choice debate in black-and-white terms.

Some people see themselves as Yes and No voters, but many do not. Thinking of people as Yes and No voters puts labels on them and boxes them into stereotypes. Refusing to do that is a freedom to see people in all their diverse, contradictory views. It is good politics in refusing to see one half of voters – who voted No in 2014 – as a homogeneous, unified entity and to instead acknowledge the varied motivations and reasons which brought people to No – and to Yes.

Equally there is an ongoing trend to present 2014 as a great moment of flux but to see the present as characterised by stasis and inertia and two great armies facing each other. *The Economist* presented Savanta ComRes data in March 2022 that showed that 73 per cent of No voters and 63 per cent of Yes put themselves on a scale of ten (as certain in their views) compared to a mere 10 per cent of respondents who had a score of six or under.[27] These figures point to a calcifying of opinions but even on the data above one-third of the electorate have not in some ways made their minds up – and the dynamics of the electorate are always subject to continual change and never fully stop.

Scotland's media and public conversations

Aspiring to the challenge of having a better public culture and conversations requires addressing the state of the media in Scotland, public sphere, and wider culture, along with issues of ethics and personal responsibility in a much more disputatious environment. Parts of Scotland's media did not have the best of experiences in the 2014 referendum. The main newspapers, with the exception of the *Sunday Herald*, all lined up behind a No vote which meant that 45 per cent of Scotland's voters were hugely under-represented in the balance of opinion in the print media. Subsequently, as a result of the interest and support for independence, Newsquest launched *The National* as a daily pro-independence title.

The broadcast media led by BBC and STV operated within the context of public service broadcasting and the requirement for 'balance' and 'impartiality'. Yet there were numerous problems which the main broadcasters encountered in the referendum campaign, most of which are still relevant in the present. The first is that in the 20 years prior to the referendum there had been a general retreat in how BBC and STV covered Scottish politics to a general public audience. Thus, despite the arrival of the Scottish Parliament in 1999 both BBC and STV reduced the amount of politics carried in their main evening news and current affairs programmes, with the commensurate rise of crime stories and sport, nearly exclusively football.[28]

A significant part of the coverage of politics on both after 1999 was put into minority interest programmes such as the

BBC's *Newsnight Scotland*, which despite being a compromise in place of the absence of a 'Scottish Six' lasted 15 years (1999–2014). Lorraine Davidson, then of *The Times Scotland*, referred to the incestuous nature of such programmes with 'a sense of looking backwards with people reminiscing about "the STUC conference in 1984" and waxing about what a public figure did in the past along the lines of "Oh do you remember when Campbell Christie did this or that?"'[29]

Secondly, the challenge of the independence question invited broadcasters to interpret the issue in a broader way which was not just about constitutional politics. This offered the possibility of having discussions on a rich array of subjects such as what kind of Scotland people wanted to live in; how they thought Scotland had changed and could do in the future; and the nature and place of where big decisions about Scotland should be made. This rich tapestry was constrained by public service broadcasting requirements for 'balance' and 'impartiality', alongside a propensity to see the campaign in terms comparable to a party election contest with a Yes and No side. This reduced the democratic and cultural potential of the referendum, and meant that the wider portrayal of the debate which was ongoing in the country was mostly missing from BBC and STV.

Thirdly, there were unique pressures and scrutiny on the BBC due to its status and funding. It was met with particular criticisms from the independence campaign and seemed at times to be on the receiving end of criticism from all sides,[30] all of which encouraged the BBC to batten down the hatches and play it as safely as possible.

The BBC had a poor referendum as did STV, but the former is the main object of criticism and worse, with STV seeming at times to get off scot-free. One exasperating problem for the BBC was the continual tensions between the BBC in Scotland and London senior figures, not helped by the reality that BBC

Scotland is not a fully autonomous body but a subset of the bigger BBC. It is therefore not accountable to the people and audiences in Scotland but ultimately at the top to the BBC high command in London which makes for a deeply dysfunctional organisation at senior levels in Scotland.

Fourthly, rather importantly the BBC and STV treated the 2014 referendum as mostly a Scottish-only story, certainly until the last few months. Missing in 2014 was any discussion on the impact on the UK, and importantly after the vote there was little sharing of experiences between BBC and STV here and their UK networks on the referendum and the Brexit vote when there were less than two years between them.

This absence of a post-2014 referendum debriefing not only had an impact on Brexit coverage and potentially result, it has consequences in the present and future. The Scottish question is alive and current but despite this the BBC and STV have not as far as anyone is aware undertaken any reappraisal of how they cover independence or seriously thought about how they might cover and report a future referendum. Given both the BBC and STV have contingency planning for numerous future news stories such as the death of the Queen, this does seem an omission.

The media landscape is changing with questions about the future of the BBC licence fee, the nature of the corporation and the regulatory framework for public service broadcasting. A vote for Scottish independence would undoubtedly bring issues about the BBC's long-term viability to the fore. The increasing multi-media, multi-platform digital age will have more 'choice' and a more fragmented audience where specialist interests can be served but will it have 'quality', and how can a connected democratic and civic culture be best nurtured?

This raises the prospect of how Scottish news and current affairs, arts and culture and the wider areas of public life have good programmes made which inform, educate and can attract audiences. In an age of diversity, niche platforms and huge global players, how can a Scottish public sphere find the space and resources?

That requires some serious thinking about the public sphere in Scotland and its relationship with the London-dominated UK public sphere in what is a kind of 'dual public sphere'.[31] This would involve looking at the role of the Scottish Government, regulatory agencies and public bodies in supporting a civic culture, championing public service broadcasting, print media and local media. It is possible to do this in other small independent countries such as Norway and Finland and it would be in Scotland.[32]

A final dimension involves the ethics and behaviour of people in public life. It is a huge positive that people now feel they can challenge and question authority, whether the government or the BBC or anyone, and it is a healthy development that people who previously were voiceless can now express themselves and engage via social media. This relatively new world comes with risks, downsides and problems and an environment without gatekeepers sometimes can seem like a world without rules and a free for all.

There is an incendiary language at the fringes of both the pro-independence and pro-Union sides which has to be called out and not tolerated. The argument sometimes put by the most fanatical true-believers on either side, that they get called out more while the other side get a free pass, is an unsustainable argument: a classic case of 'whataboutery' where as a result the rest of us all lose. All political perspectives need to up their standards and their intolerance of hatred, bigotry and bile. A culture of insults, threats, violence and abuse does little to help public debate, independence or wider participation which addresses the 'missing Scotland' and reaches out beyond the 'usual suspects' and voices. It is possible to criticise and challenge mainstream media and the narrow bandwidth of too many public conversations without reaching for invective and inappropriate behaviour.

Scotland's public sphere has a degree of autonomy and distinctiveness while being influenced by the UK's public sphere, and subject to economic, commercial and technological pressures. This could make the deepening of democratic conversations about the key issues that Scotland faces more, not less, difficult, which will necessitate some serious thinking by government and policy-makers that informs the independence question and beyond.

The importance of the radical imagination

Any expression of radical politics has to be grounded in an awareness of its past and where it comes from, rooting it in a sense of history and collective memories. However, within this for all such movement politics is the danger of 're-enactment politics' whereby activists act out the same old scripts that once had power and potency, but now have increasingly diminishing returns.

This argument has been put forward by American community organiser Michael Gecan, who through decades of experience notes that too often in radical politics too many people are increasingly playing to a narrow cast of true believers who self-police to maintain the chosen truth and engage in internal infighting hunting heretics and identifying deviation from that truth. All of this is undertaken with a degree of self-righteousness particularly in relation to those who have not yet and never will see the light: namely the vast majority of the population.[33]

For decades left and radical politics have increasingly followed a path of well-worn scripts and actions: the march, the rally, the speeches. These have reduced radicalism to a kind of performative theatre playing to an audience which knows the format; and a large part of the alternative radical political community have at times been no better. Scotland's independence movement, like most radical political forces around the world, have too often fallen into this cul-de-sac.

Speaking of such limitations, the Centre for Artistic Activism, a New York-based body set up and run by academics Stephen Duncombe and Steve Lambert, have worked for over a decade in encouraging a politics that is playful, provocative and imaginative. They aspire to create a practice of what they call an 'ethical spectacle', one which knows that it is spectacle and is aware that it can be used by the forces of reaction from the Nazis to Trump.[34] In this they are consciously trying to jump out of the limits of 're-enactment politics' and embrace interventions which champion social justice and equality which can have an impact which might involve fun and subversion, poking disrespect at the pious self-certainty and self-regard of elites and orthodox opinion.[35]

The 2014 referendum managed to combine a twin-track approach of representing an insider politics of the SNP and an insurgency politics seen in the self-organised activist initiatives which exploded onto the scene. In a future vote that balance will need to be even more worked at. The SNP will be seen by many as part of the Scottish establishment; while the insurgency side need to think about what it does and how it does it, including its relationship with the SNP and Scottish Greens.

Scottish independence is about more than the SNP but requires the SNP to have any chance of coming about. At the same time the radical imagination, which is a critical part of the edge of independence, needs careful thought and deliberation to play the part it needs to – to maximise energy, drive and imagination. All of these qualities will be needed to deal with the future landscapes of post-independence and it is to this we now focus, looking at the immediate terrain after an independence vote, followed by its implications for UK/rUK.

PART V

Future Landscapes

14

After an Independence Vote

This is the site upon which we define a new nation as one built in xenophobia, or not. This also needs to be constitutional work and is the extension of the work of membership by belonging not based on race, birth, speech, heritage etc. Its serious work for serious people. If Scotland is a nation built on xenophobia or C19 notions of ethnic purity we are doomed and I want none of it.

Alison Phipps, academic, personal communication,
February 2022

Give us our Parliament in Scotland. Set it up next year. We will start with no traditions. We will start with ideals. We will start with purpose, with courage. We will start with the aim and object that there will be 134 men and women, pledged to 134 Scottish constituencies, to spend their whole energy, their whole brain power, their whole courage, and their whole soul, in making Scotland into a country in which we can take people from all nations of the earth and say: 'This is our land, this is our Scotland, these are our people, these are our men, our works, our women and children: can you beat it?'

James Maxton, Labour MP for Glasgow Bridgeton,
St Andrew's Hall, Glasgow, May 1924

Scotland after a successful independence vote would be a changed country on nearly every level. This would be true politically but also psychologically for the nation, people and society. There are many dimensions to this concerning Scotland, rUK, the nature and process of independence, and how such events are perceived by the wider world. This chapter will look at three main areas: the wider context including beyond politics, the period between an independence vote and the formal declaration of independence, and the Scotland that then emerges onto the global stage.

A moment of history

In the event of a Scottish vote for independence, there will be a huge release of emotions and feelings across Scotland and the rest of the UK. This would be a cathartic, hyper-charged moment of history that the people of Scotland by their collective action had willed into being.

This would be an unprecedented moment in the history of Scotland and the UK, with which nothing before could be compared including Irish independence in 1921–22. This is because Scotland has been historically (unlike Ireland) an integral part of the Union and British state in a way that Ireland never fully was. Hence, Scottish independence would change fundamentally everything for Scotland and also for rUK.

Scotland immediately after the vote would contain a whole raft of powerful emotions. There would be elation and exhilaration on the independence side, surprise in many places and a feeling of anxiety and foreboding amongst some on the pro-Union side. This latter emotion would also be found in a section of the independence forces, aware at the amount of work that would now be needed to make an independent Scotland a reality.

In many parts of Scotland and rUK there would be an understandable sense of loss and confusion, bewilderment, denial and even anger and blame. There could even be some elements of pro-Union sentiment on both sides of the border who would ask the UK government to ignore the vote, or more plausibly want to stage another to 'bring the Scots to their senses'. How much traction that got would depend on the margin of victory for the forces of independence, but in most eventualities would be unlikely to garner much support. If Scotland votes for independence in a referendum that all sides agreed to and participated in, then Scotland will become an independent nation-state.

There would be in some a deep-seated sense of hurt and even in places fury and rage about what would be the death of the UK as we know it. This has to the understood and treated with a degree of respect and empathy. For some it will be the equivalent of losing someone close to them such as a member of the family, such does this debate bring up for some existential questions about identity and how we see ourselves in the world. The end of the UK as it is currently constituted would bring forth mourning and grief in some, and rightly be treated as a worldwide event of historic proportions.

Scottish independence supporters will have to be prepared for some international coverage which will amount to an elegy and sentimental attachment to what the best of the UK stood for. Thus, certain countries like the US, Canada, Australia and New Zealand will see such an event as an opportunity to replay and understand parts of British history with which they feel strongly connected like the First and Second World Wars, the defeat of Nazi Germany, and the changing nature of the UK as the sun set on the British Empire and the Commonwealth. This is an understandable reaction to the closing of a chapter in British history and the UK as it has been known.

Some international coverage will be very sympathetic to Scottish independence, as was already seen in terms of how the 2014 vote was reported. There will be much goodwill and interest in many parts including Scotland's European neighbours who have had to endure a difficult and even petulant UK over the many years of Brexit negotiations. And there will be a warm welcome from parts of the world where Scotland already has a reputation and good relationships such as within the Commonwealth.

There will be however some around the globe who portray independence in terms of post-colonialism and post-imperialism, in part because of their own experiences in gaining self-government and statehood. This does not quite fit for Scotland which was never colonised, and indeed engaged with England as a junior partner in the British imperial project at its peak.[1] But it is true that Scottish independence calls time on the last delusions of the British Empire State and hence will be seen in that light by some.

It is in the above light that Labour MP and radical socialist James Maxton's comments should be seen. Maxton was a passionate supporter of Scottish self-government which consistently expressed itself in the advocacy of home rule, but on occasions this extended to independence as in the opening quote. Even Maxton biographer Gordon Brown notes that in this 1924 intervention he 'appeared to come out in favour of independence', such was his rejection of the British Empire and imperialism and support for a 'Scottish Socialist Commonwealth'.[2] Maxton's words point to the moral values and mobilisation that would form for many a core part of the formative years of independence.

All of this will be a major opportunity for modern Scotland to reintroduce itself on to the international stage. Already the 2014 referendum provided Scotland with a similar experience, as the nation gained huge international coverage and commentary the world over. For some media and audiences this was literally an introductory crash course in the nature of the UK and Scotland, its history, previous independence, the experience of Union, and the fact that Scotland in that Union had politically and legally never gone away, and was now at the point of re-emerging as a nation, one discussing and considering its future as a self-governing state.

Any future vote and independence victory will build on that and such an eventuality would introduce a modern democratic Scottish nation-state onto the world stage. Hence the manner in which this is undertaken – the tone, voice and demeanour – will be absolutely critical. An independent Scotland will be able to draw on much goodwill, history, connections and networks including the reach and spread of the Scottish diaspora.

After a future vote, there has to be no sense of a Scotland of Yes and No, only a country where the massive majority sentiment is reconciliation and pulling together. Whichever way a vote goes that will prove to be difficult for some, as Sunder Katwala of the think tank British Future puts it:

> Advocates for Scottish independence – and for a continued UK – may focus primarily on how to get 50.1% of Scots to vote their way in any future referendum. Many will be better informed as to whether questions of voice, power and identity, or the brass tacks of currency and pensions, would prove decisive next time.

He continues:

> My hope is that some civic nationalists, along with some of their pro-Union opponents, and Scotland's civic institutions will invest some time in thinking about how a democratic society lives together while making existential political choices which can split a nation down the middle. Just as the United Kingdom found space for a much stronger Scottish political voice and a broader cultural confidence in the last quarter of a century, advocates of an independent Scotland

ought to have a post-independence reconciliation plan to recognise the British identity of many Scots too.[3]

The world after an independence vote

In the aftermath of Scotland voting for independence there will be much work to do in negotiations, preparations, organisation, scaling up and creating institutions and more. The Scottish Government will have to take steps to become the sovereign government of a sovereign nation-state and all the things that flow from this. That is a quantum leap and change from being a devolved administration in the UK state.

The UK government will have to prepare for the moment it becomes the rUK government while still making claim to the rights of being the continuing state to the UK, for which there is legal precedent. Thus, it is highly possible that rUK will claim to continue to be called 'the United Kingdom of Great Britain and Northern Ireland', but no matter. If the name remained the same it would not disguise that something fundamental had changed.

The necessary negotiations between the Scottish and UK governments will be unprecedented in the history of modern capitalist societies. At the same time there are numerous international precedents and examples that can be drawn upon, most obviously the end of the Soviet bloc and Soviet Union in the period 1989–91 including the disintegration of Yugoslavia in the mid-1990s which saw two dozen independent nation-states emerge. In those dramatic changes, as new nation-states emerged from Soviet dictatorship, there are positive examples such as Estonia, Latvia and Lithuania (which are all EU and NATO members) and the Czech Republic–Slovakia divorce (also EU and NATO members), as well as tragic examples such as Bosnia-Herzegovina's emergence in the collapse of Yugoslavia.

Numerous questions will need to be addressed in this process including how the Scottish and UK governments establish their negotiation teams and decide upon the agreed format and schedule of discussions. Thought will have to be given to such issues as:

- Does the Scottish side just contain members of the Scottish Government?
- Could it involve a more inclusive 'Team Scotland' as was floated in 2014?
- Could the negotiating team for Scotland involve formal input from people other than politicians, with perhaps an expert advisory panel?
- How does the UK government legally engage as the UK while de facto representing the future rUK?

The Scottish side will need to establish its priorities and what it wants from negotiations including issues such as how key UK-wide institutions are divided and managed, and what it feels can be left for a period to a joint Scottish/rUK authority. Any outstanding issues which remain as independence gets nearer could be parked in a transition period. Structures agreed by Scotland/rUK could be established if independence happens, such as an expert group to assess and divide assets and liabilities with an agreed arbitration process to address any disputes.

One of the biggest areas for agreement is the UK's national debt – a not inconsiderable amount and controversial in how it is addressed given the scale of monies involved. There are numerous precedents to draw on. The UK–Irish talks of 1921–22 saw the Irish accept the responsibility for a share of the UK national debt. But at the same time in the world of realpolitik the new Irish state escaped mostly debt-free, making only a series of small payments compared to the amount the UK government had initially claimed.

As well as the subject of debt there is the issue of assets and liabilities. This entails identifying the assets and liabilities of the UK some of which are fixed and immovable, while others are not fixed and moveable, and a further number exist outside of the UK's landmass and territories. In the Czech and Slovak 'velvet divorce' which legally occurred on 1 January 1993, a host of issues were left unsolved in terms of assets, such as those of the state airline and gold reserves. It took until June 2000 to finally resolve these issues, seven and a half years after the formal division into two states.

An assessment of UK assets would more than likely reveal that Scotland has a less than proportionate share of them on its own territory. It would be highly probable that this asset gap could be significant in size and worth and thus could give the Scottish Government leverage on how the overall portion of assets is divided. There has been some work done on this in the recent past. The SNP made an assessment of the National Register of Assets in 2001, a list and valuation of all the UK government assets which had been originally calculated in 1997. The SNP estimated that with Scotland having then an 8.6 per cent population share of the UK, that the UK with £273.9 billion assets produced a Scottish share of £23.5 billion; allowing for £18.85 billion in Scottish and UK government assets located in Scotland, this produced an estimate of £4.7 billion in assets which Scotland was entitled to.[4]

These figures are now over 20 years old. They illustrate that establishing a spreadsheet of the UK's assets and liabilities is a complex undertaking. It cannot just be assumed that Scotland will proportionately take a percentage of Scottish debt without seeing it in the round with other financial rights and obligations. At the very least the above gives an independent Scotland by negotiation and agreement the possibility of reducing any debt liability it agrees to undertake with the UK/rUK authorities.

After independence: Scotland and the world

The first days of Scottish independence would see Scotland retake its place on the international stage. Membership of international organisations such as the United Nations would happen, followed by economic bodies such as the IMF and World Bank, World Trade Organisation and the Organisation for Economic Co-operation and Development (OECD), and Council of Europe and Organisation for Security and Co-operation in Europe (OSCE) to name just some of the most well-known.

Scotland would be diplomatically recognised by governments around the world, formal diplomatic ties and relationships would be established, a network of embassies and trade missions representing Scotland's interests set up, and a new diplomatic corps created to staff all of this. And while this was happening governments would be coming to Scotland to establish a presence and create embassies in a process that could have quite an impact on parts of the capital city Edinburgh with the potential establishment of a diplomatic area.

Major choices would at some point have to be made about the economic and political direction of the country but the first tasks would be establishing the full institutions of an independent nation-state including a central Finance Department and central bank. The former could evolve through expansion of existing Scottish Government departments, while the role and remit of the latter would be critical including it being given 'sufficient operational independence' in the words of one assessment.[5] But Scotland would have to develop institutions and expertise in modern macroeconomic policy which it has never had to have with a direct impact on government decisions.

Once the economic and political strategy of an independent Scotland had been agreed and implemented the government would want to ensure that the country was seen as reliable in terms of international markets, investment and how it made decisions. As this environment evolved initially a new Scottish Government would have to, at least for an initial period, retain sterling which would mean that the Bank of England would continue to set interest rates for Scotland, which could easily be a source of tension; there are also significant differences between a formal and informal currency union with the UK.[6] While this set of arrangements continued there would, for the interests of both the Scottish and rUK governments, be a joint board with Scottish representation to aid policy-makers on the explicit understanding that this would be for a limited transitional period.

One of the fundamental decisions to be made at some point would be on the currency of an independent Scotland. This would include the option of setting up a new currency or deciding in principle to join the euro. The former would entail thinking about how any new currency floated on the markets, how it was pegged against the euro or sterling, estimates of currency costs in transactions and variations of the currency.

While there is a tendency of pro-Union commentary to treat the idea of an independent Scottish currency as some kind of modern-day Darien disaster and create the spectre of it being buffeted by international markets, this ignores that the world is filled with independent currencies.[7] The Danish krone with a population of just over five million operates next door to the powerful German economy with 83 million people, while the two share a land border (and of course Germany is in the euro and part of a much larger market which the Danish currency shadows).

An independent Scotland will need to make numerous other major decisions. There is the question of EU membership and the issue of whether Scottish membership should be decided by a referendum, which could underline the pro-European credentials of the majority of the population indicated in the 2016 referendum and which were run roughshod over by the UK government. The case can be made that the decision of a self governing Scotland on whether it wishes to join or not join the EU is different in principle from Scotland being a member of the EU through membership of the UK. That strengthens the case for a future referendum.

Many other strategic calls will need to be made around areas such as NATO membership, and maintenance of the Western security alliance and Scotland's contribution to that. Connected to that is the controversial subject of nuclear weapons based in Scotland and sailing in Scottish waters, as explored in Chapter 11, and upon which there will be hugely sensitive negotiations with international implications.

Other decisions of a more symbolic nature say something about what kind of country Scotland is aspiring to be. It would be highly probable that an independent Scotland would join the Commonwealth; it would situate the country in a network with which it has a shared history, common heritage and emotional bonds, and is another way for Scotland to evolve into a country which exercises soft power. And in this there would have to be at some point a nationwide conversation about the role of the monarchy and head of state which would indicate how Scotland saw its future, a decision that would more than likely happen while Charles III was on the throne.

The role of the Scottish Government

The Scottish Government as indicated above would become overnight the sovereign administration of a nation-state, and the Scottish Parliament the elected legislature of that sovereign Scotland. These institutions would thus have more legal and public policy responsibilities than before, for which they would need to develop capacity and expertise.

This would entail a fast-learning curve for the Scottish Government, that originated in the Scottish Office which was set up in 1885 as the territorial Whitehall department for Scotland. This accrued more powers and responsibilities in the 1920s and 1930s, and then in the immediate post-war era as the state expanded in Scotland and across the UK.[8] This body formed the basis of the devolved administration created by the Scotland Act 1998 which became known as the Scottish Executive under Labour and the Liberal Democrats. In 2007 when the SNP won office it was rebranded the Scottish Government, a change subsequently formalised by legislation in 2012.[9]

Underlying this short history is that the Scottish Government may now talk like such a national body, see itself in such terms and be seen by others domestically as a government, but within it are still significant shortcomings many of which have their roots in where it comes from.[10] As a Whitehall department, the Scottish Office had limited capacity for public policy and particularly for taking a lead in legislation, only having a window for one or two parliamentary bills per session. This lack of capacity in policy-making and legislative expertise can still be seen in the present, with the stretching of capacity and a lack of knowledge in certain areas which will change with time.

In 2007, the SNP reorganised government and civil service into what John Elvidge, Scottish Government Permanent Secretary at the time, called a 'relatively compact governing structure'.[11] SNP minister Shona Robison thinks that 'significant progress has been made in trying to get government out of its silos' and addressing overall strategic objectives.[12] Others would disagree that enough progress has been made; but no one would dissent from the notion that independence would require another transformation.

There is a cultural legacy from the days of the Scottish Office which paradoxically has been strengthened by becoming a government. This is about the narrow Scotland drawn into formal discussions and consultations. In the 1940s and 1950s, as the state in Scotland expanded, these processes were shaped by a closed shop of interest groups: SCDI, the STUC, business and trade organisations. In the present-day Scottish Government the talk is now of widespread consultation and participation, yet the reality of most such exercises is not that far-removed from the past order. In 2013 a Jimmy Reid Foundation report found that two-thirds of those giving evidence to Scottish parliamentary committees earned more than £34,000 with two-thirds of people coming from a professional organisation, lobbying firm or business interest.[13] There has also been observation that a large part of this world is government agencies and public bodies responding to consultations from government and Scottish Parliament in a closed cycle difficult to break into for those outside it.[14]

This raises the challenge of the scale of policy-making needed in an independent Scotland and where it will come from because it cannot realistically come from inside the system and from within the civil service machine. That would be to stretch it to breaking point. But more importantly it would not address the need for a rich, diverse ecology of policy and encouragement of competition in the realm of ideas and strategic direction. One answer to this is supporting a wider array of organisations and initiatives including think tanks, research bodies and publicly engaged academia. But this needs not just to be aided by government but for government to realise the importance of such a public culture.

As a supplement to this, if independence gives the right to decide on the strategic choices facing the country there has to be an awareness of the long-term trends which affect Scotland. That means independence itself should have a futures element and literacy about the kind of country it wants to see. This would entail going beyond the current catch-all vagueness of the current Scottish Government and SNP which is implicitly based on a centre-left social democracy, and avoids hard choices about public services, public spending and taxation for now (while admittedly the devolved government does not have a full array of powers but could still in the present signal its direction of travel when it had such powers).

This necessitates addressing this area in institutional and resource form post-independence. How does the Scottish Government, public bodies and wider society, develop a public policy culture informed by longer-term trends and factors both domestically and internationally? We have at least to begin asking this and other questions now – and think about issues of capacity and expertise – and in the concluding chapter some illustrative examples from around the world of relevance to the Scottish situation are highlighted.

The art of breaking up and staying friends

There are numerous examples of sub-state governments which became the sovereign administrations of independent nation-states which can provide an opportunity for learning. The Czechs and Slovaks in 1993; the Baltic nations in 1991 – an independent Scotland like them would not be starting from scratch but has decades of the evolution of self-government to draw from. It will be able to look at how other states made this transition, a central one being how the current civil service which is part of the UK civil service becomes a separate Scottish organisation. The scale of this change is like many multi-level challenges, not just involving establishing a new service with its own remits and processes, but nurturing the culture, ethos and normative values of the organisation and championing them throughout.

One new challenge will be the issue of becoming an internationally recognised state, for which there is no agreed clear set of processes, although becoming an independent state has several elements, one territory becoming a new state and another losing territory and authority over it. The recognition of a new state means the legal recognition of the transfer of sovereignty from one authority to another. This comes about in the case of Scotland and the UK/rUK through negotiation, mutual agreement and agreeing to a treaty between the two states.

One area where there are precedents is the legal character of an independent Scotland, and whether there are two new states created (Scotland/rUK) or one new state (Scotland) and a continuing state (UK/rUK), which automatically assumes the legal responsibilities and obligations of the UK. Such a distinction is not arcane and significant consequences flow from this. In numerous cases where one nation becomes independent from a larger entity, the latter has become the continuing state. For example, when Belgium became independent of the Netherlands in 1830, Finland from Russia in 1917, Ireland from the UK in 1922, and Singapore from the Federation of Malaysia in 1965.

The break-up of the Soviet Union in 1991 saw Russia become the continuing state. Other examples include Norwegian independence in 1905 which dissolved the union between Norway and Sweden, with each state issuing statements declaring that each would be bound by the treaties created during their union; in effect both were successor states. Another is the example of the Czechs and Slovaks in 1993 and the end of Czechoslovakia which saw both states recognised as successor states.

Scottish independence supporters have often argued that two new states could arise from the break-up of the UK. But this would face numerous obstacles across a range of international bodies, treaties and obligations and would be a subject for discussion and negotiation between the main parties. It would lead to the likely end point of the rUK state claiming the right to take on the responsibilities of being the continuing state.

These approaches can be summarised as three potential ways of breaking up:[15]

Dissolution: This is what the Czechs and Slovaks and Norwegians and Swedes undertook. In the case of Scotland, this would lead to Scotland and rUK both being successor states.

Continuation: One such example is the Irish state becoming independent from the UK, with the latter being the continuing example. This would mean in relation to Scotland that it would be the successor state and rUK would be the continuing state.

Separation: This is a third option, whereby Scotland became independent through repeal or abrogation of the Treaty of Union of 1707 returning the kingdoms of Scotland and England to their prior status. This faces the practical problem that doing so would result in the Scottish and English entities having no international legal personalities, thus leaving any real choice between the first two options.

The coming storm against independence from the right and liberal circles

The aftermath of a vote for independence will have traction, and could cause controversy, in how it is framed in rUK and in particular sections of the right-wing English media. This would matter and could have influence because the English ideological right – from the commentariat to think tanks, politicians and media – have prominent platforms and a proven record in recent times of disseminating their messages and shaping public discourse and debate.

A significant section of the English right will regard Scottish independence as an affront and virtually as an insult to how they view the world, a world defined by abrasive, aggressive capitalism, the pretence of free markets, and an anti-social possessive individualism. They will see the prospect of independence in nearly entirely negative terms about Scotland.

One strand of the English right will regard it as a joy for the English to finally get the tax-loving, subsidy-junkie Jocks off their backs. Not only in this account would it allow the English to explore the right-wing fantasyland of slashing and burning the state and public services but it would make the prospect of a Tory right-wing gridlock on the politics of England seem more feasible. And this would be how part of the English right saw it – so long, Scotland and your 'grievance culture' and hello to a world of opportunity and freedom.

Yet the dominant English right perspective would be sadness and regret both for Scotland and the UK, while still seeing the possibility of future right-wing advancement in England. There would be a feeling of rejection and of a diminishing of both Scotland and rUK. In relation to Scotland, this tradition would genuinely see it as the Scottish nation turning inward, being less cosmopolitan and less outward and internationalist, the exact opposite of how independence supporters would see things.

The English right would see Scottish independence as a vote of disapproval and disassociation with the nature of the UK over recent decades when they have been in the ascendancy. In this they would be correct, but the nature of the English right-wing project (as per ideological purists anywhere) is to avoid responsibility for their own actions, and instead to claim any shortcomings are because their zealotry has been watered down and then to double-down with even more of the same.

Scotland post-independence would need to prepare for an avalanche of criticism, attack pieces and general dismissal, not just for the general act of leaving, but for the political choices that Scots would embrace. Part of this response will not even be about Scotland directly, but seeing it as a threat to their narrow doctrinaire ideological take on the world and the affront of a majority of Scots to embark on a different political course.

Hence from the earliest days of independence, right-wing columns in the *Daily Telegraph* and *Spectator*, along with the punditry and polemic in the likes of *GB News* and the London based right-wing think tanks, would turn their attention and fire onto Scotland. An additional dimension is that this right-wing offensive will have, and already is having, an impact on elements of liberal opinion, affecting how they see the issue and its impact which is then played back by the right reinforcing their themes.

This critique will be more strident and intolerant from the English-based right, but will seep into comment from liberal and left circles, and importantly, the seeds of that assault are already present and ongoing. One prominent strand will attack the characteristic of Scottish nationalism, portraying it as anti-English, intolerant, xenophobic and not fit for the twenty-first century being still rooted in the past and the world of the nineteenth century. This will seldom get into a sociology of understanding different nationalisms or the role of British and English nationalism in decoupling the UK. This perspective can lead to reducing a large percentage of the Scots as sentimental, romantic fools who are living in the past, motivated by Bannockburn and Bruce, and not facing up to the challenges of the present.

There are many pejorative terms associated with this take: continually talking about 'separatists' and 'partitionists', 'blood and soil nationalists' and in the words of *GB News* Tom

Harwood, 'the pro-partition movement'.[16] And the spectre of this leading to violence is never far from the surface particularly when invoking Ireland, a view that spreads into liberal circles. Martin Kettle wrote in *The Guardian* in 2014 about the prospect of independence, and that 'acts of violence are not inconceivable in certain circumstances or places, as anyone with a smattering of knowledge of the Irish treaty of 1921 will grasp'.[17]

In February 2022 economist Gavin McCrone wrote in *The Times* that pent-up frustration in part of the independence movement on lack of progress towards a referendum could 'run the danger eventually of the wilder elements among those in favour trying to force the issue by non-constitutional issues. The history of Ireland should be a warning to anyone who thinks such pressure can be resisted indefinitely.'[18] Public figures like Kettle and McCrone are far removed from the politics of the right, but if they can with ease raise the prospect of violence it does make it easier for those on the right who want to do so.

A second take will paint an independent Scotland as a place beholden to political correctness, 'woke culture', 'liberal orthodoxy' and a 'nanny state' out of control crushing civil liberties and individual freedom. This is a Scotland in the grip of authoritarianism which wants to tell people what to do, think and say, whether the Offensive Behaviour at Football Act 2012 or the named persons scheme in the Children and Young People Act 2014.[19] Brendan O'Neill of the contrarian *Spiked* railed against the 2014 referendum as 'phoney democracy' and views modern Scotland as 'a hotbed of new authoritarianism' making it 'the most nannying of Europe's nanny states', and goes on: 'It's a country that imprisons people for singing songs, instructs people to stop smoking in their own homes, and which dreams of making salad-eating compulsory.'[20]

A third dimension bemoans the Scottish lack of grasp of the hard facts of life and economics, often adding to the irony of this occurring in the land of Adam Smith. Bodies such as the Centre for Economics and Business Research (CEBR) and Douglas McWilliams have a track record on an independent Scotland, commenting in 2017 that it could become a 'Third World country' within 30 years of independence if it continued with its 'addiction' to public spending which could reduce Scotland to the ignominy of being 'the new Greece' – comparing Scotland to the austerity Greece experienced at the hands of the EU.[21]

Another perspective focuses on the ideological parameters of an independent Scotland and brings forth condemnation and indignation. Broadcaster Andrew Neil has claimed that independence has peddled 'a permanent socialist nirvana'.[22] This is a common strand put forward on the right, that Scotland is a land of make-believe held afloat by English subsidies and goodwill. Related to this is the time-old prejudicial account of Scotland and the Scots, lamenting on the passing of a golden era where the Scots were an 'enterprising people', buccaneering, inventive and outward-looking. This is contrasted with recent experiences and the supposed decline of these qualities due to the rise of the 'featherbedding state'.

This view was a prevalent theme among Thatcherite Tories in the 1980s with Nigel Lawson, then Chancellor of the Exchequer, talking about the Scots and 'the culture of dependency'.[23] In 2012 Ruth Davidson, at the time leader of the Scottish Tories, told a UK party conference fringe:

It is staggering that public sector expenditure makes up a full 50% of Scotland's GDP and only 12% of households are net contributors, where the taxes they pay outweigh the benefits they receive through public spending.[24]

This led to a *Sunday Times* headline: 'It's excessive state spending that turns Scots into burden', penned by Gillian Bowditch. Commentators and journalists do not write headlines but this is all part of framing Scotland as an economic basket case, a country which cannot make or pay its own way, held down by the size of the state.[25]

An even more pronounced version of the above just lays into the character of the Scottish people, the culture of the country and the values people have, offering a sweeping dismissal of all of these. In the 2014 referendum campaign I took part in an independence debate in London run by *The Spectator* whereby one member of the audience got up and said: 'When I think of the Scots I think of Red Indians. You both have a grievance culture – drinking and abusing yourself into oblivion.'[26]

The right-wing mindset will be sent into hyperdrive by independence, launching continual border raids via numerous missives in the press, broadcast media and other platforms. Scotland's political direction and choices will be described in negative, dismissive, even apocryphal terms, articulated to constrain and curb the range of political debate in Scotland pushing it towards a right-wing agenda or more probably a timid, unsure, centre-left one.

A supplementary part of this offensive will be provided by a section of 'London Scots' – Scottish-born London based figures in political and media life, including the likes of Andrew Neil (whose main residence is in the south of France), Fraser Nelson (editor of *The Spectator*) and Andrew Marr who will use their prominence to interpret and spin a completely negative story of an independent Scotland. It will be laced with reminiscing about what it was like in the good old days of the Scottish Enlightenment, when Scots ruled the Empire, and grammar schools and education was cherished north of the border.

Scotland and the geo-political context

How independence is viewed at an international level, by those who come from or identity with the West's intelligence and security establishment including Cold War hawks, is important. There is danger from US geo-political advisers and, at the other end of the spectrum, from the Russian state and agents of disinformation using cyber-technology.

Take the view of US-based and Scottish-born analyst Azeem Ibrahim who in March 2021 authored a paper: 'Scottish Independence is a Security Problem for the United States', the rationale of which was to alert the incoming Biden administration to the danger of Scottish independence in relation to the US.[27] He wrote that it would be 'a geopolitical disaster for the United Kingdom, the United States and Scotland itself' and that 'the UK would find its nuclear deterrent in disarray'. He assessed that 'Scotland leans much more towards the European social democratic model than the Anglo-Saxon political and economic model' and hence is less likely to want to be as close to Washington as the current British state.

Ibrahim explained his thinking to me at the time: 'My piece was clearly aimed at a US audience and the Biden administration in particular. I wanted to highlight the geopolitical implications to US national security if the UK broke up.'[28] He described this in his essay in the following terms: 'Scottish independence would effectively neutralise the UK's military and diplomatic power on the global arena and deprive the United States of one of its most powerful allies', concluding that: 'The prospect of Scottish independence threatens to render the UK powerless.'

This does seem to be inflating the role and impact of Scotland, an analysis with a degree of hyperbole and at odds with some parts of the British establishment who consistently try to minimise any impact that independence will have on their geo-political priorities. Philip Rycroft was UK Permanent Secretary for Brexit from 2017 to 2019 and takes a more sanguine line about independence and relations between Scotland and rUK:

> There really is not a modern parallel to speak of... The fact that these two countries would still be sharing the same island will drive so much long term, and sensible statecraft would recognise the interests of both countries is to remain closely knitted together – one would hope to see that close collaboration in the decades beyond Scottish independence.[29]

Such florid comments (as Ibrahim's) contribute to some elements of the independence argument in dismissing the need for Scotland to have any kind of serious geo-political stance which can win friends and influence across the West, Washington and further afield. It hinders the need to have a mature conversation about Scotland's international profile and positioning on such gathering threats as disinformation by state and quasi-state actors originating in places such as Russia, China and Iran. Scotland does not need to embrace the logic of Cold War hawks or the US military intelligence establishment to recognise that these are issues worthy of serious attention.

All of these dimensions will be part of the mix in the dynamic environment of Scotland after a vote for independence, and in the early days and years of that self-governing nation-state. Numerous nation-states have become independent in living memory including the two dozen who emerged from the collapse of the Soviet bloc, alongside the successful examples in north-west Europe going further back: Norway, Ireland and Iceland. Many of these countries have lessons for Scotland and the degree of autonomy and independence for small-sized states in an age of interdependence being one of the most relevant.

This points to the need to start scaling up preparations. Addressing the missing infrastructure and networks in public life, the role and scale of government, the kind of partnerships and social concordats it wants to champion; the kind of society that public policy interventions aim to nurture; and getting government to listen, adapt and learn from success and failure. Scottish independence, as Michael Keating and Malcolm Harvey point out, is 'not merely a change to its external relations or formal status, but a rebuilding of its institutions internally'.[30] An independent Scotland will start with much goodwill in many places in the world, as well as those who wish it ill-will.

People need to start thinking, focusing and prioritising on the work and challenges of those early days to make sure that people and institutions will be as ready as possible for that eventuality. Doing so now is not some kind of optional extra, but makes the independence project more real and hence more feasible and attractive including to people who have until now not yet been convinced. All of this brings up major questions for the UK/rUK of which the next chapter is the subject.

15
The Future of the UK/rUK after Independence

I think it would be wonderful if a free Scotland and an England freed from its delusions, and with its democratic deficit repaired, following Scotland back into the EU, would come together in a new Union! Of course, it would be better still if that new Union could be built from the inside, and if it had been, then I might have to change my mind.

David Edgerton, academic and author, *The Rise and Fall of the British Nation*, personal communication, March 2022

England was, by the 1960s and early 1970s, on its ways to being a decent European country where people looked out for each other. It has become something very different. It is very hard to unwind decades where people are told to be selfish and that there is no such thing as society (just them and their families). Were Scotland to become Independent, that might help the English look a bit more thoughtfully in the mirror.

Danny Dorling, academic, personal communication, February 2022

The UK/rUK would be in a very different place, and be a very different state, as a result of Scottish independence. It would be one that many on the left and centre-left reflect on with a sense of foreboding, fear and apprehension in the belief that independence will leave them living in a state with a built-in permanent Tory majority in UK/rUK.

Others on the right and parts of the Tory Party are increasingly viewing such a possibility as one that while mostly not welcomed could have a positive side. This would revolve around in the mild version getting rid of centre-left Scotland, and swinging rUK even further to the right; in a more pronounced take this involves celebrating the exit of the 'subsidy-junky Scots' as the opportunity to progress towards a minimal state beloved by right-wing ideologues and think tanks. This chapter will consider both these perspectives while attempting to look beyond them at the terrain of the UK/rUK after independence.

A future rUK without Scotland would be an altered entity from the present state. It would have a different territory, footprint, identity and role in the world that would, by necessity, be smaller. It could allow rUK to finally be shorn of the illusions and delusions of 'Great British Powerism', and aid it finally and belatedly in the early twenty-first century to become a modern democratic state. But none of that can be taken for granted, and rather has to be argued for and won as an argument against the forces of reaction deeply embedded into the institutions which dominate English, and currently UK, society.

A rUK without Scotland would see its landmass shrink by a dramatic one-third. Its maritime waters would shrink by an even larger amount, losing the 462,315 km² defined as the 'Scottish zone' in the Scotland Act 1998, as Scotland's seas are nearly six times larger than the land area of Scotland.[1] It would lose valuable and key strategic assets – geographic, geo-political and infrastructure, including the north-west Atlantic coast of Scotland which is at least as important in the UK's strategic terms as the English Channel. Yet despite all this and more, there are still parts of the British establishment which want to underplay the scale of change and disruption, such as Philip Rycroft, previously Permanent Secretary for Brexit, cited in the previous chapter.

The reality of rUK – a 'Britain' without Scotland – is of a state that would have to confront some uncomfortable truths about the nature of itself domestically, how it operates and in whose interests, its standing in the world and what it stood for, and its relationships with others from Scotland and Ireland to nearby continental European neighbours and the wider world.

Scottish independence would be a severe shock to the system of the 'idea' of Britain – a projection internally and externally which has survived previous huge calamities and defeats – from the loss of the American colonies and Ireland, to the cumulative exhaustion, over-stretch and depletion of resources that were the First and Second World Wars, and then the long process of imperial retreat and withdrawal. Hence to some of the British establishment the Scottish debate brings forth an existential fear. For it brings into question the range of institutions and influence the UK plays a part in such as permanent membership of the UN Security Council, membership and status within the G7 and G20, the IMF, World Bank, World Trade Organisation, NATO and many other bodies, alongside its status as a nuclear weapons power, its reach diplomatically, in soft power and economically.

Not only that it would bring out into the open the mythology and fables that underpin elite versions of the UK such as the so-called 'special relationship' with the US, and the nostalgia for Empire and imperialism seen in the continual pursuit of military action and right-wing fantasies such as 'the Anglosphere' venerating an alliance of English-speaking democracies across the world.

The initial questioning of these facets post-Scottish independence would not be easy but instead entail a difficult conversation about the nature of England, Wales and Northern Ireland – the rump and their relationship with each other. In particular, it would kickstart a long overdue debate in England about its future as a nation, democracy and society. For example, within the UK, 'British' and 'English' have long been seen as synonymous and this has worked to prop up the undemocratic, unreformed, centralised Westminster system. A prime case of this is that the UK Westminster Parliament also doubles as an English Parliament making laws for England.

It is much more than this. Under the strains of dealing with the COVID pandemic, it became clear that the UK government was on many policy issues and public services acting as the de facto English government and Johnson as UK Prime Minister increasingly gave the impression by his actions and remit that he was the English Prime Minister. Similarly, UK government ministers for health, education, transport, culture and other areas, increasingly acted as English ministers nearly always without recognising this basic fact. This distinction caused all sorts of confusion and concern in the UK government and its assorted friends in the media and moreover highlights the problem with England, how it is governed, and the strange relationships it has with the other UK nations.

Not only is England badly served by the present constitutional order, it is a country which dare not speak its name across numerous areas of life. To give a couple of examples there is no English Labour Party or English Conservative Party or in broadcasting an English BBC. Thus, in the Union England is in an unsustainable position where it is subject to its own 'democratic deficit', and where Westminster wants to retain this state of affairs and cut off and stifle debate about reform and democratisation in England.

'England as Britain': a key pillar in the UK's not very democratic order

After independence these English currents would come to the fore. There would be a need to address what form an English-specific politics would and could take? Could an English Parliament finally be created? And if there remained a Union with others – such as Wales – how could an English Parliament and even more, an English-dominated Westminster, sit side-by-side? If that arrangement came to pass it does not sound like a permanent settlement, more a transition and temporary phase on the way to something else. This would go against all the instincts and traditions of Tory England which has gained numerous advantages from the English-British equation. As the conservative philosopher Michael Oakeshott put it:

> Even the English people, in spite of unique advantages, have never acquired more than an intermittent sense of being a single community, and since 1536 they have never alone composed a state; themselves manifold, they have bound once to three restless partners now to two.[2]

Tory England has known down through the centuries how to weave into a set of fables which were first about England and then about a version of Britain and England as synonymous. This has gone through many huge historic moments of expansion – 1536, 1707, 1801 – and contraction – 1922, the loss of Empire and the semi-detached nature of Northern Ireland and Scotland.

This has contributed to the recalibration of this English-British relationship, with the emergence of an 'England as Britain' school of thought which at times wants to deny the existence of other nations – and can be seen in the politics of Boris Johnson, Nigel Farage and UKIP. To take a recent example of how this is continually reproduced, the journalist Michael Crick's nearly 600-page biography of Nigel Farage contains only one index entry for England (and that is to the English Defence League) with otherwise the territory and nation posted missing – of course, being present but unnamed.[3]

This 'England as Britain' balance provides an opportunity for a predominantly English nationalism to articulate itself while disowning that it is mainly English by investing itself with pretensions to speak for all Britain/UK: a political journey that has informed the 2016 Brexit vote and its aftermath.

Labour's England problem

A fundamental part of all this is the attitude of the centre-left in England and rUK. The centre-left and Labour have long taken a self-denying ordinance about talking about England as a nation. This attitude is informed by a kind of latent fear that Englishness is somehow intrinsically susceptible to racism and xenophobia. From this unease and anxiety, it is a logical step to believe that Englishness must at all costs for the greater good (including all the liberal folk of England) be subsumed in an all-inclusive Britishness.

Hence Gordon Brown in his many interventions on the multiple nationalisms of the isles does not talk about all of them. He is more than content to talk about the different claims of Scottish and Welsh nationalisms, the contested terrain of Ulster and Irish nationalism and what he has called 'Brexit nationalism', which make up his 'five pillars of nationalism' which define the UK.[4] Leave aside that Ulster nationalism is nothing of the kind but a Northern Irish expression of British nationalism. Missing in this, as in many Brown interventions, is any reference to English or British nationalism, both of them buried in the Frankensteinian creation and nonsense of 'Brexit nationalism'.

The historian David Edgerton summarises Brown's embrace of British nationalism, while trying to be not explicit about this in actual words:

> Gordon Brown is a British nationalist in denial. His is a nationalism that cannot speak its name, because it denies that British nationalism could be like other nationalisms. He hates the nationalism of others, including that of Scots.

This puts him in a place, Edgerton assesses, where he feels that he can assert the moral superiority of his nationalism that he dares not call so, while dismissing the minority nationalisms of the UK:

> Contrasting the United Kingdom's (or the British Empire's) outward-looking patriotism with the petty inward-looking nationalism which threaten it is an old argument – for over a century the nationalist enemies of the empire and the Union were criticised for being illiberal, compared with the fair-minded, generous, multinational and multi-cultural Union and Empire. This was a very British conceit. Today such a position is perverse. In the current conjuncture Scottish, Welsh and Irish nationalisms (though not that of Ulster Unionists) are peculiarly internationalist.[5]

Gordon Brown has to be seen as an advocate of British nationalism – a state nationalism which, with its majoritarian claims and conceits, dares to think that it is not a nationalism, but cosmopolitan, internationalist and progressive. Nationalism rather, he poses, is petty, divisive, a throwback and relic from a fossilised past which has somehow managed to survive into modern times and be close to illegitimate. It has to be overcome and defeated by the forces of Enlightenment progress as represented by the likes of Gordon Brown. Yet, what Brown is doing in his choice language is actually 'othering' nationalism as being about something archaic, anachronistic and anti-modern, and not understanding the very modern variants of Scottish nationalism (as well as Welsh and Irish nationalism) and the appeal of self-government. In this he denies the very nature of what the United Kingdom is – and its complex mosaic – obstinately refusing to understand its character or at least so it seems: which is not that unusual a stand for the Westminster political classes.

This evasion goes much further than the interventions of Gordon Brown and go to the heart of how Labour has constructed its idea of Britishness, contributing to the post-war 1945 project which produced the NHS and welfare state and which sublimated England and Englishness, while even at the height of centralisation from the 1940s to mid-1960s, allowing space for distinct Scottish and Welsh strands.

A distinctly pessimistic element of the centre-left view has been the very visible anxiety that England, unbound from the Scots and the Welsh, would be forever reactionary, right-wing and Tory. In the run-up to the 2014 independence referendum, a common concern of English centre-left advocates was what would happen without Scotland. *The Guardian*'s Polly Toynbee, at a debate at the 2012 Edinburgh Book Festival with myself, concluded with this heartfelt plea to the audience: 'Don't leave us. We need you to be there' – the message being that left to their own devices they would face permanent Tory governments.[6]

It is an understandable fear that is regularly heard – and one which needs to be understood. The football and sports commentator Archie Macpherson puts as one of his main reasons for being against independence:

There is something so fundamental in my opposition that a change of mind is inconceivable. This is based on the friendship I have with people I worked with long and hard in my career, in the south, who share the same aspirational values of social improvement that have motivated us together through the years. To turn my back on them in our common fight against recurring Tory governments would be a betrayal.[7]

The basis for this fear of English centre-leftists being held against their will in a hegemonic Tory England does need to be unpacked. In 21 UK post-war general elections (1945–2019), the Conservatives won a majority of the popular vote in England on exactly one occasion: 1955 (50.4 per cent). This was the same year they won a majority of the popular vote in Scotland (50.1 per cent). It was in this year of the zenith of post-war Tory popularity, after Winston Churchill finally handed over to Anthony Eden who quickly went to the polls, only the low level of the Welsh Tory vote (29.9 per cent) preventing the Tories from securing a majority of the vote across the UK (49.7 per cent).[8]

What has given the Tories a sense of invincibility and invulnerability has been the machinations and distortions of the first-past-the-post electoral system alongside the culture of Westminster and the British state. Thus, the Tories have consistently polled well in England but have been more often than not the leading party with the biggest minority – a plurality of votes. They have won the popular vote in England on 14 out of 21 occasions since 1945 (67 per cent) – all but one with a minority of the popular vote.

What is more accurate is that Labour has an English electoral issue across those 21 post-war elections. Labour has won the most parliamentary seats across the UK, and entered office, on nine occasions (43 per cent) but has only ever won the popular vote in England on seven out of these 21 occasions (33 per cent) – 1945, 1950, 1951, 1966, October 1974, 1997 and 2001 – the last election more than 20 years ago. One of those elections (1951) even saw the aberration of Labour narrowly winning the popular vote in England as well as Wales, losing narrowly in Scotland and finishing ahead in the popular vote across the UK by 230,684, securing the highest ever Labour percentage vote (48.8 per cent) and losing office to Winston Churchill and the Tories who were returned with a parliamentary majority of 17 seats after six years of Labour government and Clement Attlee as Prime Minister.

The stark nature of Labour's English problem can be underlined by this fact. Since the invention of the Labour Party the party has entered office as the result of a UK general election on eleven occasions: adding the 1924 and 1929–31 Labour governments to the post-war periods of power to bring a total of 33 years of single-party Labour administrations. In these eleven occasions, Labour has only won the popular vote in England on six occasions – 1945, 1950, 1966, October 1974, 1997, 2001 – and failed to win the popular vote in England on five occasions and been returned to office in 1923, 1929, 1964, February 1974 and 2005.

Labour has a long-running English problem whose scale is shown by the party's historic refusal to talk about it, preferring it would go away.[9] To restate the point: it only won a bare majority in six of the eleven occasions when it was returned to office winning the English popular vote. Take the last time Labour won a UK general election when Tony Blair saw the party comfortably returned with a parliamentary majority of 66 seats: 2005. In the same election in England the Tories finished ahead of Labour by 64,613 votes (35.7 per cent to 35.5 per cent), a fact disguised by the electoral system which gave Labour a lead over the Tories in England of 92 seats (286:194).[10]

Since then, Labour has fallen off an electoral cliff in Scotland, going from 41 seats to one in 2015, then rising back to seven in 2017 and falling back to one in 2019. This makes Labour's English predicament even more acute and an issue for now not for some future unspecific date after Scottish independence.

This post-2015 situation for Labour of having to put together a winning coalition of support without having the historic banker of Scotland is an electoral mountain for the party. Labour needs to start thinking, talking and being political about England and to invoke an England of radicalism, progressivism and egalitarianism against the dominant reactionary Tory ideas. When all the electoral arithmetic shows that the party has to confront this terrain, Labour leaders such as Jeremy Corbyn and Keir Starmer working with the party's caution and conservatism, and deep-seated fear about England, have so far failed to do so.

This leads to the conclusion that the call for help from the likes of Polly Toynbee and others – while understandable – actually assists in continuing the self-denying ordinance on England that Labour and the centre-left have had through their history. It is not sustainable or defensible, and has cost the party and centre-left dear in allowing the Tories and the right to capture and be able to dare they speak for England. Therefore, Scottish independence is not the problem, but instead the evasions and lack of thinking about England across the entire centre-left need to be challenged and rectified. Perhaps an England that has to confront what it stands for post-Scottish independence could be a catalyst and wake-up call. But this historic and present silence cannot go on in perpetuity.

In recent times a rising tide of English voices on the centre-left have kicked back against this state, and tried to get Labour and the left thinking about England. This includes the likes of John Harris, Billy Bragg, Anthony Barnett, Mark Perryman and former Labour MP and minister John Denham.[11] It is not an accident that all of these thoughtful English voices (with the possible exception of Denham) are sympathetic or supportive of Scottish independence. One factor is their analysis of the Scottish independence debate and understanding of self-government, but another is that they see the misgovernance and undemocratic treatment of England as one of the central pillars for the maintenance of the existing Westminster system. The historian David Edgerton stresses the links between Scottish independence and how England is governed:

> I think an independent Scotland would benefit England in that many false notions of grandeur, which poison our politics and our ability to see ourselves properly, would evaporate and England could follow Scotland in seeing itself as a nation like so many others. The road to a refreshed democracy south of the border goes through Scottish independence.[12]

Another aspect of the weakening hold of the Union of long-term significance is the hollowing out of attachment to the Union in what anyone would expect to be one of its last redoubts – the Conservative and Unionist Party.

Even here, the multiple convulsions, tensions and break-points in the Union have affected the Tory faithful's belief in its power. A poll of Tory members undertaken by YouGov in June 2019, one month before Boris Johnson became UK Prime Minister, indicated a pent-up desire by the grassroots of the party to 'get Brexit done' at all costs which could include nearly everything else in relation to the UK – and being prepared to jeopardise the future of the Union.

The Tory members polled were willing to see the Union pass into history for the sake of Brexit – 63 per cent were prepared to see Scottish independence as a result of Brexit; 59 per cent were prepared to see Northern Ireland leave for Brexit; 54 per cent the destruction of the Conservative Party, and 39 per cent would rather that Jeremy Corbyn, then Labour leader, became UK Prime Minister than not have Brexit.[13] These are fascinating figures and one interesting takeaway is that 24 per cent gap between the near two-thirds majority of Tory members prepared to countenance independence and the two-fifths who were prepared to pay what for the Tories was the ultimate price: Corbyn in Downing Street.

The then leader of the Scottish Tories, Ruth Davidson, did not take kindly to these findings saying: 'I think there are a number of people within the Conservative Party who need to take a long, hard look at themselves.' And she went on:

> I would remind people of their obligations within the party
> – yes, we're a Conservative Party, but we're also a Unionist party, and I'd remind them that our own Union of nations is every bit as important as leaving someone else.[14]

Boris Johnson was elected Tory leader and became UK Prime Minister the following month, July 2019. The month after, in August, Ruth Davidson resigned as Scottish Tory leader. The UK left the European Union on 31 January 2020 but these problems have not gone away inside the Tory Party or the case for the Union.

Brexit and 'England outside London'

These factors would all come to fruition in an England which has to address a more English-focused politics and which was freed to champion and extend English democracy and self-government. It would bring forth numerous topics for discussion about the role of identity and the canvas of different identities in England, its history beyond the 'England speaks for Britain' account which has been so dominant for so many years, different expressions of Englishness, regionalism, the North–South divide, balance between big cities and towns and rural areas, discontent with a London-centric political system and centralisation.

As Scottish self-government has aided a slow unpacking of a homogeneous, unified Scotland and encouraged a debate on which Scotland gains the most from devolution and the decisions of the Scottish Government, so an English debate precipitated by Scottish independence could begin to unravel the conceit that there is a single entity called England and take this beyond the oft-cited cliché of referencing the North–South divide. Of the many English divides which would rise to the surface, a key one which has already emerged (and would become even more important) is the dynamic between that of the world city of London and the nation that is 'England outside London'. The divide between these two parts of the same formal nation came to the fore in the 2016 Brexit vote when London voted 59.9 per cent to 40.1 per cent to Remain (a lead of 750,287 votes) while the largest constituency of the UK – 'England outside London' – voted 55.4 per cent to 44.6 per cent to Leave (a lead of 2,684,196) and the margin that overturned London, Scotland and Northern Ireland to produce the UK-wide lead for Leave of 1,269,501 (51.9 per cent to 48.1 per cent).[15]

In the resulting years, the Brexit vote has produced more over-the-top rhetoric and claims than any other democratic exercise in recent British history and introduced new levels of intolerance and insults. Underneath all of that something profound lay in the political earthquake which produced the Brexit vote – a vote that rejected the main Westminster political parties and their main leaders and former leaders.

This popular revolt may well have been orchestrated brilliantly by the right and then hijacked by an even more virulent, disreputable right pursuing as pure a Brexit as possible, but the original causes of the revolt were manifold, some understandable. Part of this is even visible in the genius of the Dominic Cummings-inspired phrase 'Take Back Control'.

This originated in the campaign slogan against the euro, 'keep control' which became 'Let's take back control' and 'Take Back Control'. As Cummings observed after the vote: '"back" plays into a strong evolved instinct – we hate losing things, especially control'.[16] This goes beyond abstract ideas of sovereignty to wanting not to be governed by others (other nations and foreigners) and draws on the memory of pre-1973 UK to say 'we can do this'. But it also has, and this was one of its many potent strands almost of genius level, an echo of revolutionary sentiment drawing from radical traditions of self-government and self-determination once central to the left tradition.

Anthony Barnett, Founding Editor of *openDemocracy*, wrote about Brexit and Trump's ascendancy, observing: 'Large numbers in all classes did not want continuity' and went on: 'A majority in England felt the country should not carry on being governed in the way it was – it too was a wider decision than the choice on the ballot paper itself. They had had enough.'[17]

Barnett poses that five different constituencies exist inside the shell of the UK: Scotland, Wales, Northern Ireland, the world city of London and what he calls 'England without London'; although you could add a sixth – the imagined relic of the political and administrative classes ergo the state of the UK. Writing about 'England without London' and 2016, he comments that the Brexit majority created in this England was 'a cross-class, cross-party movement that overwhelmed regional differences... Something has happened in England-without-London that made it receptive to the anti-EU forces, something that knitted the arguments together and amplified them. Something national.' This was, he concludes, 'the force field of the English spirit' which 'reinforced each other in the prejudices, longing and judgements of English voters across their land to create a decisive majority for Brexit...'[18]

It has been revealing that post-2016 this English spirit has been seldom commented upon by the media or even the Leave and Remain camps; much easier and more comfortable to reach into clichés about the forgotten North of England, 'Red Wall' seats (the ultimate in insider class condescension and 'othering'), and an almost Dickensian portrayal of 'It's grim up North' but they have finally rebelled – all of which can be addressed by the repetition of such glib phrases, supplemented by the post-2016 invention, 'levelling up'.

One of the most consistently illuminating commentators on Brexit has been Irish writer Fintan O'Toole, who has dug into the layers and conceits of the English imagination. In his book on the subject, *Heroic Failure: Brexit and the Politics of Pain*, he notes that 'Brexit is essentially an English phenomenon.'[19] There then follows a coruscating polemic examining the degeneration of English politics and culture which has seen the return of an entitled Tory ruling class who barely conceal their contempt for the plebs and great unwashed and get away with it at least for now.

All fine as polemic but what is absent and unexplored in O'Toole's case are the other, different Englands and any real explanation for why this Tory reprehensible reactionary perspective has emerged triumphant. O'Toole for all his gifts as a writer and essayist is posing an essentialist England which does not and never has existed (and which the likes of Barnett avoided). And also offering no account of the marginalisation and decline of those other Englands – such as the Labour England of Clement Attlee and Harold Wilson which for brief periods looked like the progressive future. This is a fundamental point not just about history or Brexit, but about the future as another England is possible for all the degree to which the current Tory England may appear deeply dug in and impregnable.

The Irish issue

The spectre of Ireland and Northern Ireland hung over the post-2016 Brexit deliberations with Brexiteers showing their annoyance, ignorance and arrogance. Despite 30 years of 'the Troubles' and so many other aspects of Irish-British history, British politicians tended to forget about Northern Ireland as much as they could, only discussing it when forced by events.

Brexit blew that approach to pieces and the years after 2016 saw much talk of the consequences of a hard Brexit on the Irish/Northern Irish border, with Brexiteers resisting the central logic of their uncompromising Brexit stance: that it involved hard borders and had consequences for the Good Friday Agreement. All of this gave new interest to the subject of Irish reunification which was aided by other factors. There was now no automatic unionist majority in Northern Ireland; Sinn Fein are in many polls the leading party north and south in the island of Ireland; the Democratic Unionists dramatically overplayed their hand holding out for a harder Brexit in a province which voted Remain. Added to this there is little strategic, constructive thinking inside unionism about its future or that of the Union at a time when they need it most.[20] And meanwhile, the Irish Republic has gone through numerous crises and waves but emerged a distinctly more modern-looking country than the present-day UK.

A key element of Irish identity used to be 'not being British' with a sliding scale of how emphatically you rejected British-ness to affirm your Irishness. Richard Kearney notes: 'That's the dialectic. I am A because I am not B. I am Irish because I am not British. Douglas Hyde said, "The British are the people we love to hate and never cease to imitate."'[21] That relationship has been weakened in recent decades, and while Brexit brought some of the worst British attitudes to the fore, perhaps it allows the Irish a chance for accommodation and even partial escape. There is a link between Scottish independence and Irish reunification in that they are both about a Union in flux – and not in a good way. There is the small issue of timing and the interplay between the two. Whichever vote and then exit happened first would leave the other confronting some difficult issues about the nature of the Union they were left in.

The difference is that Northern Ireland's departure would be little lamented in mainland Britain and among UK political elites; the same would not be true of Scotland. 'It is hard to argue that Northern Ireland has been anything other than a bad idea to begin with that got steadily worse', notes Kevin Meagher in a history of the province, concluding, 'Northern Ireland was not built to endure. Over the next few years, that will become all too apparent.'[22] Whatever the future of Scotland and independence, no serious observer would describe Scotland's existence in such completely negative terms.

What do we do with the remnants of the Empire State?

A central issue to be confronted in the event of independence would be the remnants of the British state minus Scotland, and in particular the Empire State mindset which has domestically cost so much damage and prevented progress towards enduring progressive change – instead always acting as a bulwark for reaction and fortress ramparts against centre-left radicalism getting too carried away with itself.

The rUK political establishment would clearly try to limit any fundamental democratic change occurring after Scottish independence. Despite it being a watershed moment, they would try to present any change as minimal or use it as an opportunity to accrue even more power to themselves. They would use independence like Brexit, not as a moment of constitutional and political renewal, but as a period of constitutional retrenchment and retreat into a fantasyland past of even more absolutism and governance shorn of even the checks and balances of the old system. It could lead to a centre reasserting itself as a modern leviathan, not interested in the notion of sharing power with those bits of the UK left that it could still claim to govern.

This could produce a wake-up call for the centre-left and assist them in finally and belatedly breaking with delusions of the Empire State, centralisation and parliamentary sovereignty which have so ill-served the cause of the left. These are the myths which labourism adopted as if they were their own in 1945 when they came from the dominant reactionary Tory ideas of political power and authority. Labour have remained true to these concepts through thick and thin, and many years of disappointment. This has been the golden thread of how labourism ended up doing politics across the post-war era — from Harold Wilson and Jim Callaghan through to even Tony Blair and Gordon Brown (who showed contempt for most of the party's other traditions) — and which was mirrored on the party's left tradition from Nye Bevan through Michael Foot to Tony Benn and more recently Jeremy Corbyn.

Labour and the centre-left must create and engage with an English dimension of politics and democracy; portray and imagine England as a nation and political community, and come up with ideas, interventions and policies which speak to an English imagination and spirit. This has to have a connection to cultural politics which is a tough ask for party politics, but has to at the minimum understand that part of this English re-emergence will be fuzzy, messy and difficult to pin down, being not in shape or form conventional politics, but contributing to an informal English landscape and England of the everyday mind.

A modern enlightened Englishness is already here and visible. It is the attitude present in the best of Gareth Southgate's men's English national football team at Euro 2020 (played in the summer of 2021). But even the English football team became literally a political football, seen by many on the right as 'woke' and 'politically correct' in taking the knee in solidarity with Black Lives Matters. Being claimed by left-wingers and liberals, elite football does not and never can capture the diversity of a nation (the case of a multicultural French team winning the 1998 FIFA World Cup comes to mind). The England of multicultural, hybrid identities and multiple languages and backgrounds is out there in every community – not just in London and England's big cities but in much of the North and smaller cities and towns, but this needs a political language, expression and fearless championing against the reactionary attitudes of the monocultural English right.

England has to be encouraged to find its own voices, tones and modern-day languages but that requires a politics comfortable with nurturing its evolution, creating spaces for an emergent Englishness, and recognising that there is a political and cultural struggle here for what is part of the key terrain of English politics and public life – a terrain the right are already occupying and where they have an agenda.

The above sentiments are pivotal to what has to spring from this. Namely the political idea of democratising England and letting the different component parts of England and England overall find their voice(s) as well as different national expressions. This may sound like it is somehow easy or an add-on to real politics but it is not. A traditional Labour and left approach to the English question would be to just come up with a set of programmatic polices. This after all was the New Labour approach to English regionalism led by John Prescott which ended in the emphatic rejection by voters in the North East referendum of 2004.

To get to the point of suggesting a new set of political institutions, more politicians and more elections in England, there has to be a remaking of England and a reassertion of English democratic life. The idea of England as a political community has to be made and won, defeating the forces for whom the current limbo state of England works well, namely the Westminster governing and insider class. And that requires a multi-level approach, encouraging a cultural politics and space, naming institutions and bodies as English and about England, and then filling the political air with an understanding of England as a nation. It is not easy and will take time but the English left have to challenge their deep-seated ambivalence on England and recognise that they have to change tack. Their traditional approach to England has cost it, and most of us, dear.

Finally, Scottish independence poses a set of challenges to how relationships of the current four nations of the UK will evolve. There will be areas of political, economic and social co-operation. There will in all probability be cross-border agencies and institutions to administer pan-UK issues and contribute to pan-UK solutions. There is no realistic vision of Scottish independence which is based on actual 'separatism' and cutting Scotland off so that it sits in splendid isolation from rUK. There is no version of Scottish independence that ends up looking like 'Scexit' — a Scottish version of Brexit — pursuing an unattainable idea of absolutist sovereignty in the modern world.

While supporters of UK federalism have always had their work cut out, coming up with plausible detailed plans that address the English question and nature of the British state, paradoxically Scottish independence could entail some kind of innovative constitutional furniture such as pan-UK confederal arrangements. This would be very different from the mirage of UK-wide federalism for confederalism is a set of relationships between self-governing, independent nation-states. One scenario would see these existing between an independent Scotland and rUK but which also might have the capacity to accommodate a future Northern Ireland post-UK and a new understanding with the Republic of Ireland which would allow for an all-Ireland unity but would be aware of the needs to accommodate the concerns of Northern Ireland's unionist community in some power-sharing architecture.

Such a set of arrangements could be seen as a uniquely twenty-first-century response to the shared histories and interests of the people and nations of these islands who currently live in the UK, while also recognising the Irish dimension. This would accommodate and respect Scottish independence, alongside growing Welsh support for further self-government, and the question of Northern Ireland and Ireland. Who knows – it could, if the English left found a confidence, even develop an appropriate English contribution.

While such discussions are on some level for another day – for the days after Scottish independence – there is a need for them to be gently encouraged in some form as soon as possible. Indeed, there is a long, distinguished political tradition in Scotland of recognising the importance of sharing and pooling sovereignty at the level of the nation-state, seen in the writings of Neil MacCormick who thought and wrote about this over many years and saw the EU as an expression of such a post-national, even post-nationalist politics.[23] This position is questioned by some pro-independence left voices, with James Foley noting that: 'I think the left needs to abandon the "post-sovereignty" delusions of the old neoliberal era, as a species of nostalgia for an unremembered nineties.'[24]

The north-west of Europe and Scotland's neighbourhood has a variety of constitutional, state and semi-state arrangements and different sovereignties, as Michael Keating noted:

Europe's Atlantic periphery is home to an extraordinary variety of constitutional forms. Norway and Iceland opted for full independence in 1905 and 1944, respectively, while maintaining cultural ties to other Nordic states and remaining outside the European Union. Greenland gained home rule from Denmark in 1979 and, while remaining part of the Danish state, withdrew from the EU.

Keating goes on:

> The Republic of Ireland became a self-governing dominion in 1922 and left the Commonwealth in 1949, but over recent years has entered into common arrangements with the United Kingdom for the government of Northern Ireland... The Faroe Islands have a strong degree of self-government within Denmark but are not part of the EU and regularly contemplate the prospect of full independence. The Canaries and Azores have special status, including a distinct fiscal regime, within Spain and Portugal, respectively. The Channel Islands and Isle of Man are part of the possessions of the British Crown but not part of the United Kingdom... There is, therefore a wealth of examples of how to mix and match self-government and sovereignty claims – the product of incomplete state-building and management of this part of the European periphery.[25]

All sorts of new forms of co-operation and arrangements could be possible in the event of Scottish independence, with one caveat. One major challenge is visible in all this from afar – a kind of political iceberg – that could sink any such grand designs. That is the dominant expression of the English political tradition with its fetish for parliamentary sovereignty, indivisible power and absolutism, allowing central government (meaning the executive in the real world) to be unchecked constitutionally and politically: a tradition critiqued in *A Claim of Right for Scotland* in 1988 when it talked, borrowing from Bagehot, of 'the English Constitution – an Illusion of Democracy'.[26] Post-independence considerations of co-operative arrangements between all of the peoples and nations will come up against this tradition and in particular the Tory right-wing's virulent fixation on such ideas – along with Labour's historic attachment to them without fetishising them to such an extent.

This right-wing take has been successful because it has down the years found echoes – if less dogmatically – on the left. When the writer Bernard Crick talked about this subject and called it 'the English ideology', he was not just posing it as a problem of the right, but of the left in England as well.[27] Crick's articulation of this drew upon his understanding of the delusions of British absolutist sovereignty which, alongside imperialist hubris, saw the humiliation of the UK in the American War of Independence in 1775–76 and struggle for Irish independence in 1921–22. He took the view that the UK was at its core held together by smoke and mirrors aided by myth and that: 'Our rulers have ended up believing their own rhetoric, and therein often lies ruin and disaster.'[28]

Hence, any talk of pan-UK arrangements post-independence while desirable come back to the English question and the need for a democratic English politics. And for this the centre-left in England need to start thinking and talking about what England means and what it could mean to be English in all its many different facets. They need to stop their silences, evasions and feeling embarrassed about such a subject – England – which is of direct consequence and import to millions upon millions of people up and down the country, as well as indirectly the inhabitants of Scotland, Wales and Northern Ireland.

Many Englands can also be characterised not just by territory but also identity and different scales of English and British identity. The Future of England Survey found in England 42 per cent support for Northern Ireland leaving the UK, 23 per cent for Scottish independence and 17 per cent for Welsh independence. These findings led academics Ailsa Henderson and Richard Wyn-Jones to state:

> While there remains strong support for the Union with Scotland and Wales, this is simply not the case with regard to Northern Ireland… Those who feel exclusively or predominantly English are less supportive of the maintenance of the Union, including that with Scotland and Wales, than those who feel exclusively or predominantly British.

They assess about the future of England and the Union that 'if majority opinion in England were ever to have its way, then the Union would continue on a radically revised basis', and that if Scotland decided to choose the path of independence 'attitudes in England towards the newly independent state would be punitive – particularly so among the exclusively and predominantly English.'[29]

That is one distinct possible future: a punitive, bitter England kicking out against those it perceives as betraying and undermining it. But that is also a political contest and struggle about the kind of England which will exist in the future, the balance between different forces and opinion, and the power and influence of a reactionary right-wing Englishness searching for others to blame and stigmatise. There is no guarantee of its triumph or defeat.

One word of observation about the dynamic in England and rUK after Scottish independence. This would not be a non-event to which the ruling circles could just respond by burying their heads in the sand, and carrying on regardless. In this sense this would be of more historical import than the seismic moments of the breakaway of the American colonies in 1775–76, and the birth of the Irish Free State in 1922. These were not and never were seen as intrinsic parts of the British Union that was the core UK. The loss of the American territories was a colonial defeat, while Ireland (despite being part of the UK) was always seen as other and as distinct, a place to be ignored when the history or politics proved too difficult or problematic for the British state.

None of those descriptions accurately fit Scotland. Scottish independence is not the loss of a colony or another distant territory. Instead, it would represent withdrawal from the UK of a territory which is part of the homeland that is the UK and mainland that is Britain, and whose union with England in 1707 is as close as the UK has got to fundamental law. It would be unprecedented in the history of Scotland, England, Wales and Northern Ireland, and in the history of the UK. And in that sense, it could elicit many varieties of emotions, responses and confusions, some of which might not be very attractive and others which might surprise us in their imagination and thought. We should at the very least start preparing to think about the unthinkable.

16
Scotland's Right to Decide

The mere setting up of a bourgeois Parliament at Edinburgh without sturdy local self-government to control it will simply make new jobs for Edinburgh lawyers and Glasgow business men – and the real people of Scotland will have as little liberty and self-government as at present.

Tom Burns, 'Giving Government Back to the People of Scotland', in Neil Maclean (ed.), *The New Scotland: 17 Chapters on Scottish Reconstruction*, 1942

Supporters of independence need to focus less on the when of a referendum and much more on developing a clear, compelling and positive case for self-determination. That should be rooted in attentive listening to the aspirations and concerns of those who live here, identifying common ground in values and principles, and doing the careful work of responding thoughtfully to anxieties and criticisms. We need to build alliances to challenge the current rather sterile narrative – whether coming out of Westminster, or from the flag waving nationalists – with an achievable vision of the kind of nation we want to be. This needs to be the settled will of the Scottish people in order to provide fertile soil for growing a mature, progressive and caring society.

Lesley Orr, activist and theologian,
personal communication, March 2022

Neal Ascherson ended a powerful polemic in the *London Review of Books* when looking back on the 2014 independence vote by saying that:

> In Scotland's 2014 referendum campaign, one apparently humble word became the deadliest weapon. The word was 'normal'. Again and again, at pro-independence gatherings, I heard people say: 'I just want my kids to grow up in a normal wee nation, like other countries.' By this they meant a country which took its own decisions for better or worse, which could feel that its future was in its own hands.[1]

This was written six years after Scotland voted in the 2014 referendum and in a political climate in which so much had changed, was in flux or in doubt. Not only had the UK not reformed in a more democratic or progressive direction, not embraced more constitutional reform or really faced up to its broken economic and social model. In many respects, the UK had gone backwards – and this after the twin 'big bangs' of the 2014 Scottish and 2016 Brexit votes – which in different ways were insurgencies against the status quo. Anthony Barnett described the latter as showing that 'willed change is possible' and that 'voters can take a risk' – a take with some resonance to Scotland if people are given the chance.[2]

The independence question over this time has not only not gone away; it has not been settled; and is still an active and live issue which needs to be discussed and a formal decision made about it. Public opinion is undoubtedly still in play on the question, with, in 2022, neither Yes or No having built up a sustainable lead and majority. But what can be observed is that the 2014 campaign permanently transformed the prospects of independence support – and that while independence has not yet become a decisive majority – gains made in the 2014 campaign have not been temporary but proved to be long-term and enduring.

It is understandable that large parts of the pro-Union case want to ignore this reality. They did not of their own free choice want the 2014 vote and campaign. It was not a debate of their choosing and for understandable reasons is not their terrain and what motivates many, if not most, of them.

Former Scottish Labour leader Johann Lamont reflected after the 2014 vote that she had found the experience of leading Scottish Labour during the campaign unpleasant. She subsequently said that 'I want to lead this party into the battles over equality and social justice which have been put on hold too long'[3] and resigned as leader one month later.

Despite Lamont's lament, this is an active, ongoing issue that has to have at some point some kind of closure and that can only happen with another vote. The late Nigel Smith – cited previously – who advised Better Together, observed: 'This is not a settled issue, but rather a live one which has to be concluded one way or another by at some point having another independence referendum.'[4]

The belief in Scotland's right to decide its own future is widely recognised as popular as a principle – one which people can relate to and identify across the political divide – although it has not yet translated into widespread support for a second independence referendum. Pamela Nash, Chief Executive of Scotland in Union, said at the These Islands conference in February 2020 that 'the SNP's right to choose campaign' was 'very carefully pitched and reaching out'.[5]

The Scottish debate has to tap into and recognise the desire to be normal – to be a mainstream, modern, democratic nation-state. Yet this on its own is not enough and it is also salutary to recognise that there are many expressions of what normal is for a nation-state – and that there is a crisis about what passes for normal and mainstream across much of the world's politics.

Scotland has to embrace not just the desire of some to be normal, but to go beyond this and embrace the imaginative, bold and unique, both in terms of how we think and act in Scotland and beyond, and in the relationships of the people and nations of what is currently the UK.

This could involve the prospect of a very new kind of partnership within Scotland and across the current UK in terms of political power, sovereignty and institutions which, rather than having its roots in nineteenth-century absolutism, charts out a new diffuse, adaptable twenty-first-century set of arrangements. This would have the prospect of drawing on older Scottish traditions of authority and legitimacy with roots in the idea of Scotland, the community of the realm and the source of formal power springing from the people, not from the top downwards which is the English tradition. The challenge in this would be how to make it real and lived, and how it is accommodated or sits next to the influence of 'the English ideology' of indivisible authority we saw in the previous chapter.

The terrain of being imaginative and bold includes looking at how Scotland does politics, public policy and institutions and the stories we tell ourselves which shape and define public life. For example, in too many places and areas of life there has been a propensity to institutional groupthink and lack of diversity and dynamism in thinking, in political discussion and in legislation passed by the Scottish Parliament. This latter point can be seen across the board, from education, health, local government and democracy, community empowerment and much more.

The reach and relevance of self-government

The idea of self-government has been a powerful one through the ages, but it should not just stop at Scottish self-determination at the level of the nation. Instead, it could have the potential of being a defining principle for a future independent Scotland and how it organises and governs itself not just at the national, but local and community. Self-government as an organising principle of society could be a means by which Scotland looked to run public services instead of the current mix of paternalist, managerial and technocratic delivery systems. This principle is at least worthy of consideration when we reflect on the exhaustion of those traditions to express the common good. How do we make public services 'public' and what principles and values do we base them on? What is the scope for self-government to be widened from the national to the local and communities? And in what ways could self-government be a principle used by professional groups and sectors to advance thinking about how to spread democratisation more widely throughout society?

It is worth recalling that the idea of self-government is one of the central principles of the socialist movement, linked to the goal of greater economic democracy, which became less influential as socialism in Britain became more statist and about central control. This tradition was associated with the Rochdale pioneers and co-operative movement; Robert Owen after New Lanark; G.D.H. Cole; guild socialism; and had a brief renaissance in the late 1960s and 1970s, shaped by the trade union shop steward movement.[6] It draws from the ideas of self-determination taking them beyond the nation to become an organising principle for communities and society.

Holding power to account and self-organising Scotland

Scotland needs to be more imaginative in how we hold power to account in a practical way. This is a basic prerequisite for a society with ambition to be bold and more radical. In the history of modern Scotland and the extension of the state from late Victorian times, too often institutional authority and opinion has managed to avoid being held to account or even scrutinised too closely. This has been because of the nature of Scottish elites, the establishment and how professional groups have looked after their own self-interests, whether business groups, the legal profession or sections of the media.

One recent example of not holding institutional power to account was Rangers FC's administration in February 2012, followed by liquidation in July 2012. This saw them have to start again from the fourth tier of senior Scottish football after reconstituting the club. The events which led to this saw the mainstream media not asking pertinent questions about how Rangers were being run financially. When Rangers went into liquidation it took the self-organisation of football fans beyond the big two Glasgow clubs to prevent the football authorities engaging in a typical old-fashioned stitch-up and allowing the newly constituted Rangers to remain in the top league as if nothing had happened (apart from the possibility of a points deduction).

This is not just a story about football, but about power in Scotland and the capacity in today's world for accountability, checking power and self-organisation. I put these points to one of SNP's leading strategists who played a major role in the 2014 referendum just after the vote, saying that this episode sowed the initial seeds of DIY activism which exploded into the flowering of activism in 2014. They responded with a look of surprise: 'You are not just talking about football are you? You are talking about power and who holds it in society.'[7]

This does point to the perils of living through fast-changing history and all of us, including some of the leading participants, not always grasping the scale of change underway. Scotland's independence referendum came about as a result of long-term changes about how people think and feel about the 'idea' of Scotland. And this surge of support and interest for independence and democratic engagement has altered the terrain of public life and is something fundamental which is beyond the SNP and party politics.

It also positions Scotland's 2014 referendum in the tradition of 'referendums from below' which have grown up around the world as a challenge to mainstream politics: another being the 2011 Italian referendum which rejected water privatisation.[8] Scotland has a long tradition of such votes from the rich history of local temperance ballots in the 1920s which saw 1,131 votes on whether neighbourhoods should be 'dry' or 'wet', to more recently the Strathclyde water privatisation vote in 1993.[9] This is a tradition which deserves nurturing and support in the future.

A major dimension in the expression of popular power is invoking popular sovereignty in Scotland versus parliamentary sovereignty as we have already seen in previous chapters.[10] It is most commonly cited in Scotland in relation to Westminster absolutism – the threat being posed as external and the traditions north of the border as more democratic. Yet it is also true that the promoting of popular sovereignty has ramifications for power and authority and how it is dispersed within Scotland, on which work is needed. The language of popular sovereignty has been shrouded in mythology and folklore, but has so far had little practical consequences domestically.[11] It could be persuasive if this tradition were linked not only to critiquing Westminster, but how power is more widely shared across Scotland.

A practical element in learning from the above and other examples is that there has to be some consideration of the culture and ecology of the public sphere in Scotland – namely the arena of public life in which politics and ideas are discussed and considered – and which includes the media but is much larger than that. There is the need to consider how best to support public interest journalism, local media and public service broadcasting. These are challenging topics across the developed world with the rise of digital platforms and multi-media consumption. All of this is particularly acute in small-sized nation-states, although there are examples that can provide inspiration. The Norwegian Media Authority for one was set up in 2005 and has a remit to 'promote freedom of expression, the process and a vibrant democracy'.[12] It runs a number of initiatives such as subsidising newspapers and specialist publications including those representing minority languages, funding user-orientated media and continuing education along with local broadcasting grants.

Thinking long

One future strand which needs addressing is the capacity to develop and research the scale of policy interventions required in an independent Scotland. At the moment the policy environment is dominated by the Scottish Government and civil service (as we saw in Chapter 14), but in an independent Scotland thought will have to be given to how to nurture a more pluralist, competitive policy landscape.

There is currently a paucity of conventional think tanks in Scotland. Those that exist are small and under-resourced, while examples such as the hybrid Common Weal have made an impact but not developed a sustainable model financially and in other ways. There are numerous ways in which this paucity of resources for thinking about policy can be addressed. The Institute for Public Policy Research (IPPR) Scotland produced a report in March 2021 on this lack of think tanks and research organisations, looking at different ways government and public agencies could support a more diverse policy environment; this would require government to recognise the need to change particularly in the event of independence but so far this is not the case.[13]

There are other approaches which do not need to go down this conventional road. A plethora of think tanks does not of itself lead to better ideas and government. The two most crowded think tank environments in the world are London and Washington, DC and as this world has become an industry in the past couple of decades, so the corporate think tank has arisen as the dominant model connected to the corporate capture of public policy.[14] That is without getting into the rise of the right-wing think tank world around Westminster based on secretive funders and lack of transparency.[15] Yet at the same time a policy environment such as Scotland with hardly any such agencies means that most policy development is done by government in-house.

The Welsh government has faced a similar set of challenges in an even smaller policy environment and responded in a way different from the conventional response. It passed a Well-Being of Future Generations Act in 2015. This was advocated by former Welsh Environment, Sustainability and Health minister Jane Davidson, who had grown increasingly disillusioned with the high talk and platitudes of sustainability from public bodies who then failed to deliver with little comeback. UN Sustainable Development goals were used as a starting position and structure which led to the creation of a Future Generations Commissioner for Wales – the first person appointed being Sophie Howe who started in 2016. She is tasked with examining proposed legislation and development with a mind to the future and has said she sees her work as being to act as 'the guardian of the interests of future generations in Wales'.[16]

Democratising the future and challenging 'the official future'

This raises the subject of futures literacy and how to democratically think and create our collective future. This has been perhaps surprisingly a terrain which 'official Scotland' has mostly remained completely silent on since the advent of the Scottish Parliament, despite the existence of the Scottish Parliament's Futures Forum which has mostly undertaken narrow policy work, and being connected to the Parliament is circumscribed on being able to get into more controversial subjects.

This has left this important territory to think tanks and individuals with initiatives including the *Scotland 2020* and *Glasgow 2020* programmes that I led,[17] and more recently the publication of *Scotland 2070*.[18] Hillary Sillitto, one of the co-authors of *Scotland 2070*, told me: 'There is very little long-term thinking and the 50-year view is missing altogether – no one else seems to be thinking this *far* ahead.'

He summarises his credo as:

Telling new stories about Scotland's future. Scotland can succeed in the new world if we act decisively and ambitiously to take advantage of new opportunities that we can see emerging.

Our dream would be that Scots love to look to the future positively, post-COVID, post-Brexit, post-oil, with the 'can-do' attitudes that so characterised it in the past. Scottish scientists, engineers, administrators, academics and entrepreneurs have set the pace before. We still have those latent skills.[19]

The *Scotland 2020* and *Glasgow 2020* programmes embraced much of this terrain. They started with the premise that 'official stories' and 'official future' on offer from government, public bodies and corporate business were increasingly threadbare and increasingly problematic while becoming increasing dogmatic and doctrinaire. This was for the reason that institutional opinion has already decided the big questions about the future for the rest of us: a world of endless economic growth and conspicuous consumption while lecturing the masses about globalisation and that 'There is no Alternative'.[20]

Both *Scotland 2020* and *Glasgow 2020* posed that the creation of new stories which profoundly broke with these 'official' perspectives was critical. The two initiatives embraced the idea of futures literacy and mass imagination, based on the premise that people have the capacity to imagine and create alternative futures if aided and encouraged and given respect and space to do so.

One illuminating difference between the world of 'the official future' and the stories of the future which emerged in *Scotland 2020* and *Glasgow 2020* was that the vision of the future presented in the former in formal documents was often sectoral (i.e. about the economy, culture or tourism), value-free (with any values implicit rather than explicit), and devoid of people outside of institutions (with endless photographs of tidy and empty public spaces).

The future created in *Scotland 2020* and *Glasgow 2020* was all-encompassing and connected (not being about one area or sector but rather how life is lived), explicitly about values and wanting an open conversation about the trade-offs between them, understanding the fabric of society as a social contract, and wanting to see this explicitly recognised in an open honest discussion where institutions talked about difficult challenges and choices, rather than (as many people felt) treat them as stupid and reduce everything to glib phrases and soundbites.

Running through these discussions was a deep-seated awareness of the need for society to embrace an exploration of philosophical conversations and values – and a belief that these should underpin long-term choices about government policy and the direction of society. Many of the observations across these projects – with more than 5,000 people contributing to the *Glasgow 2020* project – felt that the 'official future' did somewhere have a set of values, but often chose to hide it and not be explicit for fear that people would register their disapproval. This all contributed to a climate of suspicion and distrust towards government and public agencies, which has only built from the supposed 'golden era' of globalisation of Blair and Clinton to the present.

The politics of time

Connected to this is nurturing a politics of change which recognises that bringing about real lasting progress cannot be, in most cases, instant and has to have an understanding of the politics of timescales in it. To take one example already cited, an independent Scotland will not be able within a very short period of time to eradicate all child poverty in the country. Such issues are complex and multidimensional and involve structural, societal, generational, geographical and individual factors. And then there is the issue of prioritising in government policy, identifying and delivering resources and spending, and the limits of government in a world of interdependence and virulent capitalism. The debate on such topics has to have a sense of a timescale of change, otherwise the reality of an independent Scotland will be of immediate disappointment for some and for others engender a sense of betrayal.

The political writer Bernard Crick nearly 40 years ago wrote about this very subject, offering some recommendations for socialists and radicals. He put forward the case that much of the rhetoric and language of what passes for radical politics is unreflective and based on an 'instant gratification culture' on the left, and what others have subsequently called 'a Pot Noodle radicalism: just add water and hey presto', believing that if radical positions are taken by the right leadership then somehow change will happen. Crick poses that such a mindset represented an immaturity, and inherently has the seeds of its own self-destruction and built-in disappointment, retreat and defeat.

To avert this, Crick stated that radicals should adopt a policy that was more nuanced and 'campaign on three different levels'. These were first, 'short-term tactical reforms within the system to build a basis of popular confidence for advance'. Second, 'middle-term strategies to change the system'. Third, 'long-term persuasion to work a new system in a new spirit.' Crick concludes: "Those levels do not contradict, they complement each other so long as the distinctions about time are clear.'[21]

The insight of Crick on radical intent and the importance of timescales is a salutary one for the politics of independence and mapping out the future direction of Scotland. A politics of timescales should be explicit to independence, laying out different horizons while trying to maintain progress, and has been noticeably missing since 2014. Take a specific example such as private education. To build up a momentum and alliance to consider their eventual abolition – as, for example, happened in Finland in the 1960s – would be aided by slowly removing all of their financial advantages (some of which happened in April 2022) and eventually removing their charitable status and financial reliefs that they claim – to produce a level playing field in education. At the same time, the case would be made for education and health as public goods which should be publicly owned and not have services for profit – all of which would make the case for the eventual abolition of private education and its role in perpetuating privilege.

The growing pains of growing up

The rich tapestry of thinking longer-term has been only notionally engaged with by 'official Scotland'. One of the paradoxes of the Scottish independence project as presented by the Scottish Government and SNP has been to leave the ground of futures thinking about Scotland unexplored and, in the words of Pat Kane, to implicitly say let's leave all that important stuff until after independence:

> I think it's to do with the maintenance of what one (now disgraced) minister once described to me as 'the golden thread of competence' throughout SNP Government. The idea is that you show you know how to run and manage things properly under devolution, and that builds up confidence in the voters that Scotland can manage more ambitious forms of government, like full independence.
>
> It aspired to be just as good as Norway, Ireland or Finland, in their mild prosperity and sensible world status. Let us get to the starting block of nation-statehood, goes this mentality, and we'll worry about the future when it comes.
>
> Well the future's already here – whether it's biosphere disruption in its many forms (pandemic, global warming), or technological displacement of human labour, or nuclear self-termination – and we can't wait for a period of 'normality' before we engage with it.[22]

A fundamental in addressing these issues beyond the abstract is linking such observations to understanding the psychologies, mindsets and attitudes of Scottish public opinion, allowing for the many differences and divisions within it. This is a truism about all nations across the world and how they continually imagine and remake themselves. Fintan O'Toole observed this looking from his experience of Ireland and looking at Scotland in 2014:

> Scotland also has the opportunity to become more mature and take responsibility without the baggage of national unity

and the heady rush of illusions that quickly become the toxic sludge of post-independence disillusionment. This is the art of growing up: far more important than any formal constitutional standing.[23]

This brings us to the need for Scotland and Scottish public life to look honestly and with candidness at the state of our country and measure it against who we are, what we profess our values to be, and ask if this really is the best we can do. In so doing, it is not good enough to find ourselves short in what we would like to be and just blame external forces such as Westminster, the Union and faraway Tories. Rather, any genuine self-reflection has to address where we as a society have fallen short, including institutionally many of which are autonomous, and look at how we change that rather than blame others.

Scotland is a society scarred by endemic child poverty, appalling health inequalities, educational apartheid which excludes many of the brightest working-class children, and has the highest drug death total anywhere in Western Europe. As damning, too much of society works as a self-preservation society for middle-class entitlement while pretending it is shaped by egalitarian values, social justice and progressive ideals.

Such an attitude will prove difficult for some because it is easier to look for simple solutions and try to put the blame on to others rather than reflect on ourselves. Embracing Fintan O'Toole's 'the art of growing up' is not some luxury or add-on. It is fundamental to embracing an independence of the Scottish mind and embodying the spirit and practice of self-government. Independence in this sense is about the pains of growing up and maturing, and accepting individual and collective responsibility. That process of maturity allows people to have the self-confidence, honesty and self-awareness, to look around

Scotland and assess where we fall short of what we say we are, and to have a conversation about changing things

But it is also true that growing up is frightening. The act of maturing was never ever going to be one that everyone in Scotland embraces and this is true of independence supporters as well as others. For some people this evolution will see them refuse to mature and instead embrace immaturity, cling to the mindset of victimhood and blame others for the state of Scotland. Sometimes these forces are even the most vocal in independent circles, but what it illustrates is that the 'art of growing up' and maturity was never going to be tidy and linear, but messy and filled with contradictions. That is what real change often looks like.

A Scotland beyond nationalisms

There is the need in this debate to go beyond just emphasising the civic and benign nature of Scottish nationalism. Rather there is also the dynamic that a debate about Scotland's future which is defined by the competing claims of two nationalisms – Scottish and British – is narrow and suffocating. At times it can reduce the debate at its worst to the charge that 'my nationalism is better than your nationalism' which is not a good place to be.

This is an asymmetrical contest in one respect. Scottish nationalism is out and proud as to what it is – a nationalism; but unionism (British state nationalism) is in near-complete denial about its own nature and in many respects ashamed of being a nationalism. This latter stance is a fairly common phenomenon the world over where 'official' and majority state nationalisms refuse to see themselves in such terms posing themselves as the 'official' story of a country or as patriotism.

A contest reduced to the claims and counter-claims of two nationalisms is by its very nature constraining. This is true on several fronts. First, many people in Scotland do not see themselves as either nationalists or unionists but think of themselves in other terms as left, right, green, feminist, Christian, Muslim, old, young, for example. A recent survey in Northern Ireland for the 2019 UK election found that, in a politics defined by stark binary choices, 28 per cent saw themselves as unionists, 25 per cent nationalists and 40 per cent as neither unionist nor nationalist.[24] These terms have less historic baggage and rigidity in Scotland and it is possible we would find an even larger constituency in the 'neither' constituency. No one has, as we speak, asked the question.

Second, not all pro-independence sentiment is 'Scottish nationalist'; the Scottish Green Party are pro-independence but not nationalists. Similarly, it is possible to support the Union and not think of oneself as a 'British nationalist' or 'unionist'. Each political tribe likes to label the other as 'nationalist' or 'unionist' (or worse) while professing the wide array of support they claim to their own side. Instead of trying to force the debate into a binary straightjacket, it would be better to acknowledge the multitude of political traditions which sit under being pro-independence and pro-Union, and indeed other constitutional options.

Third, a politics reduced to being about two nationalisms not only minimises choice. It reduces all politics to being about constitutional change and a narrow range of identities. It puts up barriers to a wider discussion of topics and the kind of Scotland we want to live in – a debate ignited on the Yes side in 2014 but which needs careful nurturing if this is to happen again.

Finally, another philosophical reason taps into the last point about the kind of Scotland people aspire to and that links to the power and limits of nationalism. Fintan O'Toole closely followed the 2014 referendum campaign and observed something he found in equal parts impressive, mature and of historic importance. At the same time, drawing from experience and knowledge of Irish independence, he offered the following words of advice for Scotland and its future trajectory:

> Nationalism is a rocket fuel that can get you out of the orbit of the old order but burns quickly and leaves you dependent on much more complex and subtle systems of guidance to get you through the lonely expanses of historic space.

O'Toole concludes:

> Nationalism on its own is never enough. Look at Ireland. Look at anywhere in the world. It does not matter how 'civic' and inclusive your nationalism is, and this is the prevailing story of contemporary Scottish nationalism – it is still a nationalism – it can only take you so far.[25]

Taking these well-intended words Scotland would be well advised to begin that conversation on the limits of nationalism and of Scottish nationalism as soon as possible rather than waiting until the morning after a victorious independence referendum. Undertaking this would make the debate richer, more pluralist and relevant, prepares for the future, and as an added bonus, it probably at the margins aids the likelihood of a Yes vote.

One dimension of Scottish public life that needs reflecting upon is the nature of British identity in an independent Scotland. No feasible, desirable version of independence represents a complete divorce in relations between Scotland and rUK. There is no such thing as full-blown 'separation', sometimes invoked by the most passionate voices on Yes and No – one as aspiration, the other as frightening dystopia.

In a world of Scottish independence the role of British identity, tradition and history will still have relevance – as will different facets of Britishness. Such eventualities will be an affront to a section of independence supporters who imagine a Scotland renewed (and even cleansed) by the calling of time on Britishness, equating it only with Empire, colonialism and reaction.

This ignores the fact that an independent Scotland does not start out as a blank canvas, exorcising 300 years of union history. To try to do so would be an act of denial of the importance of Britishness in Scotland – past, present, future. It deliberately glosses over that not all aspects of Britishness are about Empire and right-wing ideas; other interpretations exist. And just as importantly, an independent Scotland should be comfortable in its multi-cultural and multi-national make-up, and not want to go near any sense of monocultural identity.

The nature of Britishness would undoubtedly change under independence and that requires further deliberation. For some people it would become extinct and external, but for others it would still have resonance – and that has to be respected. In all probability some elements of political co-operation across the territories of the current UK in the event of Scottish independence will remain, alongside the possible continuation of a political dimension to Britishness in Scotland. As relevant is the acknowledgement of the cultural aspect of Britishness – from arts, culture and creative sectors, to the shared legacy and values of three centuries of union.

A Scotland aware of these factors, identities and tensions – and able to acknowledge and face up to them in an open, generous way – would be a country all the better for having done so; part of 'the art of growing up' which is a continuous process. We now conclude with a brief overview of the contours and possible themes of the stories which could define a future independent Scotland and why they matter.

17
Future Stories of Scotland

It takes us a while to adjust to the nervous energy of the Scots. Their society is constantly bombarded with information – not from above, but from below, from the grassroots... The Scots are post-money. They live for experience, for collaboration, for networking, for the intense sociability of the art opening, for the pleasures of the moment.

Momus, *The Book of Scotlands*, 2009

We need some story about a new Scottish state as our tool, or our platform, to help us cope with major incoming crises: primarily the effects of climate disorder, the automation of routine labour (mental and physical), the migration of populations (000's of millions) fleeing the unliveable South to the liveable North.

Pat Kane, writer and musician,
personal communication, February 2022

In offering some concluding thoughts, I want to turn to two areas: Scotland and the UK and the prospects for change in a future Scotland. The first is the terrain of contemporary Scotland and the constraints of devolution: not just over the past 20 years, but as a mechanism for change in the future. Every so often, voices in the pro-Union side turn to the possibilities of 'devo max' – meaning a third option between independence and the Union. It is portrayed by many advocates as an escape out of binary choices reducing everything to Yes versus No.

There are pitfalls in the supposed nirvana of 'devo max'. An obvious one is that it requires the agreement of the British political system to allow Scotland to take more powers and unilaterally create its own constitutional settlement within the UK. Another is that it does not deal with the problem of the British state and how it sees Scotland and the UK. 'Devo max' leaves the political power centre of the UK unreformed and undemocratised, and importantly leaves the Tory built-in advantage and dominance unchecked. All of which would contribute to an unstable settlement unlikely to have much longevity. This was understood by Nigel Smith, the chair of the cross-party campaign for the Scottish Parliament in the 1997 referendum, who noted in 2019:

> You cannot reform the UK by continual Scottish constitutional coups – just taking more powers unilaterally in the UK.[1]

The objections about federalism are more practical as has already been discussed. The continual use of the mantra of 'federalism' from the likes of Gordon Brown are always without detail, often underlined by talking vaguely about such terms as 'near federalism', 'quasi-federalism' or 'moving towards federalism' without being specific about what this entails.

The second dimension is that of the 'idea' of Scotland which is more than a nation but also a political community, society, shared histories, memories and stories, and a communicative and social set of spaces. The rise in awareness and consciousness of differing interpretations of Scotland, and myriad possible futures, are one of the important backdrops that have driven the debate to achieve a Parliament and informed the independence debate, along with wider perceptions of the role of government, the importance of arts and culture, and the role of identities.

Particularly relevant to contemporary debates is the scale and vision of post-war Scotland, the society after 1945 which dared to tackle some of the huge challenges of society. This version of Scotland had a sense of imagination, boldness and practicality.[2] It created a NHS and post-war welfare state, it engaged in huge slum clearances of urban centres, it built new homes and towns for working people, it engaged in huge public health campaigns and interventions seeing the eradication of diseases such as polio, it galvanised the power of hydro-electricity to change the Highlands, and built road bridges across the Tay and Forth rivers connecting Dundee and Edinburgh to nearby Fife.

All of this was done in the name of progress, enlightenment and modernity, using government in partnership with experts and business to physically change the environment of Scotland and improve the lived experiences of millions of Scots.[3]

It is true that this version of Scotland's future was undertaken in the UK. It was a version of Scottishness connected to a vision of a Britain which was collectively linked to the future. This future was what could be described as the high point of 'Labour Scotland 1945–65' and part of the zenith of 'Labour Britain' – the era of Clement Attlee, Nye Bevan and Harold Wilson – a political project which remade society and believed it had the skills to make the future.

This past Scotland has pointers for the outline of a future Scotland – one of similar ambition and reach. The scope of this should be about doing big things, making a real difference to the lives of millions and having a legacy and lasting impact that lasts down the decades. It should also involve a national mobilisation of energy, drive and hope, and draw from different areas of public life – government, professionals, experts, business.

That future Scotland should be a society that aims to heal divisions and inequalities that have scarred society with widespread child, pensioner and working age household poverty which should shame a country of unparalleled wealth and prosperity, where no one should go without the basics and live in hardship.

This has to be future-focused, embracing carbon net zero and the climate crisis, the need for new technologies in work and life, and the rise of AI. This has to be connected to the creation and articulation of new stories based upon the belief that we can collectively imagine and build that future Scotland.

That future Scotland is inherent to the appeal and rationale of independence, while independence has to be shaped by the collective power that we can together create a different future. Central to this is the principle of Scotland's right to decide and putting it at the heart of the independence cause. This vision of a dynamic, motivated Scotland can help advance self-government and self-determination across Scottish society, and offer a blueprint of independence that is not just abstract but connected to a powerful and persuasive idea of what Scottish society could look like if we agree this is the kind of Scotland we want to live in.

Daring to tell new stories of Scotland's future

How this scale and vision is mobilised and brought into being has to involve more than thinking about policies, politicians and the abstract idea of independence. Instead, it has to aid the creation and articulation of new stories talked about earlier. A first step is recognising the past stories and myths which have defined Scotland. The term 'myth' is used in this context to denote 'an idea or set of ideas whose importance lies in being believed or accepted by a significant body of people sufficient to affect behaviour or attitudes whether grounded in fact or fiction'.[4]

Tom Nairn wrote in 1967 about 'the Great Scottish Dream' invoking 'tartanry, militarism, Burns and Scott' in the context of the Edinburgh Festival.[5] The following year 'he wrote of three great dreams of Scottish nationalism', citing in the making of Scotland, the Reformation, romanticism and bour-geois nationalism.[6] Writing in response to Nairn, the political scientist James Kellas wrote: 'There is a Scottish Dream or Scottish myth, and it is part of Scottish national consciousness (or unconsciousness?).' This he elucidates is the story of egal-itarianism which he connected to the appeal of Robert Burns:

> His simple and lyrical defence of the inherent dignity of man, unbent by privilege; his defiance of the 'unco guid' or affectedly righteous; above all his attitude towards romantic love, which must prevail despite Calvinist morality – all have expressed the Scottish Dream directly to the Scottish people...[7]

This might seem, more than a half a century later, a romantic take but Kellas is talking about myths. To this he adds the principles of 'egalitarianism and democracy' which can be identified in how the education system and Presbyterian Church present themselves; he notes that 'rigid social conser-vatism' and the power of elites contradict 'the democratic and egalitarian myths of Scottish life'.[8]

Fast-forwarding to the present there would be many who would agree with an updated version of the above and that 'Scotland's Dream' now follows similar principles. This would include a sense of egalitarianism in everyday life seen in the phrase 'Jock Tamson's Bairns' and Burns's 'For a' that and a' that'.

The former is so steeped into folklore to almost defy definition but was described by David Murison as representing a commitment to 'the human race; common humanity; also with less universal force, a group of people united by a common sentiment, interest or purpose'.[9] There is a radical version of this spirit of equality stressing greater material equality, but a minimal more conservative interpretation which just means individual common decency and an expectation of treating everyone the same.

There is the belief in education and 'the democratic intellect' – the potential of access to educational opportunity, less social class inequality and a greater dissemination of knowledge and ideas. And finally, there is the democratic impulse and idea that power and legitimacy emanate from the people seen in popular sovereignty.

These three myths – egalitarianism, education and popular sovereignty – have had great currency in Scotland and contributed to how we see ourselves and perceive ourselves as different. Stephen Maxwell, writing in 1976, pointed out the importance of myths in Scottish nationalism:

> To criticise the cherished nationalist myths of Scottish democracy is not to deny them all significance. They reflect real, though, partial, elements in Scottish society which in the past probably has been more democratic than English society and which even today has a more democratic ethos. A political programme for an independent Scotland must, however, be built on a more substantial base than that which dream of Scottish democracy provides.[10]

Two observations flow from the above discussion on myths. First, if this is who we want to say we are collectively, then we have to have a rigorous hard look at ourselves, what we do and then agree if we want to act differently. Scotland is not a society that acts and defines itself by these ideals. There is no evidence that Scotland is more egalitarian, better and more open at education, or more democratic than elsewhere. But given the centrality and backstory of these values we could choose to act upon them.

This would require having an honest conversation which involved government, public bodies, professions and businesses, about the degree to which Scotland falls short of these myths and how we could go about rectifying them. Academic Hannah Graham notes of the stories of modern Scotland and its politics: 'Where are the women?' and that: 'If Holyrood is a modern people's Parliament, who is and isn't telling, narrating, co-editing our story?'[11]

This would not be an easy task, as elements of Scottish society have through the years been quite comfortable perpetuating some of these myths, such as the belief that we are more egalitarian and not acting on it, but rather presiding over a deeply unequal society of endemic privilege and poverty. This would require not just honesty, action and building a popular alliance of change, it would necessitate digging up the foundations of the aforementioned 'Scottish Dream'.

Here we face a profound choice. We could choose to continue in our present state of believing 'wha's like us' while not acting upon it and still feeling good about ourselves. Or we could choose to act. Taking the latter course would have difficulties and even some pain; it would entail (like Ireland did after the crash) confronting the fact it was not really 'the republic' it said it was, but rather a host of conceits offering cover for cronyism, corruption and dishonest authority. As Fintan O'Toole observed: 'The task is not to rediscover or reinvent a lost republic. It is to build something we have never had.'[12]

Second, related to the above if we choose this course we have to animate and inhabit this course of action. This includes creating relevant collective stories, drawing upon diverse and previously excluded voices, and nurturing self-organisation beyond the 'official Scotland' and the potential of agency. Stories are central to how we understand and interpret the world and are fundamental to being human and how we communicate, connect and remember. And the collective stories we create when we come together define societies and nations down the ages.[13] There are inherent dangers in stories, the peril of 'the official future' colonising story, demagogues from Trump to Putin invoking potent dark stories, and the brilliant observation from the writer Chimamanda Ngozi Adichie about 'the danger of the single story' reducing the world into the simplicity of 'Them' and 'Us'.[14]

Scotland faces deep-seated choices not just about independence, but about the future direction and nature of society. Fundamental to this is the notion that independence is about making decisions on the strategic choices we face. That requires understanding and talking about the issue of risk, and exploring transitional difficulties that will be inevitable and which will involve some degree of temporary pain to then get to the gains.

All this has to be brought out into the open, rather than left implied or only for the select few to mull over. Scotland for too long was characterised by power in the darkness where the vast majority were kept as far away from decision-making as possible. These new discussions should involve respect and inclusion, facts and opinions, imagination and dreams, accord and disagreements, principles and values, and recognise that technocratic managerial politics from any perspective are unlikely to provide the road map to our future.

We should all recognise that Scottish independence is a demanding debate for some. It poses tough questions which are fundamental to society, democracy and who we think we are collectively. Fortunately, for all the talk of binary choices this is not as black and white as is sometimes made out, and certainly nothing in comparison to what people face every day in parts of the world.

The independence debate is about important questions: how we make decisions as a society, how we decide our future, and how we make our relationships in society and internationally. It is important that we get this right and do it with respect for our fellow citizens – here in Scotland, across the UK and internationally – and are given respect in return. It is too important to do otherwise.

Notes

Chapter 1

1. James Kellas, *The Scottish Political System*, Cambridge University Press 1973; Arthur Midwinter, Michael Keating and James Mitchell, *Politics and Public Policy in Scotland*, Palgrave Macmillan 1991.

2. *Royal Commission on the Constitution: Minutes of Evidence: Volume IV: Scotland*, HMSO 1973, pp. 32–33.

3. *The Scotsman*, 29 August 2016.

4. See: Our Scottish Future, 'Poll Shows UK-Wide Shared Priorities and Values', *Our Scottish Future*, 16 September 2021.

5. Alex Massie, 'Scotching a Myth: Scotland is Not as Left-Wing as You Think It Is', *The Spectator*, 21 May 2014.

6. Alan Cochrane, 'The Case for No', in George Kerevan and Alan Cochrane, *Scottish Independence: Yes or No*, The History Press 2014, p. 117.

7. Chris Deeming, 'Is Scotland More Nordic than Liberal?', in Elizabeth Clery, John Curtice, Sarah Frankenburg, Hannah Morgan and Susan Reid (eds), *British Social Attitudes: The 38th Report*, National Centre for Social Research.

8. All UK and Scottish election data taken from: Colin Rallings and Michael Thrasher, *British Electoral Facts 1832–2012*, Biteback Publishing 2012; 2019 figures: Robert Ford, Tim Bale, Will Jennings and Paula Surridge, *The British General Election of 2019*, Palgrave Macmillan 2020.

9. Mark Diffley, 'Public Services Reform and Public Opinion', in Ipsos MORI Scotland, *Spotlight on Scotland*, 2013.

10. John Curtice and Ian Montagu, 'Do Scotland and England & Wales have Different Views about Immigration?', British Social Attitudes, December 2018, accessed 4 January 2022 https://natcen.ac.uk/

media/1672027/Do-Scotland-and-England-and-Wales-Have-Different-Views-About-Immigration.pdf

11. Neil Davidson, Minna Liinpaa, Maureen McBride and Satnam Virdee (eds), *No Problem Here: Understanding Racism in Scotland*, Luath Press 2018.
12. Personal communication, 6 March 2022.
13. On the idea of closed tribes and the possibility of open tribes, see Sue Goss, *Open Tribe*, Lawrence and Wishart 2014.
14. *Scottish Liberal Democrats Press Release*, 10 December 2019.
15. *i*, 13 March 2017.
16. *The Guardian*, 29 August 2014.
17. John Curtice, 'The Scottish Independence Referendum of 2014', in Julie Smith (ed.), *The Palgrave Handbook of European Referendums*, Palgrave Macmillan 2021.
18. Gerry Hassan and Eric Shaw, *The People's Flag and the Union Jack: An Alternative History of Britain and the Labour Party*, Biteback Publishing 2019.
19. See John Denham, *The Rebuilding of England*, Biteback Publishing 2022.

Chapter 2

1. SNP, *Self-Government in Practice: A Report of a delegation appointed by the Scottish National Party to visit Northern Ireland, the Irish Free state and the Isle of Man to study certain aspects of self-government*, SNP 1934.
2. Richard J. Finlay, 'For and Against? Scottish Nationalists and the British Empire, 1919–1939', *Scottish Historical Review*, Vol. 71 No. 191/192, 1992, pp. 184–206; *Independent and Free: Scottish Politics and the Origins of the Scottish National Party*, John Donald 1994.
3. Colin Kidd, *Union and Unionisms: Political Thought in Scotland, 1500–2000*, Cambridge University Press 2008.
4. *The Scotsman*, 15 February 1950; quoted in James Mitchell, *Conservatives and the Union: A Study of Conservative Party Attitudes to Scotland*, Edinburgh University Press 1990, p. 50.

5. Conservative and Unionist Central Office, *The Campaign Guide: The New Political Encyclopaedia*, Conservative and Unionist Central Office 1955, p. 308.

6. Gordon Pentland, 'Edward Heath, the Declaration of Perth and the Scottish Conservative and Unionist Party 1966–70', *20th Century British History*, Vol. 26 No. 2, 2015, pp. 249–273.

7. David Torrance, *'We in Scotland': Thatcherism in a Cold Climate*, Birlinn 2009.

8. Department for Levelling Up, Housing and Communities, *Levelling Up the United Kingdom*, HMSO CP 604, 2022.

9. Alister Jack, 'Union is Strength', in Andrew Bowie (ed.), *Strength in Union: The Case for the United Kingdom*, Centre for Policy Studies 2021.

10. James Davies, 'Building a Better Wales Crosses Borders', in Bowie, ibid.

11. David Torrance, *'Standing Up for Scotland': Nationalist Unionism and Scottish Party Politics, 1884–2014*, Edinburgh University Press 2020.

12. Michael Billig, *Banal Nationalism*, Sage 1995.

13. Constitutional Steering Committee, *A Claim of Right for Scotland*, Campaign for a Scottish Assembly 1988.

14. Richard Finlay, *Scottish Nationalism: History, Ideology and the Question of Independence*, Bloomsbury Academic 2022, chapter 2: Nationalism.

15. Gordon Brown and Douglas Alexander, *New Scotland, New Britain*, Smith Institute 1999.

16. Douglas Alexander, 'A Better Post-Brexit Path for Scotland', in Gerry Hassan and Russell Gunson (eds), *Scotland, the UK and Brexit: A Guide to the Future*, Luath Press in association with the Institute for Public Policy Research Scotland 2017.

17. William L. Miller, 'Modified Rapture All Round: The First Elections to the Scottish Parliament', *Government and Opposition*, Vol. 34 No. 3, 1999, pp. 299–322.

18. Clement Attlee, 'Foreword', in Thomas Burns, *Plan for Scotland*, London Scots Self-Government Committee 1937.

19. Ernie Ross, 'Devolution', in Jon Lansman and Alan Meale (eds), *Beyond Thatcher: The Real Alternative*, Junction Books 1983, p. 191.

20. Gerry Hassan, 'The Legacy of Donald Dewar and Scotland's Stories: Past, Present and Future', *Sunday National*, 12 October 2020.

21. Tom Nairn, 'Upper and Lower Cases', *London Review of Books*, 24 August 1995.

22. *The Scotsman*, 9 March 2018; *Scottish Daily Express*, 12 January 2022; *Twitter*, 7 August 2019.

23. Keir Starmer, *The Road Ahead*, Fabian Society 2021, p. 19.

24. Jess Phillips, *Everything You Really Need to Know about Politics: My Life as an MP*, Gallery Books 2021, p. 215n.

25. Ben Okri, *Birds of Heaven*, Phoenix 1986, p. 21.

26. Yuval Noah Harari, 'Vladimir Putin Has Already Lost the War in Ukraine', *The Guardian*, 1 March 2022.

27. Gerry Hassan, 'That Was Then and This is Now: Imagining New Stories about a Northern Nation', in Gerry Hassan, Eddie Gibb and Lydia Howland (eds), *Scotland 2020: Hopeful Stories for a Northern Nation*, Demos 2005.

28. Albert O. Hirschman, *Exit, Voice and Loyalty: Responses to Decline in Firms, Organisations and States*, Harvard University Press 1970, p. 98.

29. Margaret Thatcher, *The Downing Street Years*, HarperCollins 1993, p. 619.

Chapter 3

1. On elite concerns on the 'ungovernability' of the UK, see Anthony King (ed.), *Why is Britain Becoming Harder to Govern?*, BBC Books 1976.

2. Colin Rallings and Michael Thrasher, *British Electoral Facts 1832–2012*, Biteback Publishing 2012.

3. David Butler and Richard Rose, *The British General Election of 1959*, Macmillan 1960, p. 173.

4. Kenneth Roy, *The Invisible Spirit: A Life of Post-war Scotland*, Institute of Contemporary Scotland 2013, p. 241.

5. *Report on the Scottish Economy: Committee of Inquiry into the Scottish Economy Under the Chairmanship of J.N. Toothill*, Scottish Council (Development and Industry) 1961.

6. Ibid.
7. Jack Brand, *The National Movement in Scotland*, Routledge, Kegan and Paul 1978, pp. 67, 88.
8. Brian P. Jamison, 'Scotland and the Trident System 1979–1999', PhD University of Glasgow, 2004, chapter 5: 'Scotland and the Disarmament Movement'.
9. J.M. Reid, *Scotland: Past and Present*, Oxford University Press 1959, pp. 146–147.
10. Moray McLaren, *The Shell Guide to Scotland*, Ebury Press 1965, p. 57.
11. James G. Kellas, *Modern Scotland: The Nation since 1870*, Pall Mall 1968, p. 7.
12. Duncan Glen (ed.), *Whither Scotland? A Prejudiced Look at the Future of a Nation*, Victor Gollancz 1971; James McMillan, *Anatomy of Scotland*, Leslie Frewin 1969.
13. Vince Cable, 'Glasgow: Area of Need', in Gordon Brown (ed.), *The Red Paper on Scotland*, Edinburgh University Student Publications Board 1975, p. 244.
14. Roger Davidson and Gayle Davis, *The Sexual State: Scotland 1950–1980*, Edinburgh University Press 2012.

Chapter 4

1. Gerry Hassan and Simon Barrow (eds), *A Nation Changed? The SNP and Scotland Ten Years On*, Luath Press 2017.
2. *Daily Mail*, comments, 18 August 2021; *Daily Telegraph*, 31 March 2021.
3. Martin Laffin and Alys Thomas, 'The United Kingdom: Federalism in Denial?', *Publius*, Vol. 29 No. 3, Summer 1999, p. 89.
4. On this tradition in Labour, see Barry Jones and Michael Keating, *Labour and the British State*, Clarendon Press 1985.
5. Seán Patrick Griffin, *Remaking the British State: For the Many, Not the Few*, Red Paper Collective 2020.
6. James Foley and Pete Ramand, *Yes: The Radical Case for Scottish Independence*, Pluto Press 2014, p. 3.
7. George Kerevan, Neoliberalism and Scotland', in Gregor Gall (ed.), *A New Scotland: Building an Equal, Fair and Sustainable Society*, Pluto Press 2022, pp. 38, 43.

8. Stephen Maxwell, *Arguing for Independence: Evidence, Risk and the Wicked Issues*, Luath Press 2012, p. 20.

9. Scottish Government, *Scotland's Future: Your Guide to an Independent Scotland*, Scottish Government 2013.

10. Personal communication, 24 February 2022.

11. Personal communication, 23 February 2022.

12. Personal communication, 22 February 2022.

13. Personal communication, 22 February 2022.

14. Paul Mason, 'The British Left, Neoliberalism and the Potential of Scottish Independence', in Gerry Hassan and Simon Barrow (eds), *A Better Nation: The Challenges of Scottish Independence*, Luath Press 2022.

15. Hélène Landemore, 'Inclusive Constitution Making and Religious Rights: Lessons from the Icelandic Experiment', *Journal of Politics*, 2017, Vol. 79 No. 3, pp. 762–779, accessed 14 December 2021 doi:10.1086/690300; Silvia Suteu, 'Constitutional Conventions in the Digital Era: Lessons from Iceland and Ireland', Boston College International and Comparative Law Review, 2015, Vol. 38 No. 2, pp. 251–276, accessed 14 December 2021 https://lawdigital commons.bc.edu/iclr/vol38/iss2/4/.

16. Personal communication, 6 March 2022.

Chapter 5

1. *The Fog of War: Eleven Lessons from the Life of Robert S. McNamara*, Sony Pictures Classics 2003.

2. *The Courier*, 12 February 2021.

3. The subtitle of Scottish Office, *Scotland in the Union: A Partnership for Good*, HMSO 1993, Cm 2225.

4. For an outlier view on this, see Azeem Ibrahim, 'Scottish Independence: Why is Vladimir Putin a Supporter?', *The Scotsman*, 22 July 2020.

5. Alan Cochrane, 'The Case for No', in George Kerevan and Alan Cochrane, *Scottish Independence: Yes or No*, The History Press 2014, p. 117.

6. Jamie Maxwell and David Torrance, *Scotland's Referendum: A Guide for Voters*, Luath Press 2014.

7. Tony Blair, 'We'd All Be Losers If the Union Fell', *Daily Telegraph*, 16 March 2007; Daniel Sanderson and Simon Johnson, 'Scots Benefit from "Union Dividend" of More than £2,500 per Person', *Daily Telegraph*, 28 April 2021.

8. Personal communication, 2 March 2022.

9. Personal communication, 25 February 2022.

10. Ben Jackson, 'Scottish Independence: Denial is No Way to Ward Off Divorce', *Prospect*, 14 July 2020; *The Case for Scottish Independence: A History of Nationalist Thought in Modern Scotland*, Cambridge University Press 2020.

11. Johann Lamont, 'Constitutional Change is Not Enough', in Maria Fyfe (ed.), *Women Saying No: Making a Positive Case Against Independence*, Luath Press 2014, p. 15.

12. Gordon Brown, *Our Scottish Future* event, 12 January 2022.

13. Gordon Brown, 'The Britain of Emma Raducanu Shows Why Nationalists are Losing the Argument', *New Statesman*, 16 September 2021.

14. *Twitter*, 14 January 2022.

15. John Home Robertson, Letters, *New Statesman*, 22 September 2021.

16. Gordon Brown, Hugo Young Memorial Lecture, Chatham House, London, 13 December 2005.

17. Gordon Brown, *My Scotland, Our Britain: A Future Worth Sharing*, Simon and Schuster 2014, p. 239.

18. *Scottish Daily Express*, 13 July 2021.

19. John Lloyd, *Should Auld Acquaintance Be Forgot: The Great Mistake of Scottish Independence*, Polity Press 2020, p. 165.

Chapter 6

1. Tony Benn, 'Britain is a Colony', *New Socialist*, September/ October 1981, p. 62.

2. Centre for Contemporary Cultural Studies (eds), *The Empire Strikes Back: Race and Racism in 70s Britain*, Hutchinson 1982.

3. Caroline Elkins, *Legacy of Violence: A History of the British Empire*, Bodley Head 2022.

4. Ian Cobain, *The History Thieves: Secrets, Lies and the Shaping of a Modern Nation*, Portobello Books 2016, p. 67.

5. Christopher de Bellaigue, *Patriot of Persia: Mohammad Mossadegh and a Very British Coup*, Bodley Head 2012; Michael Axworthy, *Revolutionary Iran: A History of the Islamic Republic*, Oxford University Press 2013.

6. Keith Kyle, *Suez*, Weidenfeld and Nicolson 1991; Martin Woollacott, *After Suez: Adrift in the American Century*, I.B. Tauris 2006.

7. John Darwin, *Unfinished Empire: The Global Expansion of Britain*, Allen Lane 2012, p. 378.

8. *BBC News*, 19 November 1967.

9. Richard Crossman, *The Diaries of a Cabinet Minister: Volume Two: Lord President of the Council and Leader of the House of Commons 1966–68*, Jonathan Cape 1976, p. 639.

10. Margaret Thatcher, *The Downing Street Years*, HarperCollins 1993, p. 161.

11. Radhika Natarajan, 'Ties of Blood: How Thatcher Altered "British"', *openDemocracy*, 13 April 2013.

12. *Royal Commission on the Constitution 1969–1973: Volume One: Report*, Cmnd 5460, HMSO 1973.

13. David Olusoga, 'Britain's Shameful Slavery History Matters – That's Why a Jury Acquitted the Colston Four', *The Guardian*, 6 January 2022.

14. David Olusoga, *Black and British: A Forgotten History*, Macmillan 2016.

15. Kris Manjapra, 'When Will Britain Face Up to Its Crimes against Humanity?', *The Guardian*, 29 March 2018.

16. Bagehot, 'The Tiger Under the Table', *The Economist*, 3 December 2009.

17. David Edgerton, *Warfare State: Britain, 1920–1970*, Cambridge University Press 2006, p. 9.

18. On the British and French experience and 'legacy' of decolonisation, see Robert Gildea, *Empires of the Mind: The Colonial Past and the Politics of the Present*, Oxford University Press 2021.

19. Edward Shils, *The Intellectuals and the Powers*, University of Chicago Press 1972, p. 135.

20. Patrick Wright, *On Living in an Old Country: The National Past in Contemporary Britain*, Oxford University Press 2nd edn 2009.

21. *Twitter*, 25 January 2019.

22. Wright, op. cit.
23. Neal Ascherson, 'Ancient Britons and the Republican Dream', reprinted in *Games with Shadows*, Radius Books 1988, pp. 156–157.
24. On the Nairn thesis, see Tom Nairn, *After Britain: New Labour and the Return of Scotland*, Granta Books 2000; Jamie Maxwell and Peter Ramand (eds), *Old Nations, Auld Enemies, New Times: Selected Essays Tom Nairn*, Luath Press 2014. For a left-wing critique of class and nation: Neil Davidson, Patricia McCafferty and David Miller (eds), *Neoliberal Scotland: Class and Society in a Stateless Nation*, Cambridge Scholar Publishing 2010; and for a more recent left-wing pro-independence text: Bob Fotheringham, Dave Sherry and Colm Bryce (eds), *Breaking Up the British State: Scotland, Independence and Socialism*, Bookmarks Publications 2021.

Chapter 7

1. David Seawright, *An Important Matter of Principle: The Decline of the Scottish Conservative and Unionist Party*, Ashgate 1999.
2. Gerry Hassan, '"It's Only a Northern Song": The Constant Smirr of Anti-Thatcherism and Anti-Toryism', in David Torrance (ed.), *Whatever happened to Tory Scotland?*, Edinburgh University Press 2012, p. 78.
3. All UK and Scottish election data taken from: Colin Rallings and Michael Thrasher, *British Electoral Facts 1832–2012*, Biteback Publishing 2012; 2017 and 2019 figures from: Philip Cowley and Dennis Kavanagh, *The British General Election of 2017*, Palgrave Macmillan 2018; Robert Ford, Tim Bale, Will Jennings and Paula Surridge, *The British General Election of 2019*, Palgrave Macmillan 2021.
4. Vernon Bogdanor, *Devolution in the United Kingdom*, Oxford University Press 1998.
5. House of Lords website. Of the 769, 656 are life peers (85.3 per cent), 87 hereditary peers (10.4 per cent) and 26 bishops (3.4 per cent): accessed 4 February 2022, www.parliament.uk/lords/
6. David Torrance, *The Crown and the Constitution*, House of Commons Library, 4 February 2022, accessed 10 February 2022, https://commonslibrary.parliament.uk/research-briefings/cbp-8885/

7. *Channel Four News*, 23 July 2013.
8. Speech by the Queen to Parliament on her Silver Jubilee, 4 May 1977.
9. *BBC News*, 14 September 2014.
10. David Laws, *Coalition: The Inside Story of the Conservative-Liberal Democrat Coalition Government*, Biteback Publishing 2016, p. 442.
11. *BBC News*, 19 September 2019.
12. *BBC News*, 23 September 2014.
13. Vernon Bogdanor, *The Monarchy and the Constitution*, Oxford University Press 1995.
14. Ibid., p. 144.
15. Peter Hennessy, 'Foreword to the Diamond Jubilee Edition', in Ben Pimlott, *The Queen: Elizabeth II and the Monarchy*, Harper Press 2012, p. xv.
16. Andrew Marr, *The Diamond Queen: Elizabeth II and Her People*, Macmillan 2011, inside cover.
17. *The Guardian*, 9 February 2021.
18. *Twitter*, 14 June 2019.
19. Gwyneth Hochhausler, 'Who Decides When Britain Goes to War? The War Prerogative in the United Kingdom', *Chicago Journal of Public Policy*, 1 April 2019.
20. Adam Tomkins, 'Crown Privileges', in Maurice Sunkin and Sebastian Payne (eds), *The Nature of the Crown: A Legal and Political Analysis*, Oxford University Press 1999, pp. 171–172.
21. Stephen Haseler, *The End of the House of Windsor: Birth of a British Republic*, IB Tauris and Co. 1993, p. 23.
22. This version of Britain and its progress democratically and as a society is still alive. See as an example: Andrew Marr, *The Making of Modern Britain: From Queen Victoria to V.E. Day*, Macmillan 2009.
23. Mike Ratcliffe, 'The History of University Representation', *WONKHE*, 28 January 2015.
24. Gordon F. Millar, 'Walter Elliot', *Oxford Dictionary of National Biography*, 2004.
25. F.W.S. Craig, *British Parliamentary Election Results 1918–1949*, Parliamentary Research Services, 3rd edn 1983.
26. James Callaghan, *Time and Chance*, HarperCollins 1987, p. 271.

27. Paul Foot, *The Vote: How It Was Won, and How It Is Undermined*, Viking 2005.
28. David Torrance and Graeme Cowie, *Devolution: The Sewel Convention*, House of Commons Library Briefing Paper, 13 May 2020, accessed 28 January 2022, https://researchbriefings.files. parliament.uk/documents/CDP-8883/CBP-8883.pdf
29. Carwyn Jones, Welsh Senedd, 22 January 2020.
30. James Mitchell, *Devolution in the UK*, Manchester University Press 2009.
31. Tom Mullen, 'Brexit and the Territorial Governance of the United Kingdom', *Contemporary Social Science*, Vol. 14 No. 2, pp. 276–293.
32. Personal communication, 26 February 2022.
33. Personal communication, 23 February 2022.

Chapter 8

1. Andrew Gamble, *Britain in Decline: Economic Policy, Political Strategy and the British State*, Macmillan 1981.
2. Stephen G. Cecchetti, M.S. Mohanty and Fabrizio Zampolli, *The Real Effects of Debt*, Bank for International Settlements: BIS Working Papers No. 352, 2011.
3. Brett Christophers, *Rentier Capitalism: Who Owns the Economy and Who Pays for It?*, Verso Books 2020.
4. Adapted and revised from Kevin Albertson and Paul Stepney, '1979 and All That: a 40-year Reassessment of Margaret Thatcher's Legacy on Her Own Terms', *Cambridge Journal of Economics*, Vol. 44 No. 2, 2020, pp. 319–342, https://doi.org/10.1093/cje/bez037; 2015 onward figures are for 2015–19 up to pre-COVID and calculated by Kevin Albertson.
5. Tom Devine, *The Scottish Nation 1700–2000*, Allen Lane 1999; David McCrone, *The New Sociology of Scotland*, Sage 2017.
6. Gavin McCrone, *After Brexit: the Economics of Scottish Independence*, Birlinn 2022, p. 78.
7. Scottish Government, *Gross National Product Quarterly National Accounts: 2021 Quarter 3 (July–September 2021)*, Scottish Government 2022.

8. John McLaren, 'How Scotland Ranks', *Sceptical Scot*, 1 October 2019, accessed 4 February 2022, https://sceptical.scot/2019/10/how-scotland-ranks/

9. Alex Massie, 'Levelling Up is Vague But Asks Vital Questions about Nationalism', *Sunday Times*, 20 February 2022.

10. James Mitchell, *Governing Scotland: The Invention of Administrative Devolution*, Palgrave Macmillan 2003.

11. Alan Trench, 'The 2012 Olympics and the Barnett Formula: an End to the Row', *Devolution Matters*, 23 December 2011.

12. Craig Dalzell, 'Beyond GERS: Scotland's Fiscal Position Post-Independence', *Common Weal*, 2016, p. 1.

13. Office for National Statistics, *UK Government Debt and Deficit: September 2021*, Office for National Statistics 2021.

14. David Heald, 'The Politics of Scotland's Public Finances', in Michael Keating (ed.), *The Oxford Handbook of Scottish Politics*, Oxford University Press 2020, p. 522.

15. Jim Cuthbert, 'Fiscal Policy in Scotland: Under Devolution and Under Independence', in Gregor Gall (ed.), *A New Scotland: Building an Equal, Fair and Sustainable Society*, Pluto Press 2022, p. 138.

16. Dalzell, op. cit., p. 6.

17. Graeme Roy and David Eiser, 'What are the Implications of Independence for Public Revenues and Spending?', in Eve Hepburn, Michael Keating and Nicola McEwen (eds), *Scotland's New Choice: Independence After Brexit*, Centre for Constitutional Change 2021, p. 100.

18. United Nations Development Programme, *Human Development Report 2020: The Next Frontier: Human Development and the Anthropocene, United Nations 2020*, accessed 31 January 2022, https://hdr.undp.org/sites/default/files/hdr2020.pdf

19. Human Development Indices, *Global Data Lab*, accessed 31 January 2022, https://globaldatalab.org/shdi/shdi/GBR/.

20. *Scottish Natural Capital Accounts 2021*, Scottish Government 2021, accessed 4 February 2022, www.gov.scot/binaries/content/documents/govscot/publications/statistics/2021/06/scottish-natural-capital-accounts-2021/documents/scottish-natural-capital-accounts-2021/scottish-natural-capital-accounts-2021/

govscot%3Adocument/scottish-natural-capital-accounts-2021.
pdf.

21. *World Inequality Database 2020*, United Kingdom, accessed 10 December 2021, https://wid.world/country/united-kingdom/.

22. Personal communication, 19 August 2020.

23. *Financial Times*, 23 December 2021.

24. James Marriott and Terry Macalister, *Crude Britannia: How Oil Shaped a Nation*, Pluto Press 2021; Christopher Harvie, *Fool's Gold: The Story of North Sea Oil*, Hamish Hamilton 1994.

25. David Manley and Keith Myers, 'Did the UK Miss Out on £400 Billion Worth of Oil Revenue?', *National Resource Governance Institute*, 5 October 2015, accessed 4 January 2022, https://resourcegovernance.org/blog/did-uk-miss-out-%C2%A3400-billion-worth-oil-revenue.

26. Chris Rhodes, David Hough and Louise Butcher, *Privatisation*, House of Commons Library Research Paper, 18 November 2014, accessed 30 November 2021, https://commonslibrary.parliament.uk/research-briefings/rp14-61/.

27. James Meek, *Private Island: Why Britain Now Belongs to Someone Else*, Verso Books 2014, pp. 105–106, 149.

28. Craig Dalzell, 'Scotland Deserves Much More than the Growth Commission's "Soft Independence"', *The Herald*, 27 April 2019.

29. See Katherine Trebeck, George Kerevan and Stephen Boyd, *Tackling Timorous Economics: How Scotland's Economy Could Work Better For Us All*, Luath Press 2016.

30. Victoria Pinoncely and Mario Washington-Ihieme, *Culture Club: Social Mobility in the Creative and Cultural Sectors*, Centre for London 2019.

31. CAMEo Research Institute for Cultural and Media Economies, *Workforce Diversity in the UK Screen Sector: Evidence Review*, University of Leicester 2018.

32. Ian Fraser, *Shredded: Inside RBS, The Bank That Broke Britain*, Birlinn 2014.

33. *BBC News Scotland*, 25 February 2022.

34. *The Guardian*, 11 September 2021.

35. STUC Friends of the Earth Scotland, *Just Transition Partnership Manifesto 2021*, accessed 4 January 2022, https://foe.scot/wp-content/uploads/2020/09/JTP-Manifesto-2021-final.pdf.

36. Scottish Government, *Scotland's National Strategy for Economic Transformation*, Scottish Government 2022, accessed 4 March 2022, www.gov.scot/publications/scotlands-national-strategy-economic-transformation/.

Chapter 9

1. Gwilym Pryce and Meng Le Zhang, 'Inequality in Scotland: Despite Nordic Aspirations, Things are Not Improving', *The Conversation*, 7 November 2018.

2. Organisation of Economic Co-operation and Development (OECD), *Income Inequality*, 2021, accessed 31 January 2022, https://doi. org/10.1787/459aa7f1-en.

3. Scottish Government, *Gini Co-efficient by UK Nation*, Scottish Government 2020, accessed 31 January 2022, www.gov.scot/publications/additional-poverty-statistics-2020.

4. Mike Danson and Francis Stuart, 'Income, Wealth and Inequality in Scotland', in Gregor Gall (ed.), *A New Scotland: Building an Equal, Fair and Sustainable Society*, Pluto Press 2022, p. 121.

5. Save the Children Fund Scotland, *Child Poverty in Scotland: The Facts*, Save the Children Fund 2013.

6. *BBC News*, 30 July 2021.

7. *The Guardian*, 31 July 2021.

8. National Records of Scotland, *Drug-related Deaths in Scotland*, 30 July 2021.

9. Personal communication, 26 February 2022.

10. James McEnaney, *Class Rules: The Truth about Scotland's Schools*, Luath Press 2021, p. 70.

11. 'St Andrews Second Only to Oxford', *St Andrews QV*, 22 February 2019. Subsequently on numerous indicators St Andrews University has emerged as second only to Durham University in its intake of privately educated UK students. I am grateful to Danny Dorling of Oxford University for pointing this out.

12. 'The Tatler Guide to the University of St Andrews', *The Tatler*, 2017.
13. Henry McLeish, interview, 14 September 2010.
14. Glasgow School of Art, private information, 2 November 2013.
15. On the latter two figures, *The Herald*, 10 February 2016.
16. *The Times*, 11 January 2018.
17. *Sunday Times* 'Rich List', 23 May 2021.
18. Mike Danson and Francis Stuart, op. cit., pp. 121–122.
19. 'Scotland's Land Barons and their Connections to Global Capitalism', *Global Justice Now*, August 2016.
20. William Astor, 'Should We Fear a Mugabe-style Land Grab in Rural Scotland?', *The Spectator*, 23 May 2015.
21. Jeffrey Meeks, *Queer Voices in Post-War Scotland: Male Homosexuality, Religion and Society*, Palgrave Macmillan 2016.
22. Deborah Orr, *Motherwell: A Girlhood*, Weidenfeld & Nicolson 2020, pp. 43–44.
23. Darren McGarvey, *Poverty Safari: Understanding the Anger of Britain's Underclass*, Luath Press 2017.
24. Ibid., p. 205.

Chapter 10

1. H.J. Hanham, *Scottish Nationalism*, Faber & Faber 1969.
2. James Mitchell, *Strategies for Self-Government: The Campaigns for a Scottish Parliament*, Polygon 1996.
3. Private communication, 8 February 2011.
4. *BBC News*, 8 December 2021.
5. *A Culture Strategy for Scotland*, Scottish Government, February 2020.
6. Philip Schlesinger, 'The SNP, Cultural Policy and the Idea of "the Creative Economy"', in Gerry Hassan (ed.), *The Modern SNP: From Protest to Power*, Edinburgh University Press 2009.
7. Nathalie Olah, *Steal as Much as You Can: How to Win the Culture Wars in an Age of Austerity*, Repeater Books 2019.
8. Personal communication, 13 January 2022.
9. Personal communication, 13 January 2022.

10. Angus Calder, *The People's War: Britain's War 1939–1945*, Jonathan Cape 1969; Paul Addison, *The Road to 1945: British Politics and the Second World War*, Jonathan Cape 1975.

11. David Butler and Dennis Kavanagh, *The British General Election of 1979*, Macmillan 1980.

12. Andrew Gamble, *Britain in Decline: Economic Policy, Political Strategy and the British State*, Macmillan 1981.

13. Tom Devine and Carol Craig, 'Scotland's Velvet Revolution', in Gerry Hassan, Eddie Gibb and Lydia Howland (eds), *Scotland 2020: Hopeful Stories for a Northern Nation*, Demos 2005.

14. Gerry Hassan and Eric Shaw, *The Strange Death of Labour Scotland*, Edinburgh University Press 2012.

15. Steve Richards, *The Rise of the Outsiders: How Mainstream Politics Lost its Way*, Atlantic Books 2017. More relevant and understanding of alternative politics from an American perspective is: Alissa Quart, *Republic of Outsiders: The Power of Amateurs, Dreamers and Rebels*, New Press 2014.

16. Jeremy Gilbert, *Anticapitalism and Culture: Radical Theory and Popular Politics*, Berg Publishing 2008; Mark Fisher, *K-Punk: The Collected and Unpublished Writings of Mark Fisher from 2004–2016*, Repeater Books 2018.

17. Mark Fisher, quoted in Mick McStarkey, 'Exploring the Culturally Significant Life of Mark Fisher', *Far Out*, 13 January 2022.

18. Carol Craig, *The Scots' Crisis of Confidence*, Big Thinking 2003.

19. Christopher Peterson, Steven F. Maier and Martin F.P. Seligman, *Learned Helplessness: A Theory for the Age of Personal Control*, Oxford University Press 1995.

20. Eleanor Yule and David Manderson, *The Glass Half-Full: Moving Beyond Scottish Miserablism*, Luath Press 2014.

21. Ibid., p. 74.

22. Carol Craig, 'Why This Optimist is Voting No', *Scottish Review*, 9 September 2014.

23. Iain Macwhirter, *Divided Kingdom: How Westminster Won a referendum but Lost Scotland*, Cargo Books 2014, p. 59.

24. Eleanor Yule, 'Begbie's Belief; Miserablism Behind Bars: No Longer a Nation of Trainspotters', in Gerry Hassan and Simon

Barrow (eds), *A Nation Changed? The SNP and Scotland Ten Years On*, Luath Press 2017, p. 273.

25. Scott Hames, *The Literary Politics of Scottish Devolution: Voice, Class, Nation*, Edinburgh University Press 2019.

26. *Radical Scotland*, February–March 1987.

27. Constitutional Steering Committee, *A Claim of Right for Scotland*, Campaign for a Scottish Assembly 1988.

28. This is not to ignore the continual impressive efforts of those who have continued to beaver away at these ideas in recent times, such as the pro-independence site Bella Caledonia. On which, see Mike Small (ed.), *Bella Caledonia: An Anthology of Writing from 2007–2021*, Bella Caledonia 2022.

29. On 'the third Scotland', see Gerry Hassan, *Caledonian Dreaming: The Quest for a Different Scotland*, Luath Press 2014, chapter 13: 'The Emergence of "the Third Scotland": Values, Voice and Vessels.'

30. Peter Geoghegan, *Democracy for Sale: Dark Money and Dirty Politics*, Apollo 2020; Tom Burgis, *Kleptopia: How Dirty Money is Conquering the World*, William Collins 2020.

31. Chris Harvie, *Scotland and Nationalism: Scottish Society and Politics 1707–1977*, George Allen and Unwin 1977, p. 283.

Chapter 11

1. Winston S. Churchill, 'Conservative Mass Meeting: a Speech at Llandudno', 9 October 1948, in *Europe Unite: Speeches 1947 and 1948*, Cassell 1950, pp. 416–418. See on this: Michael Harvey, 'Perspectives on the UK's Place in the World', Chatham House, December 2011.

2. Andrew Gamble, *Between Europe and America: The Future of British Politics*, Palgrave Macmillan 2003.

3. *The Herald*, 11 February 2022.

4. Paul Mason, 'The British Left, Neoliberalism and the Potential of Scottish Independence', in Gerry Hassan and Simon Barrow (eds), *A Better Nation: The Challenges of Scottish Independence*, Luath Press 2022.

5. Marco Buti, Servaas Deroose, Vitor Gaspar and Joao Nogueira Martins (eds), *The Euro: The First Decade*, Cambridge University Press 2010.

6. Personal communication, 25 February 2022.

7. *The Times*, 16 November 2004.

8. *Daily Telegraph*, 23 July 2014.

9. National Intelligence Council, *Global Trends 2040: A More Contested World*, March 2021, p. 96.

10. Steel Commission, *Moving to Federalism: A New Settlement for Scotland*, Scottish Liberal Democrats 2006.

11. UK Government, 'Delivering for Scotland: Scotland in the UK: Global Influence', n.d. [2021], www.deliveringforscotland.gov.uk/scotland-in-the-uk/global-influence/.

12. Stephen Gethins, *Nation to Nation: Scotland's Place in the World*, Luath Press 2021, pp. 124–125, 176.

13. Daniel Kenealy, 'What Kind of International Role and Influence Would an Independent Scotland Have?', in Eve Hepburn, Michael Keating and Nicola McEwan (eds), *Scotland's New Choice: Independence after Brexit*, Centre on Constitutional Change 2021, p. 204.

14. Tim Marshall, *Prisoners of Geography: Ten Maps that Tell You Everything You Need to Know about Global Politics*, Elliott and Thompson 2015, p. 92.

15. Ibid., p. 92.

16. Sustainable Growth Commission, *The New Case for Optimism: A Strategy for Inter-generational Economic Renaissance: Report of the Sustainable Growth Commission*, SNP 2018.

17. US Senate Committee on Foreign Relations, *Minority Report, Putin's Asymmetric Assault on Democracy in Russia and Europe: Implications for U.S. National Security*, 2018.

18. Intelligence and Security Committee of Parliament, *Russia*, House of Commons July 2020, HC 632.

19. Claire Mills, Ali Shalchi, Melanie Gower, Neil Johnston and John Woodhouse, *Countering Russian Influence in the UK*, House of Commons Library Research Briefing, 25 February 2022, accessed 28 February 2022, https://commonslibrary.parliament.uk/research-briefings/cbp-9472/.

20. *Press and Journal*, 21 July 2020.

21. Oliver Letwin, *Apocalypse How? Technology and the Threat of Disaster*, Atlantic Books 2020, pp. 12–13.
22. *The Herald*, 12 March 2012.
23. *The Herald*, 25 October 2021.
24. Andrew Neal, 'Security Matters', in Gerry Hassan and Simon Barrow (eds), *Scotland the Brave? Twenty Years of Change and the Future of the Nation*, Luath Press 2019, p. 310.
25. *UK Defence Journal*, 9 August 2019.
26. Trevor Royle, *Facing the Bear: Scotland and the Cold War*, Birlinn 2019, chapter 5: 'Ding Dong Dollar: Opposing Armageddon'.
27. Jack Brand, *The National Movement in Scotland*, Routledge and Kegan Paul 1978, pp. 257–261.
28. CND Scotland, *Disarming Trident, A Practical Guide to De-activating and Dismantling the Scottish-based Trident Nuclear Weapon System*, CND Scotland 2012.
29. Hugh Chalmers and Malcolm Chalmers, *Relocation, Relocation, Relocation: Could the UK's Nuclear Force Be Moved after Scottish Independence?*, Royal United Service Institute 2014, p. 21n.
30. Ibid., p. 22.
31. Colin Fleming, 'Defence and Security', in Michael Keating (ed.), *Debating Scotland: Issues of Independence and Union in the 2014 Referendum*, Oxford University Press 2017, p. 131.
32. *Daily Record*, 2 September 2021.
33. Paul Canning, 'Yet Another Failure for Appeasement? The Case of the Irish Ports', *International History Review*, Vol. 4 No. 3, 1982, pp. 371–392.
34. Malcolm Chalmers and William Walker, *Uncharted Waters: The UK, Nuclear Weapons and the Scottish Question*, Tuckwell Press 2001.
35. William Walker, 'Defending Scotland', in Gerry Hassan and Simon Barrow (eds), *Scotland the Brave? Twenty Years of Change and the Future of the Nation*, Luath Press 2019, p. 304.
36. Malcolm Chalmers and William Walker, 'Preparing for Negotiations on Nuclear Weapons', in Gerry Hassan and Simon Barrow (eds), *A Better Nation: The Challenges of Scottish Independence*, Luath Press 2022.
37. Ibid.

38. Anthony Salamone, *The Global Blueprint: Prospectus for Scotland's Foreign Policy Institutions under Independence*, European Merchants 2021; Anthony Salamone, *The EU Blueprint: Pathway for Scotland's Accession to the European Union under Independence*, European Merchants 2021.

39. Personal communication, 12 March 2021.

40. Personal communication, 11 March 2021.

41. Stephen Gethins, op. cit., p. 193.

Chapter 12

1. The full title of the 'Edinburgh Agreement' was the Agreement between the United Kingdom Government and the Scottish Government on a referendum on independence for Scotland.

2. Aileen McHarg, 'The Referendum: Memorandum of Agreement and Draft Section 20', *Scottish Constitutional Futures Forum*, 16 October 2012; Christine Bell, 'The Legal Status of the "Edinburgh Agreement"', *Scottish Constitutional Futures Forum*, 5 November 2012.

3. Andrew Tickell, 'No Magic Bullets: Legal Issues in Achieving Independence and a Referendum', in Gerry Hassan and Simon Barrow (eds), *A Better Nation: The Challenges of Scottish Independence*, Luath Press 2022.

4. Ciaran Martin, *Resist, Reform or Re-Run? Short and Long-Term Reflections on Scotland and the Independence Referendums*, Blavatnik School of Government, University of Oxford, April 2021, p. 5.

5. Ibid., p. 7.

6. Ibid., p. 18.

7. This is the position taken by the site Wings Over Scotland. See: Scott Hames and Dominic Hinde, 'The Rise and Fall of Wings Over Scotland', *New Statesman*, 18 May 2021.

8. Personal communication, 22 September 2019.

9. Adam Tomkins, 'Why We Need a New Act of Union – and What to Put in It', *The Spectator*, 21 April 2021.

10. Tom Devine, *BBC Newsnight*, 19 September 2014.

11. James Forsyth, 'To Save the Union, Negotiate Scotland's Independence', *The Spectator*, 5 September 2020.

12. Tim Shipman, *All Out War: The Full Story of How Brexit Sank Britain's Political Class*, William Collins 2016.

13. James Mitchell, 'The Referendum Campaign', in Aileen McHarg, Tom Mullen, Alan Page and Neil Walker (eds), *The Scottish Independence Referendum: Constitutional and Political Implications*, Oxford University Press 2016, p. 81.

14. Personal communication, 24 April 2012.

15. The James Callaghan Labour government fell after it lost a vote of no confidence on 28 March 1979, 311–310 – with the eleven SNP MPs and 13 Liberal Party MPs voting against Labour. Margaret Thatcher won the resulting UK general election on 3 May 1979.

16. Personal communication, 18 October 2019.

17. Colin Kidd, 'A Future No Campaign: Terrain and Challenges', in Gerry Hassan and Simon Barrow (eds), *A Better Nation: The Challenges of Scottish Independence*, Luath Press 2022.

18. Survation, January 2020; Panelbase, June 2020, *What Scotland Thinks*, accessed on 8 February 2022, https://whatscotlandthinks.org/questions/should-the-scottish-parliament-or-the-uk-parliament-ultimately-have-the-power-to-decide-whether-there-should-be-a-second-independence-referendum/.

19. Survation: September and November 2021, *What Scotland Thinks*, accessed 8 February 2022, https://whatscotlandthinks.org/questions/should-there-or-should-there-not-be-a-referendum-on-scottish-independence-within-the-next-two-years/.

20. Panebase, April and November 2021, What Scotland Thinks, accessed on 8 February 2022, https://whatscotlandthinks.org/questions/do-you-think-another-scottish-independence-referendum-should-be-held-in-the-next-12-months-in-the-next-2-5-years-or-there-should-not-be-another-referendum-in-the-next-few-years/.

21. ComRes, January 2022, *What Scotland Thinks*, accessed 8 February 2022, https://whatscotlandthinks.org/questions/when-if-ever-do-you-think-there-should-be-another-scottish-independence-referendum/.

22. Tickell, op. cit.

23. Margaret Thatcher, *The Downing Street Years*, HarperCollins 1993, p. 624.

24. Sarah Priddy, 'Claim of Right for Scotland: Debate Pack', House of Commons Library Research Briefing 2016, accessed 30 November 2021, https://commonslibrary.parliament.uk/research-briefings/cdp-2016-0158/.

Chapter 13

1. On the issues of 2014 as they were happening, see: Andrew Goudie (ed.), *Scotland's Future: The Economics of Constitutional Change*, Dundee University Press 2013; Charlie Jeffrey and Ray Perman (eds), *Scotland's Decision: 16 Questions to Think About for the referendum on 18 September*, David Hume Institute and the Hunter Foundation in association with Birlinn 2014; Royal Society of Edinburgh, *Enlightening the Constitutional Debate*, Royal Society of Edinburgh/British Academy 2014. For a less institutional and less conventional analysis, see: Gerry Hassan and James Mitchell (eds), *After Independence*, Luath Press 2013.
2. Rob Johns, 'It Wasn't "the Vow" Wot Won It: The Scottish Independence Referendum', in Philip Cowley and Robert Ford (eds), *More Sex, Lies and the Ballot Box: Another 50 Things You Need to Know About Elections*, Biteback Publishing 2016, p. 188.
3. *Twitter*, 2 September 2014.
4. Robert Linera, Ailsa Henderson and Liam Delaney, 'Voters' Response to the Campaign: Evidence from the Survey', in Michael Keating (ed.), *Debating Scotland: Issues of Independence and Union in the 2014 Referendum*, Oxford University Press 2017, p. 182.
5. Lord Ashcroft, 'How Scotland Voted, and Why', *Lord Ashcroft Polls*, 19 September 2014.
6. Gordon Brown, 'The Britain of Emma Raducanu Shows Why Nationalists are Losing the Argument', *New Statesman*, 16 September 2021.
7. See, for example: Neil MacCormick, *Questioning Sovereignty: Law, State and Nation in the European Commonwealth*, Oxford University Press 1999; Kenny MacAskill, *Building a Nation: Post-Devolution Nationalism*, Luath Press 2004.

8. Colin Kidd, 'A Future No Campaign: Terrain and Challenges', in Gerry Hassan and Simon Barrow (eds), *A Better Nation: The Challenges of Scottish Independence*, Luath Press 2022.

9. Ibid.

10. Marco G. Biagi, 'The New Strategic Challenges of Securing a Yes Vote', in Gerry Hassan and Simon Barrow (eds), *A Better Nation: The Challenges of Scottish Independence*, Luath Press 2022.

11. Gerry Hassan, *Caledonian Dreaming: The Quest for a Different Scotland*, Luath Press 2014, pp. 82–83.

12. Ipsos MORI Scotland Focus Groups: Dundee and Glasgow: December 2013–January 2014.

13. Willie Sullivan, *The Missing Scotland: Why Over a Million Scots Choose Not to Vote and What It Means for Our Democracy?*, Luath Press 2014.

14. Frances Fox Piven and Richard A. Cloward, *Why Americans Still Don't Vote and Why Politicians Want It That Way*, Beacon Press, 2nd edn 2000.

15. Arianna Introna, 'Nationalist and Institutional Horizons in (Post-) Referendum Scottish Politics', *Renewal: A Journal of Social Democracy*, Vol. 23 Nos 1–2, 2015.

16. Gordon Brown, 'Many Scots Don't Want Independence, but a More Co-operative Union', *The Guardian*, 9 May 2021.

17. Personal communication, 30 October 2014.

18. Personal communication, 4 July 2020.

19. Personal communication, 19 July 2020.

20. Personal communication, 11 July 2020.

21. Personal communication, 19 July 2020.

22. Personal communication, 9 July 2020.

23. Personal communication, 14 July 2020.

24. Personal communication, 11 July 2020.

25. Personal communication, 24 February 2022.

26. Personal communication, 27 October 2018.

27. 'The Fight Over Scottish Independence Appears to Be Deadlocked', *The Economist*, 5 March 2022.

28. Gerry Hassan, 'Minority Interest Nation: The Changing Contours of Reporting Scotland on BBC and STV', *Political Quarterly*, Vol. 89 No. 1, 2017.

29. Gerry Hassan, *Independence of the Scottish Mind: Elite Narratives, Public Spaces and the Making of a Modern Nation*, Palgrave Macmillan 2014, p. 100.

30. Pat Anderson, *Fear and Smear: The Campaign against Scottish Independence*, Snowy Publications 2015; G.A. Ponsonby, *London Calling: How the BBC 'Stole' the Referendum*, NNS Press 2015.

31. Philip Schlesinger, 'Scotland's Dual Public Sphere and the Media', in Michael Keating (ed.), *The Oxford Handbook of Scottish Politics*, Oxford University Press 2020, pp. 156–177.

32. Christopher Silver, *Demanding Democracy: The Case for a Scottish Media*, Word Power Books 2015.

33. Michael Gecan, *Going Public: An Organiser's Guide to Civic Action*, Anchor Books 2004.

34. Stephen Duncombe, *Dream or Nightmare: Re-imagining Progressive Politics in an Age of Fantasy*, OR Books 2019.

35. Steve Duncombe and Steve Lambert, *The Art of Activism: Your All-Purpose Guide to Making the Impossible Possible*, OR Books 2021.

Chapter 14

1. Tom Devine, *Scotland's Empire: 1600–1815*, Allen Lane 2003; Michael Fry, *The Scottish Empire*, Tuckwell Press 2001.

2. Gordon Brown, *Maxton*, Mainstream Publishing 1986, p. 161.

3. Personal communication, 28 February 2022.

4. HM Treasury, *National Register of Assets 2001*, Stationery Office 2000; SNP Westminster Parliamentary Group, *An Analysis of the National Register 2001 and the Missing Millions that Scotland Has Contributed to the UK*, SNP 2001.

5. Gemma Tetlow and Thomas Pope, 'What New Institutions of Economic Policy Would an Independent Scotland Need?', *Economics Observatory*, 25 January 2022.

6. Much of this ground is explored in the SNP's Growth Commission: The Sustainable Growth Commission, *Scotland: The New Case for Optimism: A Strategy for Inter-generational Economic Renaissance: Report of the Sustainable Growth Commission*, SNP 2018.

7. Julie Orr, *Scotland, Darien and the Atlantic World: 1698–1700*, Edinburgh University Press 2018.

8. George Pottinger, *The Secretaries of State for Scotland 1926–76*, Scottish Academic Press 1976.

9. This was undertaken in the Scotland Act 2012.

10. Richard Parry, 'The Civil Service and Government Structures', in Michael Keating (ed.), *The Oxford Handbook of Scottish Politics*, Oxford University Press 2020.

11. John Elvidge, *Northern Exposure: Lessons from the First Twelve Years of Devolved Government in Scotland*, Institute for Government 2011, p. 33.

12. Aron Cheung, Akash Paun and Lucy Valsamidis, *Devolution at 20*, Institute for Government 2019, p. 37.

13. Larry Flanagan and Stephen Reicher, *Not By the People: The Commission on Fair Access to Political Influence*, Jimmy Reid Foundation 2013. Also see: David Torrance, 'Has Devolution in Scotland Delivered What Was Promised before 1999?', in Akash Paun and Sam Macrory (eds), *Has Devolution Worked? The First 20 Years*, Institute for Government 2019.

14. Darren Halpin, Iain MacLeod and Peter McLaverty, 'Committee Hearings of the Scottish Parliament: Evidence Giving and Policy Learning', *Journal of Legislative Studies*, Vol. 18 No. 1, 2020, pp. 1–20.

15. See Robert Lane, 'Scotland in Europe: An Independent Scotland in the European Community', in Wilson Finnie, Christopher Himsworth and Neil Walker (eds), *Edinburgh Essays in Public Law*, Edinburgh University Press 1991.

16. *GB News*, 2 September 2021.

17. Martin Kettle, 'Scottish Referendum: the UK is on Shifting Sands – We Can't Assume Survival', *The Guardian*, 16 April 2014.

18. Gavin McCrone, 'Economic Reality of Scottish Independence has Altered since Brexit', *The Times*, 12 February 2022.

19. Both of these pieces of legislation faced much criticism when passed when the SNP had a parliamentary majority between 2011 and 2016, and when the party lost it in 2016 the Offensive Behaviour at Football Act was repealed along with the named person scheme part of the Children and Young People Act.

20. Brendan O'Neill, 'Scotland: Once Again the Demos Save the Day', *Spiked*, 19 September 2014; 'Scotland: The Most Nannying of Europe's Nanny States', *Reason*, 4 June 2015.

21. *The Scotsman*, 19 February 2017.

22. *BBC Sunday Politics*, 19 October 2013.

23. *The Herald*, 24 November 1987.

24. *BBC News*, 8 October 2012.

25. *Sunday Times*, 13 October 2012.

26. 'It's Time to Let Scotland Go', *Spectator* Debate, London, 24 May 2012.

27. Azeem Ibrahim, 'Scottish Independence is a Security Problem for the United States', *Foreign Policy*, 8 March 2021.

28. Personal communication, 12 March 2021.

29. Philip Rycroft and Kirsty Hughes, 'Scotland's Independence Will Impact the UK's Global Role', *Chatham House*, 10 May 2021.

30. Michael Keating and Malcolm Harvey, *Small Nations in a Big World: What Scotland Can Learn*, Luath Press 2014, p. 140.

Chapter 15

1. Marine Scotland Information: Facts and Figures about Scotland's sea area (coastline length, sea area in sq kms), accessed 4 February 2022, https://marine.gov.scot/data/facts-and-figures-about-scotlands-sea-area-coastline-length-sea-area-sq-kms.

2. Michael Oakeshott, *On Human Conduct*, Oxford University Press 1975.

3. Michael Crick, *One Party After Another: The Disruptive Life of Nigel Farage*, Simon & Schuster 2022.

4. Gordon Brown, 'Opening Address', These Islands: Our Past, Present and Future Conference, Newcastle upon Tyne, 20 January 2020.

5. David Edgerton, 'Gordon Brown and British Nationalism', *David Edgerton blog*, 28 June 2019.

6. Edinburgh International Book Festival, 25 August 2012.

7. Personal communication, 21 February 2022.

8. Colin Rallings and Michael Trasher, *British Electoral Facts 1832–2012*, Biteback Publishing 2012, pp. 37–38.

9. Gerry Hassan and Eric Shaw, *The People's Flag and the Union Jack: An Alternative History of Britain and the Labour Party*, Biteback Publishing 2019.

10. Rallings and Thrasher, op cit., pp. 57–58.

11. Billy Bragg, *The Progressive Patriot: A Search for Belonging*, Transworld Publishers 2007.

12. Personal communication, 2 March 2022.

13. *YouGov*, 18 June 2019.

14. *BBC Scotland News*, 18 June 2019.

15. BBC election figures.

16. Dominic Cummings, 'How the Brexit Referendum was Won', *The Spectator*, 9 January 2017.

17. Anthony Barnett, *The Lure of Greatness: England's Brexit and America's Trump*, Unbound 2017, p. 36.

18. Ibid., pp. 103, 113.

19. Fintan O'Toole, *Heroic Failure: Brexit and the Politics of Pain*, Apollo Books 2018.

20. John Wilson Foster and William Beattie Smith (eds), *The Idea of the Union: Great Britain and Northern Ireland*, Blackstaff Press 2021.

21. *Irish Times*, 8 September 2012.

22. Kevin Meagher, *What a Bloody Awful Country: Northern Ireland's Century of Division*, Biteback Publishing 2021, pp. 235, 278.

23. Neil MacCormick, *Questioning Sovereignty: Law, State and Nation in the European Commonwealth*, Oxford University Press 1999.

24. Personal communication, 28 February 2022.

25. Michael Keating, *The Independence of Scotland: Self-government and the Shifting Politics of Union*, Oxford University Press 2009, pp. 176–177.

26. Walter Bagehot, *The English Constitution* [1867], Fontana 1963; Constitutional Steering Committee, *A Claim of Right for Scotland*, Campaign for a Scottish Assembly 1988.

27. Bernard Crick, 'In Conversation', Changin' Scotland weekend, Ullapool, 15 March 2008.

28. Bernard Crick, 'On Devolution, Decentralism and the Constitution', in *Political Thoughts and Polemics*, Edinburgh University Press 1990.

29. Ailsa Henderson and Richard Wyn Jones, *Englishness: The Political Force Transforming Britain*, Oxford University Press 2021, pp. 71, 78.

Chapter 16

1. Neal Ascherson, 'Bye Bye Britain', *London Review of Books*, 24 September 2020.
2. Anthony Barnett, *The Lure of Greatness: England's Brexit, America's Trump*, Unbound 2017, p. 44.
3. *Labour Hame*, 8 October 2014.
4. Personal communication, 18 October 2019.
5. These Islands: Our Past, Present and Future conference, Newcastle upon Tyne, 22 February 2020.
6. Anthony Wright, *G.D.H. Cole and Socialist Democracy*, Oxford University Press 1979; Evan Luard, *Socialists without the State*, St Martin's Press 1979; Ken Coates (ed.), *Can the Workers Run Industry?*, Spokesman Books 1972.
7. Personal communication, 10 October 2014.
8. Donatella Della Porta, Francis O'Connor, Martin Portos and Anna Subirats, *Social Movements and Referendums from Below: Direct Democracy in the Neoliberal Crisis*, Policy Press 2017.
9. Callum G. Brown, *Religion and Society in Scotland since 1707*, Edinburgh University Press 1997, p. 146.
10. On the idea of popular sovereignty, see: Edmund S. Morgan, *Inventing the People: The Rise of Popular Sovereignty in England and America*, W.W. Norton and Company 1988.
11. Ben Jackson, *The Case for Scottish Independence: A History of Nationalist Thought in Modern Scotland*, Cambridge University Press 2020, chapter 5: 'Sovereignty and Post-Sovereignty'.
12. Norwegian Media Authority website, accessed 21 January 2022, www.medietilsynet.no/
13. Jack Fawcett, Doug Sloan and Russell Gunson, *Strengthening the Think Tank Sector in Scotland*, Institute for Public Policy Research Scotland 2021.

14. Hartwig Pautz, *Think-Tanks, Social Democracy and Social Policy*, Palgrave Macmillan 2012.

15. Peter Geoghegan, *Democracy for Sale: Dark Money and Dirty Politics*, Head of Zeus 2020.

16. Sophie Howe, *Future Generations Commissioner for Wales*, accessed 4 January 2022, www.futuregenerations.wales/team/sophie-howe/.

17. Gerry Hassan, Eddie Dick and Lydia Howland (eds), *Scotland 2020. Hopeful Stories for a Northern Nation*, Demos 2005; Gerry Hassan, Melissa Mean and Charlie Tims, *The Dreaming City: Glasgow 2020 and the Power of Mass Imagination*, Demos 2007.

18. Ian Godden, Hillary Sillitto and Dorothy Godden, *Scotland 2070: Healthy, Wealthy, Wise: An Ambitious Vision for Scotland's Future without the Politics*, College Publications 2020.

19. Personal communication, 2 January 2021.

20. Richard Eckersley, *Well and Good: How We Feel and Why It Matters*, Text Publishing Company 2004.

21. Bernard Crick, *Socialist Values and Time*, Fabian Society 1984, p. 37.

22. Private communication, 28 December 2020.

23. Fintan O'Toole, 'The Art of Growing Up: A Foreword', in Gerry Hassan, *Caledonian Dreaming: The Quest for a Different Scotland*, Luath Press 2014, p. 11.

24. Jonathan Tonge, 'Northern Ireland', in Robert Ford, Tim Bale, Will Jennings and Paula Surridge, *The British General Election of 2019*, Palgrave Macmillan 2021, p. 450.

25. Fintan O'Toole, 'The Art of Leaving and Arriving: Brexit, Scotland and Britain', in Gerry Hassan and Simon Barrow (eds), *Scotland the Brave? Twenty Years of Change and the Future of the Nation*, Luath Press 2019, p. 327.

Chapter 17

1. Personal communication, 12 October 2019.

2. Richard Finlay, *Modern Scotland 1914–2000*, Profile Books 2004; Catriona MacDonald, *Whaur Extremes Meet: Scotland's Twentieth Century*, Birlinn 2009.

3. James A. Bowie, *The Future of Scotland: A Survey of the Present Position with some Proposals for Public Policy*, W & R Chambers 1939.

4. James Mitchell, *The Myth of Dependency*, Scottish Centre for Economic and Social Research 1990, p. 4.

5. Tom Nairn, 'The Festival of the Dead', *New Statesman*, 1 September 1967.

6. Tom Nairn, 'The Three Dreams of Scottish Nationalism', *New Left Review*, no. 49, May–June 1968. See: Neil Davidson, 'In Perspective: Tom Nairn', *International Socialism*, No. 82, March 1999.

7. James G. Kellas, *Modern Scotland: The Nation since 1870*, Pall Mall 1968, p. 8.

8. Ibid., p. 11.

9. David Murison (ed.), *Scottish National Dictionary: Volume Five*, Aberdeen University Press 1986, p. 337.

10. Stephen Maxwell, 'Can Scotland's Political Myths Be Broken?' [1976], reprinted in Stephen Maxwell, *The Case for Left-Wing Nationalism*, Luath Press 2013, pp. 19–20.

11. Personal communication, 4 October 2020. See, on a similar theme: Sara Sheridan, *Where are the Women? A Guide to an Imagined Scotland*, Historic Environment Scotland 2019.

12. Fintan O'Toole, *Enough is Enough: How to Build a New Republic*, Faber & Faber 2010, p. 39.

13. Christopher Booker, *The Seven Basic Plots: Why We Tell Stories*, Continuum Publishing 2004.

14. Chimamanda Ngozi Adichie, 'The Danger of a Single Story', TED talk, 7 October 2009.

Index